LOTS OF LEHMANS

The Family of Mayer Lehman

of Lehman Brothers

———◆———

Remembered by His Descendants

The Mayer Lehman family in Tarrytown, New York, c. 1888. Front row, kneeling: Herbert (left) next to Irving. In the second row seated (left to right): Hattie Lehman Goodhart holding daughter Helen, Mayer Lehman with grandson Howard Goodhart, Babette with grandson Allan Lehman, Settie Lehman Fatman with daughter Margaret. Back row (left to right): Philip J. Goodhart, Harriet Lehman (Sigmund's wife), Sigmund M. Lehman, Clara Lehman (later Clara Lehman Limburg), Morris Fatman, Arthur Lehman. (Herbert H. Lehman Suite & Papers, Columbia University)

LOTS OF LEHMANS

The Family of Mayer Lehman
of Lehman Brothers

Remembered by His Descendants

Edited with Introduction & Notes by Kenneth Libo

FOREWORD
William L. Bernhard and John L. Loeb Jr.

AFTERWORD
June Rossbach Bingham Birge

CENTER
FOR JEWISH
HISTORY

PUBLISHED BY CENTER FOR JEWISH HISTORY

Editor and Compiler	Kenneth Libo
Editorial Consultant	Kathy Plotkin

EDITORIAL, DESIGN, AND PRODUCTION SERVICES BY MTM PUBLISHING, INC.

President	Valerie Tomaselli
Editorial Coordinator	Tim Anderson
Design and Layout	Annemarie Redmond
Copyediting	Janine Stanley-Dunham
Proofreading	Zach Gajewski; Paul Scaramazza

GENEALOGY AND FAMILY TREES BY OUR LIVING TREE

President	Bob Breakstone
Genealogist	David Kleiman
Designer	Scott Citron

Distributed by Syracuse University Press
ISBN # 978-0-9792336-0-9
Library of Congress Cataloging-in-Publication data in progress.
Manufacturing supervised by Active Concepts, Inc., N.Y.

Printed in Canada

Table of Contents

—◆—

Lots of Lehmans:
The Family of Mayer Lehman of Lehman Brothers
Remembered by His Descendants

EDITED WITH INTRODUCTION & NOTES   Kenneth Libo
FOREWORD   William L. Bernhard and John L. Loeb Jr.
AFTERWORD   June Rossbach Bingham Birge

CONTRIBUTORS (in alphabetical order)

Dorothy L. Bernhard
Robert A. Bernhard
William L. Bernhard
Jonathan B. Bingham
June Rossbach Bingham Birge
Stephen Birmingham
Ann Loeb Bronfman
Helen L. Buttenwieser
Lawrence B. Buttenwieser
Paul A. Buttenwieser
Peter L. Buttenwieser
Judith Loeb Chiara
Julius Edelstein
Carolin Flexner
Gabrielle Forbush
Peter Friedman
Hans Gerst
Ann Straus Gertler

Sir Philip Goodhart
Lord William Howard Goodhart
John D. Gordan III
Phyllis Goodhart Gordan
Joan Morgenthau Hirschhorn
Peter Josten
Wendy Lehman Lash
Adele Lewisohn Lehman
Arthur Lehman
Babette Neugass Lehman
Edith Altschul Lehman
Herbert Lehman
Irving Lehman
Mayer Lehman
Orin Lehman
Penelope Lehman
Wendy Vanderbilt Lehman
Marjorie Lewisohn
A. Myles Limburg

Peter Limburg
Arthur L. Loeb
Frances L. Loeb
John L. Loeb Jr.
John L. Loeb Sr.
Eileen Josten Lowe
William Mayer
Henry Morgenthau III
Robert M. Morgenthau
Franklin Delano Roosevelt
Camilla Master Rosenfeld
Isadore Rosenfeld
Mabel Limburg Rossbach
Deborah Jane Wise Sheridan
Irving Lehman Straus
Louise Blumenthal Sulzberger
Duane Tananbaum
Peter Lehman Wise

Foreword

By William L. Bernhard and John L. Loeb Jr.

Great-grandsons of Mayer Lehman and Babette Neugass Lehman
Grandsons of Arthur Lehman and Adele Lewisohn Lehman

The genesis of these Lehman family memories took place in Hyde Park, New York, in October 2004. A one-day seminar on Herbert Lehman's four-term governorship of New York State was being held at the Franklin and Eleanor Roosevelt Institute under the auspices of Lehman College with the help of William Bernhard.

The previous evening, our cousin June Rossbach Bingham Birge—now the ranking female member of the Mayer Lehman clan—gave a talk describing Herbert Lehman not as a great governor but as a great uncle.

June's first memory of her Uncle Herbert was when she was about four: "I was in his arms as we bobbled up and down at the shallow end of his swimming pool. Men's bathing suits in those days had a top, but even so, I could see how furry he was. I asked why he had so much more hair on his chest than on his head. He told me he didn't know but he was sure that I would not inherit this distinction."

John was so taken by June's speech that he said to her afterward, "You've got to write a family history!" to which she replied, "Not in a thousand years."

June was busy with her own writing projects, but the idea of a book about the Lehman family stayed alive and evolved. In 2005 the three of us (June, Bill, and John) met to discuss producing an anecdotal history of Herbert Lehman, his six siblings, and their spouses as recalled by their descendants.

To compile and edit such a book, we chose Ken Libo, a National Book Award recipient and a professor of history at Hunter College. Ken was also known to us as the researcher, editor, and writer of John L. and Frances Lehman Loeb's oral memoir, *All in a Lifetime*. One of Ken's ideas was to include letters from the Herbert Lehman Archives at Columbia, as well as *New York Times* articles recognizing Herbert and his siblings for their enormous contributions to public service, a Lehman tradition going back several generations in Germany before its continuation in America. Public service remains an important hallmark of our family.

Meetings of the four of us followed for the next year, along with countless phone calls and e-mails among us and the rest of our far-flung Lehman family, soliciting their interest as well as their memories. We have used all the sources and resources we could think of to contact every member of the family. If we have committed any sins of omission or commission, please forgive us, for we have done our utmost to make this book all-inclusive. To those who have responded to our requests for participation, we are truly grateful.

Over several months the family responses became a manuscript; now they are a book we hope will provide both pleasure and insights, not only for a wide-ranging number of Lehman family members but also for other readers who find fascinating the anecdotes and recollections of well-known families. May all our readers enjoy what follows.

—*WLB and JLL*

Acknowledgements

———❖———

In compiling and editing *Lots of Lehmans*, I enjoyed working closely with June Rossbach Bingham Birge, John L. Loeb Jr., and William L. Bernhard—with whom the idea for this book originated. This project could not have been undertaken without a rich assortment of Lehman memories they shared, along with other contributors who, cumulatively, make up the heart and soul of this book. I also owe an enormous debt of gratitude to Wendy Lehman Lash, president of the Edith and Herbert H. Lehman Foundation, both for her invaluable genealogical contributions and for her commitment to the Herbert H. Lehman Suite & Papers at Columbia University. There, with the able assistance of Tamar Dougherty, I discovered a wealth of letters, photographs, and oral and written accounts. These materials, together with others from the family archives of Henry Morgenthau III, Dorothy Treisman, Frances Dinkelspiel, and John D. Gordan III, provided a perfect complement to the family recollections of Mayer and Babette Lehman's three dozen and more living descendants who take us back to the world of "Our Crowd."

At John Loeb Jr.'s office, Kathy Plotkin contributed not only a meticulous line-by-line reading of the text but also an uncanny ability for problem solving, often after raising the right questions. To Valerie Tomaselli of MTM Publishing, MTM's editorial coordinator Tim Anderson, and MTM copy editor Janine Stanley-Dunham a very special thank you for exercising impeccable taste and care in helping to produce this book. Bob Breakstone of Our Living Tree deserves much praise for making the genealogical charts both attractive and functional.

Special thanks also to photo archivists Phyllis Collazo of the *New York Times* and Joan Carroll of AP/Wide World Photos, and researchers Daniel Scott, Dennis Raverty, and Michael Skakun. Finally, thank you to the University of Syracuse Press for permission to quote from Stephen Birmingham's *"Our Crowd": The Great Jewish Families of New York*.

—KL

LOTS OF LEHMANS

Rimpar, Bavaria, where the Lehmans lived in 1845, five years before Mayer Lehman immigrated to the United States. (cover photo in The Lehmans: From Rimpar to the New World, A Family History, *Mainfränkisches Museum Würzburg)*

The Lehmans:
A Family and a Firm

———⊰◆⊱———

By Kenneth Libo

BY 1950 LEHMAN BROTHERS, the sixth largest investment banking house in the country, had become to
investment banking what Levi Strauss, by then, had long
been to blue jeans—quite an achievement for a family
enterprise organized in 1850 by three German Jewish
immigrant brothers with little more going for them

than determination, family loyalty, and a background in the cattle trade. Their economic rise began in the antebellum South. The exhaustion of the soil in the Atlantic seaboard states coupled with the removal of the indigenous Indians precipitated a sizable migration into western Georgia, Alabama, Mississippi, and Louisiana. The chief attraction to this vast area of rich black soil was a new staple crop that promised quick profits—cotton. Almost overnight thriving communities came into being along the Yazoo, Alabama, and Mississippi rivers.

Word of this reached the family of Eva and Abraham Lehman. Abraham was a prosperous Jewish cattle dealer living in Rimpar, Bavaria (Germany). At the time the Catholic prince-bishops of Bavaria permitted only one male child of a Jewish family to receive a license to marry and work in his place of birth. Because it was the tradition that the eldest son would receive such a license, Abraham and Eva's younger sons Henry, Emanuel, and Mayer were encouraged to move, and the eldest, Seligmann, stayed. (A detailed account of the Lehmans in

18th- and 19th-century Rimpar—set against the historic backdrop of Jewish life in Bavaria—can be found in *The Lehmans: From Rimpar to the New World, A Family History* by Roland Flade.)

Just when many young German Jews as well as non-Jews began immigrating to America, Henry, at twenty-one, the eldest of the three younger brothers, heard the "call of cotton." Landing in Mobile, Alabama, in 1844, Henry contacted a member of his extended family named Goldschmidt, who provided him with peddlers' supplies, probably on credit, before he set out with a wagonload of merchandise for sale to farmers, plantation owners, and their families.

Peddling was the Harvard Business School of that day. Moving north along the Alabama River, Henry, within a year, had his start. He had accumulated enough savings to open a small store on Commerce Street in the booming town of Montgomery. Beginning with a modest stock of foodstuffs, kitchenware, and general merchandise, he lived alone in the back of the store, working long and tedious hours, frequently deep into the night. In 1846

Henry was one of sixteen German Jewish founders of Hevra Mavaker Holim, a society for visiting the sick. Three years later the group voted to form itself into a congregation, which on April 12, 1852, was legally incorporated as Kahl ("Congregation") Montgomery.

Home for 4,000 whites and 2,000 slaves, Montgomery was linked to Atlanta by rail and to Mobile and New Orleans by waterway. The city was already an important storage and trading point for cotton. In 1847 a younger brother, Emanuel, joined Henry. A year later, with savings they had stowed away, they built a new two-story general store on Montgomery's Court Square bearing the legend "H. Lehman & Bro."

A third brother, twenty-year-old Mayer, arrived in 1850. Mayer had strong political reasons for leaving Germany. "He felt it was a completely undemocratic country," according to an oral memoir dictated late in life by his youngest son, Herbert, who would later become a New York governor and U.S. senator, "and he never got over this distrust of Germany and the German ruling classes." When Mayer left, he may have already met his future wife, Babette Neugass, the daughter of a weaver from nearby Rieneck whom he would marry in New Orleans several years later. In the spring of 1850 Mayer boarded the *Admiral* in Hamburg and on July 17 reached New York. Soon after his arrival in Montgomery, H. Lehman & Bro. changed its name to Lehman Brothers.

Directly opposite Montgomery's main slave auctioning block, their store was well stocked with everything from sheeting, shirting, and yarn to cotton rope and ball thread. "It was largely a barter arrangement," recalled Herbert. "The farmers would come in with their cotton and trade it for shirts and shoes and fertilizer, such little as was used in those days, and seed, and all the necessities. That's how they got started in the cotton business." By 1852 the brothers were also buying and selling real estate and extending long-range credit to planters, settling accounts in bales more often than dollars. For some 40 years to the end of the century, following the unexpected death of Henry in 1855 from yellow fever, Emanuel and Mayer *were* the firm. Emanuel was considered conservative, Mayer adventurous. According to family tradition, Mayer made the money, and Emanuel made sure they didn't lose it.

Early on, Lehman Brothers established an informal banking operation in Montgomery based on loans to cotton growers secured by crop liens. They also bought cotton outright and before long became cotton dealers, keeping their store as an adjunct. Every year Emanuel went to New York City to replenish supplies and negotiate with cotton manufacturers and exporters while Henry headed the Lehman operation in New Orleans, the major receiving point for the cotton crops. After Henry's death, Babette's brother Benjamin Neugass took over in New Orleans. Meanwhile, Mayer, in addition to managing the Montgomery store, dealt with planters and farmers in the surrounding area. Mayer became the cotton expert in the family, mastering every intricacy and nuance of the trade with the same patience and persistence his ancestors had applied to the Talmud.

In 1858, when the brothers decided to open a permanent New York City office, Emanuel headed north for good and established Lehman Brothers, a cotton brokerage, at 119 Liberty Street, center of the largest market for cotton in the country and just a few blocks from the brokerage and banking operations of the Kuhns, Loebs, Goldmans, Sachses, and Seligmans.

Besides heading operations in Montgomery, Mayer made frequent trips to New Orleans, where Babette Neugass was then living with relatives. A few days before his twenty-eighth birthday, he married twenty-year-old Babette. In Montgomery they occupied a substantial residence, where their first four children were born—Sigmund in 1859, Hattie in 1861, Settie (Lisette) in 1863, and Benjamin (who died in infancy) in 1865. Mayer by now owned seven slaves—four women and three men. Some helped at the residence, while others worked in the firm. One, a nursemaid, voluntarily accompanied the Lehmans to New York after the Civil War and took care of not only Settie but also Clara, who was born in New York in 1870.

Home of Mayer and Babette Lehman at South Court Street in Montgomery, Alabama,
c. 1855. (Robert M. Morgenthau)

A staunch supporter of Alabama's leading Democratic politicians, Mayer was also a member in good standing of Montgomery's Masonic lodge, as well as a leading contributor to a building fund for Montgomery's first Jewish house of worship built expressly for that purpose. The synagogue building was completed in 1862, one year after Jefferson Davis was sworn in as president of the Confederacy on the balcony of the Montgomery statehouse just a few blocks away.

Lehman Brothers suffered huge costs following the outbreak of the Civil War, which virtually cut off relations between Montgomery and New York. "*Alles ist beendet!*" ("Everything is over!") Emanuel wrote desperately from New York to his wife's relatives in Liverpool. Yet the firm's business went on. While Mayer remained in Montgomery, Emanuel, with his family, returned to Europe, where he oversaw the arrival of shiploads of cotton from New Orleans to Liverpool, London, and other European ports. All this the Lehman brothers did through various alliances, mostly with Babette's kinfolk, the Neugasses and Sterns.

Babette's brother-in-law Abraham Stern belonged to a group that bought the cotton that was shipped either from New Orleans or New York to Liverpool, where the great cotton factories were. As for the descendants of the Sterns, a great-grandson of Mayer Lehman, John Loeb Jr., recalls:

One has recently retired as head of the Liverpool Cotton Exchange, and another one, totally Anglican, has for many years been the sheriff of Cheshire County. The relations with the Lehmans get even more complicated when Abraham Stern's younger brother moves to New Orleans and becomes partners with Babette's younger brother, Benjamin Neugass, and the Lehmans in New Orleans. The firm was originally called Lehman, Neugass. With the arrival of young Mr. Stern, the name was changed to Lehman, Stern.

Meanwhile, back in Montgomery, Mayer formed a partnership with John Wesley Durr,

Lehman, Durr & Co. in Montgomery, Alabama, c. 1865. Mayer Lehman and John Wesley Durr owned and operated one of Montgomery's biggest storage centers for cotton. (Robert M. Morgenthau)

the managing director of Montgomery's principal cotton center, the Alabama Warehouse. With Lehman money, Mayer's know-how, and Durr's background and connections, the Alabama Warehouse soon became Montgomery's leading storage center for cotton probably shipped by gunrunners to Liverpool via New Orleans. Lehman and Durr remained partners throughout the war. In the final months of the Confederacy, Mayer was authorized by the Alabama governor, Thomas Hill Watts, to negotiate $500,000 from sales of non-Lehman owned cotton in New York for the relief of Alabama soldiers in Northern prison camps. Mayer wrote directly to General Grant for permission to pass through the lines. His request, however, went unanswered.

After the war, Mayer and Emanuel resumed operations of Lehman Brothers in New York while continuing the partnership between Lehman and Durr in Montgomery.

In the *New York Times* obituary of Rosa Parks (October 25, 2005), the mention of Virginia Durr, granddaughter-in-law of John

Wesley Durr, elicited the following recollections from John Loeb Jr.:

Virginia Durr and her husband Clifford were two leading white members of Montgomery's Civil Rights community. After Rosa Parks was arrested for sitting in the front of a city bus, the Durrs went to the police station with the president of the local branch of the NAACP and got her released. They knew her personally; she had done some seamstress work for Virginia.

I met Virginia Durr in Montgomery when she was quite elderly. We had a lovely dinner together, talking among other things of her activity in the Civil Rights movement and her support of Martin Luther King and Rosa Parks. For many years Virginia was ostracized for her stand on civil rights by the top social figures of Montgomery. Her sister was married to Hugo Black, an associate justice of the Supreme Court from 1937 to 1971.

Mayer Lehman on a visit to his family in Bavaria, 1867. Seventeen years earlier he had immigrated to the United States. He came back as a successful businessman. (Henry Morgenthau III)

Toward the end of the Civil War, the Lehman–Durr Warehouse was burned by the owners to keep the cotton supply from being confiscated by Union soldiers, but even so, the co-owners had managed to save a considerable sum of money which they somehow parlayed into gold. Virginia told me that when the Union troops occupied Montgomery the only safe place for their gold to be hidden was in Mrs. John Wesley Durr's petticoats, and that after the Union troops left, the gold was divided equally between the two families.

In 1868 Mayer moved from Montgomery to New York City with his family. A few months before the family's arrival in New York, Lehman Brothers moved to Pearl Street, close to Hanover Square, the heart of the flourishing cotton trade. Though Lehman Brothers would do a sizable business on the coffee and petroleum exchanges, the core of the business remained cotton. By turn of the century, the firm was widely regarded as the country's largest futures and spot cotton house. Its success in the cotton trade was in no small way facilitated by the American cotton crop having more than doubled (in revenue earned) from 1859 to 1899.

After they moved to New York, Mayer and Babette had four more children—Clara born in 1870, Arthur in 1873, Irving in 1876, and Herbert in 1878. The year Irving was born Mayer had a five-floor brownstone residence built at 5 East 62nd Street. The Lehman family occupied the house until the turn of the century, when a widowed Babette moved with her youngest son, Herbert, to an apartment at 175 West 58th Street, where her eldest son Sig, his two boys Allan and Harold, and their families also lived.

Many years later when Herbert was a U.S. senator, his secretary took the following notes as he recalled the house on East 62nd Street:

Front door in middle—Enter hall—at right long parlor furnished in light gold satin—late Victorian furniture. (Children never were in this room).

The three youngest Lehman boys—Herbert, Irving, and Arthur— all students at Dr. Sachs's school, c. 1885. (John L. Loeb Jr.)

"My father-in-law Arthur Lehman [right], senior partner of Lehman Brothers, with his brothers—Herbert [middle], governor of New York, and Irving, justice of the New York State Court of Appeals, the highest court in the state—on December 31, 1934, the day Irving swore in Herbert for another term as governor. They are three of the most different men I've ever known. Arthur was a hardheaded banker. Herbert was a great humanitarian. Irving was a leading jurist and a deeply religious man. They were all outstanding in their particular fields." — John L. Loeb Sr., All in a Lifetime *(John L. Loeb Jr.)*

Children used library on second floor. Bay window in front (no window seat). Furnished in late Victorian furniture—stiff walnut frames—upholstered in mixed green and black brocade. On the right was a mantel (dark wood). Opposite was a door to small room in which the bookcases were.

Governor Lehman's and Judge Lehman's [the future governor's brother Irving, who served as chief judge of the New York State Court of Appeals] bedroom was at back of the house in which there was a double bed. Very plain, simple furniture. This room was very hot in summer and very cold in winter as there was no upper story above it. A second roof, however, was built over it to try to relieve this situation.

The key to the flourishing of this remarkable family lay in its taking full advantage of educational and economic opportunities in the New World that had not existed for Jews in Europe.

Like most German Jews in the America of their day, Mayer and Babette reared their children differently from the way they had been brought up themselves. Mayer had received, in addition to a secular education, a traditional Jewish upbringing, which included reading, writing, and speaking Hebrew, as well as learning German written in Hebrew script. Babette had received an equivalent education given to Jewish girls. Although the couple remained true to their Jewish heritage by eschewing non-kosher food, observing Jewish holidays, attending religious services regularly, and using Hebrew and Judeo-German expressions as a matter of course, their children received little if any formal Jewish education beyond weekly home-based Bible classes.

Instead, their daughters were raised by black nursemaids, who inculcated them with folk wisdom, and European governesses, who taught them German and French. The Lehman boys, after years of a totally secular education at Dr. Sachs's School, went on to Ivy and "Little Ivy" League schools: Sigmund to Cornell, Arthur to

Harvard, Irving to Columbia, and Herbert to Williams. Had Babette and Mayer remained in Europe, in the face of limited social and economic opportunities, they might not have stressed secular studies for their boys as much as they did in America, where, instead of Hebrew, the boys studied Homer, Cicero, and Schiller.

A strong emphasis on secular culture and education made sense to Mayer and Babette—and other "Our Crowd" families as well. Governesses and Ivy League schools were, as they well knew, a trade-off for the Jewish religious learning they would have received in the Old Country. Here in America, where everyone was a fellow American, little time remained for learning even the rudiments of Judaism. Thus, in the 1920s, when Settie Lehman Fatman's grandson Henry Morgenthau III asked his mother, Elinor (Mrs. Henry Morgenthau Jr.), what he should tell the kids at school when they asked him what his religion was, she replied, "Tell them you're an American."

All conformed to the dictates of Reform Judaism, which urged its members to assimilate into the American scene, not religiously but in most other ways. When young Herbert heard his father intoning a prayer in Hebrew over a family Passover seder, he had to leave the room for giggling uncontrollably at what struck him as a totally foreign language.

Herbert nonetheless recalled growing up in a house in which "both my parents' family and my Uncle Emanuel's family would always meet at Passover, on the Jewish high holy days, and on January 1." Herbert adds, "They didn't celebrate Christmas in those days, but celebrated Chanukah. Gifts were always given on January 1, never on Christmas Day"; however, once Babette accepted the first Christmas tree in the family of her daughter Clara, around the turn of the century, the green light was given to Christmas presents on Christmas Day.

When Babette and Mayer moved to New York in 1868, they may very well have expected to continue their free and easy relations with the gentile elite they had enjoyed in the South, where by and large Jews were well received as a people sharing a common European origin.

Mayer Lehman after moving to New York City, c. 1870.
(Henry Morgenthau III)

Babette Neugass Lehman in New York City, c. 1870.
(Henry Morgenthau III)

Jews were accepted as allies on the side of slavery. In the North, by contrast, banks, law firms, and hospitals as a matter of course did not accept Jewish partners or directors. What resulted, in an atmosphere of anti-Semitism not experienced in Montgomery, was the formation of an elite of a few hundred New York German Jewish families of wealth inhabiting a largely self-contained "Our Crowd" world, a universe parallel to that from which they had been excluded.

Living in an inherently exclusionary world, it is hardly surprising that every one of Mayer and Babette's seven children who reached adulthood married fellow Jewish Americans of German origin. Their family names—Altschul, Fatman, Goodhart, Lehman, Lewisohn, Limburg, Straus—are right out of "Our Crowd," as are, with very few exceptions, their children's spouses—the forebears of this book's principal contributors.

What resulted, in the words of Arthur and Adele's daughter Frances (Peter) Lehman Loeb, "was socializing entirely with other Jewish families. This is the way it was when my parents grew up and this is the way it was for me. I don't think there was one non-Jewish boy or girl at the dancing classes at Grandpa Lewisohn's. Unquestionably, we were brought up in a Jewish society even though we were so assimilated there wasn't much Jewish about us."

Although similar in appearance, demeanor, and education to their WASP counterparts, "Our Crowd" families were nonetheless excluded from elite WASP circles simply because they were Jewish. Invariably, this encouraged feelings of discomfort over their religious heritage. "In my parents' home," Frances Lehman Loeb recalled, "one lowered one's voice when one used the word *Jewish*. All sorts of terms were used instead. Once at the dinner table the name of the wife of a well-known personality came up and someone said in a whisper, 'She's Jewish.' And I said in a loud voice, 'Why do you all lower your voices when you say *Jewish*? We are all Jewish here.' They looked at me as if I were crazy."

Perhaps to compensate for providing their children with so little in the way of Jewish learning, Babette and Mayer encouraged them to look upon Jewish philanthropy (*tsedaka*) as their religion, which their oldest child, Sig, did as a founder of Montefiore Hospital, now Montefiore Medical Center, in the Bronx. As a major supporter for many years of the Jewish Home and Hospital for the Aged (still located at West 106th Street and Columbus Avenue), Babette served as an example to her eldest daughter, Hattie, who carried on her mother's work at the Home for the Aged as a trustee and at Mount Sinai Hospital, where Babette had replaced Mayer as a member of the board of trustees after Mayer's death in 1897 and where Hattie's husband, Philip Goodhart, served as a board member from 1907 to 1933. In addition to his interest in Mount Sinai, Philip became a trustee of Temple Emanu-El in 1919 and as a member of the building committee was active in formulating the design of the present edifice. (Modeled after a cathedral in Marseilles, it features a rose window facing Fifth Avenue donated by the Mayer Lehman family.)

Every Sunday without fail, Mayer would take his three youngest children—Arthur, Irving, and Herbert—through the wards of Mount Sinai Hospital to see for themselves both the fruits and the challenges of Jewish philanthropy. All three boys became major philanthropists—Arthur a co-founder of the Federation of Jewish Philanthropies and the Museum of the City of New York, Herbert a staunch supporter of Lillian Wald's Henry Street Settlement House and a founder of the Joint Distribution Committee, and Irving a longtime president of the 92nd Street Y and Temple Emanu-El as well as a frequent and anonymous contributor to a wide range of charitable causes. Through example, Mayer and Babette passed on to their children and grandchildren the rich Jewish tradition of *tsedaka*.

Another tradition passed on to the family was dedication to family. The Lehman brothers and their wives established a set of rules, a pattern of behavior, a hierarchy of values that offered no choice for their offspring but to love, honor, and obey "Papa" and "Mama." Especially "obey." Especially Babette.

"Our Crowd" at play in Elberon, New Jersey, c. 1923. (Left to right): unknown (far left), Edith Limburg, Adele Lehman, Max Rossbach, Arthur Lehman, Franz Lewisohn, Mabel Rossbach. (June Rossbach Bingham Birge)

Babette's youngest son, Herbert, recalled his mother "as near a matriarch as anyone I've ever known." She exercised enormous authority over her family. All of her children were expected to maintain a daily regimen conforming to Babette's needs and whims. In addition to the house at 5 East 62nd Street, her domain included a summer home in Elberon, New Jersey, and, as a part of a prevailing pattern among the German Jewish elite, a camp in the Adirondacks. Babette's children and their families were expected to live nearby, or visit regularly, or at least write to Babette wherever she might be. There were also visits every few years to relatives in Germany, with an entourage of children and grandchildren in tow. To those left behind the only solace were letters from Mama reminding them to be first in everything, to take care of themselves and, lest they forget, to tell Mama "everything." On June 22, 1895, she wrote home from Cunard Steamship Co.'s HMS *Campania*:

My Dear Children, Only a few lines to let you know that thank God we are well and happy. We just left Queenstown. The water is magnificent. . . . Dear Papa looks well, touch wood, and the ocean voyage did him good. Had an excellent stewardess. I can assure you that I didn't once miss Ellen. More than likely she would have been seasick. Meyersohn's maid was sick three or four days. I'm surprised Mrs. Borg's wasn't. Sorry that my children, especially my boys, aren't as good and smart in everything as hers. Am glad it is Friday so that dear Irving will be finished with his exams. . . . I'm anxious to hear if you dear Clara are in Long Branch with the children and how you like it; tell me everything. Be careful in the evening after sundown especially now when it is still cool. . . . Should Irving come to you for a few days don't let him go out at night if possible. Kiss the dear children from me and remind them frequently of us, what you must do that the little ones don't forget us. . . . Have you decided dear Hattie and Settie where you are going and when? Hope you have a very pleasant summer and that you Dear Sigi don't always worry unnecessarily. Dear Harriet [Sig's wife], give your dear Daddy [Emanuel] many cordial greetings. . . . Please dear Settie tell Mrs. Einstein that I thank her for her fruit basket. Has my dear Arthur and little Ella not yet forgotten their grandmother?

In Manhattan all of Babette's children remained close at hand with their growing families. Hattie and Settie lived just across the park in adjoining houses on West 81st Street built for them by their father. Clara, with her husband Richard Limburg and a growing family, resided with Babette and Mayer at 5 East 62nd Street until Mayer's death in 1897. Arthur and Adele were not far off, having been given a house on West 56th Street east of Sixth Avenue, built on a plot of land provided by Adele's father, copper and real estate tycoon Adolph Lewisohn.

Irving lived at home while going to college. Herbert also lived at home until 1895, when he left for Williams College in Massachusetts. After graduating, he lived with his widowed mother until 1910, when he married Edith Altschul. Edith's brother Frank also married into the Lehman family. He married Hattie Lehman Goodhart's daughter Helen. Even after Babette's death in 1920, members of the family stayed in close proximity to one another. Until her death in 1932, Clara resided at the Ambassador Hotel at Park Avenue and 51st Street, just blocks away from the Savoy-Plaza at 59th Street and Fifth Avenue where Settie resided, and The Sherry-Netherland also at 59th Street and Fifth Avenue, where Harriet lived. This was within walking distance of the Herbert Lehmans, who resided at 820 Park Avenue at 75th Street, and the Irving Lehmans, who lived in the West Sixties before moving to the East Seventies. Living in close proximity to one another was a significant factor in maintaining strong family ties.

With Mayer's death in 1897 at the age of sixty-seven and Emanuel's death ten years later, the firm passed into the hands of a second generation of Lehmans. These included Henry's son, Meyer H.; Emanuel's son, Philip; and Mayer's sons, Sigmund, Arthur, and Herbert, the latter joining the firm after Sig retired in 1908. Until 1924, nearly seventy-five years after the firm was founded, all the partners were named Lehman. Even if you were a descendant, you couldn't join the firm if your name wasn't Lehman. John L. Loeb Jr. recalls that his father "couldn't get a job at Lehman Brothers when he wanted to work on Wall Street. They wouldn't hire any in-laws, and in fact for years I don't think there was even a descendant who had a name other than Lehman who got a job."

During much of its rise to prominence, Lehman Brothers had been occupied with trading in basic commodities such as sugar, grain, cotton, petroleum, and coffee. It wasn't until the second generation took over that the character of Lehman Brothers was altered from "merchant" to "investment" bankers. This was done through the financing by Lehman Brothers of Jewish-owned and Jewish-run businesses—such as Philip Morris and Sears, Roebuck as well as numerous department stores, textile manufacturers, clothing manufacturers, and five-and-ten cent operations—that private bankers had hitherto passed by.

The results were extremely profitable. Riding the crest of a burst of technological innovation, the Lehmans were destined to take the high road that led the firm inexorably into the ranks of America's foremost banking institutions. A major step in that direction resulted from a fateful meeting over a backyard fence between Emanuel's son, Philip, and his counterpart at Goldman, Sachs.

Robert Bernhard, great-grandson of Babette and Mayer Lehman and a former partner of Lehman Brothers, was told about that momentous event, which occurred in 1903:

Lehman Brothers got into the investment banking business at the turn of the century. Goldman, Sachs & Co. was then in the commercial paper business, and Lehman Brothers was in the cotton-trading business. A senior partner of

Babette and Mayer Lehman, progenitors of the seven siblings who are the subjects of this book. (Portraits by C. Volkman, photographed by Richard Valencia, London; courtesy of Lord and Lady William Goodhart)

Goldman, Sachs and his family had a summer place in Elberon, New Jersey, and so did Philip Lehman and his family. They were back-to-back neighbors.

In the course of looking for clients for commercial paper, the fellows at Goldman, Sachs ran into a new and emerging retail company called Sears, Roebuck. They wanted to do a public offering. Goldman had been doing commercial paper with Sears, but did not have the capital to do the underwriting. So across the fence in Elberon, Philip was asked to go into the investment banking business, with Goldman the main partner and Lehman supplying the money.

Between 1903 and 1926 they did a number of deals, some brought in by Goldman and some by Lehman. Their clients included many leaders in the garment and retail industries of German Jewish origin, such as the Gimbels and the Lazaruses, who formed Federated Department Stores and who were also friends of the Lehman family.

In 1926 a new generation of partners in both firms decided that Goldman didn't need Lehman any longer to supply the capital and Lehman didn't need Goldman to bring in the clients. So a letter of agreement was signed dividing the business into four parts—Goldman clients, Lehman clients, and clients in which either Goldman or Lehman would be the principal partner.

A generation separates the oldest from the youngest of Mayer and Babette's seven children. Sig was born in 1859, and Herbert almost twenty years later. They divide coveniently into an older group—Sig, Hattie, Settie, and Clara—and a younger group—Arthur, Irving, and Herbert.

The groups—including their spouses—differ radically from one another. The women of the older group (Harriet, Hattie, Settie, and Clara), with the exception of philanthropic work, confined their activities mostly to the home; however, the women of the younger group—Adele, Sissie (wife of Irving Lehman), and Edith—widened their horizons by entering the public arena as staunch supporters of their husbands or by developing public images in their own right as philanthropists and patrons of the arts.

Major differences also existed between the older sisters—Hattie, Settie, and Clara—and the younger brothers—Arthur, Irving, and Herbert. The women are remembered almost invariably as difficult and demanding, their younger brothers as warm, friendly, and funny.

Many of the recollections that follow come from the grandchildren, grandnieces, and grand-nephews of Mayer and Babette Lehman's seven children and their spouses. Some were written for this book, a few were quoted from published sources, others were taken from oral histories and private memoirs of family members no longer living; many more were based on taped interviews.

Collectively they constitute a major link to the world of "Our Crowd." When the last of our contributors goes, a vital connection with the past goes with them. All the more reason to benefit from what the Mayer Lehman family has to say about a rich and vibrant world that is no more.

CHAPTER ONE

Mayer Lehman & Babette Neugass Lehman

———◈———

IN 1850 MAYER LEHMAN TRAVELED as a twenty-year-old from Rimpar, Bavaria, to Montgomery, Alabama, to join his brothers Henry and Emanuel in the cotton trade. On a business trip to New Orleans, Mayer courted Babette Neugass, who had immigrated to the United States from Rieneck, a neighboring town of Rimpar. Mayer and Babette were married in New

Orleans in 1858. The Lehmans became prosperous within a short time.

Their four eldest children—Sigmund, originally named Sigismund (1859), Hattie (1861), Lisette, but always known as Settie (1863), and Benjamin, who died in infancy (1865)—were born in Montgomery and lived in a large house in the best part of town. In 1868 the Lehmans moved to New York City, where Clara (1870), Arthur (1873), Irving (1876), and Herbert (1878) were born. Mayer was a brilliant businessman: Among his many accomplishments, he was one of the founders of the New York Cotton Exchange. As philanthropists, Mayer and Babette set an example for their children, with Mount Sinai Hospital, Temple Emanu-El, and the Jewish Home and Hospital for the Aged high on their list of priorities.

Mayer Lehman & Babette Neugass Lehman

Mayer
Lehman
1830 - 1897

| Sigmund Lehman 1859 - 1930 | Harriet Lehman 1861 - 1944 | Hattie Lehman 1861 - 1948 | Philip Goodhart 1857 - 1944 | Settie Lehman 1863 - 1936 | Morris Fatman 1858 - 1930 | Benjamin Lehman 1865 - 1865 |

Babette
Neugass
1838 - 1919

Clara   *Richard*   **Arthur**   *Adele*   **Irving**   *Sissie*   **Herbert**   *Edith*
Lehman = *Limburg*   **Lehman** = *Lewisohn*   **Lehman** = *Straus*   **Lehman** = *Altschul*
1870 - 1932   *1857 - 1916*   **1873 - 1936**   *1882 - 1965*   **1876 - 1945**   *1879 - 1950*   **1878 - 1963**   *1889 - 1976*

Mayer Lehman: husband, father, businessman, philanthropist, c. 1890. (John D. Gordan III)

Mayer Lehman

1830–1897

———◆———

New York Times, June 22, 1897

MAYER LEHMAN IS DEAD

Was Taken Ill Last Friday and Succumbs to an Operation Performed on Sunday.

Mayer Lehman, a prominent merchant of this city and a member of the firm of Lehman Brothers, 22 William Street, died yesterday afternoon at 4 o'clock after an illness of only four days, at his residence, 5 East Sixty-second Street. He was taken ill last Friday, and Sunday Dr. Gerster performed an operation on him for gangrene. He sank rapidly and death followed.

Mr. Lehman was born Jan. 9, 1830, at Rimpa[r], near Würzburg, Bavaria, and was educated in the public schools of Würzburg. At the age of [twenty] he came to this country and settled with his brothers in Montgomery, Ala., where [they] started the firm of

Lehman Brothers. . . .[He went into business for himself but again joined his brothers in 1863.] The following year Mr. Lehman was appointed by the Governor of Alabama a Commissioner to visit the Confederate soldiers confined in the Northern prisons.

In 1867 Mr. Lehman came to New York, and has lived here ever since, for the past twenty years in the house where he died. Aside from his active interest in the firm of which he was a member, he has been largely identified with railroad, mining, and industrial enterprises, and was one of the twenty men who established the first iron furnace in the South before the war.

Mr. Lehman was a member of the Harmonie Club and a number of charitable organizations, taking especial interest in the Mount Sinai Hospital and Training School, to which he frequently contributed large sums. He was also a Director in the Hamilton Bank and in the N. K. Fairbank Company.

In 1858 Mr. Lehman married Miss Babett[e], daughter of Isaac Newgoff [sic] of New Orleans. She survives him, as do four sons–Sigismund M., Arthur, Irving, and Herbert–and three daughters–Mrs. Hattie Goodhart, Mrs. S. Fatman, and Mrs. Clara Limburger.

Funeral services will be held at Temple Emanu-El next Thursday morning at 9:30, the Rev. Dr. Gustav Gottheil officiating. Interment will be at Cypress Hills.

—◦—

New York Times, June 25, 1897

MAYER LEHMAN BURIED

. . . . Funeral Services for Mayer Lehman, who died Monday, were held yesterday morning at Temple Emanu-El, Forty-third Street and Fifth Avenue, the Rev. Dr. Gustav Gottheil officiating.

Shortly before the time appointed for the public services, Dr Gottheil held a special service at the family home, 5 East Sixty-second Street.

After music had been rendered by the full choir, Dr. Gottheil delivered a eulogy upon the life and achievements of Mr. Lehman, choosing for his text the verse, "As the whirlwind passeth by the wicked, but the righteous are the foundation of the world."

"Our brother here," said Dr. Gottheil, "easily saw that the righteous are the foundation of the world, for he and his brothers by the work of their hands and by using their natural abilities with economy and foresight, and especially with justice, secured the fortune which they deserved. The crown of a good name shineth forth from this casket. 'Tis a heritage of which his sorrowing relatives and friends may well be proud.

". . . How many hearts he has made glad! How many sufferers send their mute appeal to God for him to-day! He toiled and labored in the field of charity with all the zeal that he did elsewhere. He was also a pious man. He leaned on his people's God and on his God's people. His death leaves a painful void that can never be filled."

Prayer was then offered, and the casket was carried out, the twenty pallbearers preceding it and standing with uncovered heads as it was placed in the hearse. The casket, as well as the altar, was covered with flowers. Among the floral pieces were wreaths from the Cotton Exchange, Mount Sinai Hospital, and the Whitney National Bank of New Orleans.

The Temple was crowded with the many friends and relatives of the Lehman family. Delegations were present from the Cotton Exchange and other institutions with which Mr. Lehman was connected. The Cotton Exchange closed at 10 o'clock A. M. as a mark of respect to his memory.

The burial was in the cemetery at Cypress Hills. There were simple services at the grave. Five carriage loads of flowers and more than a score of carriages filled with mourners accompanied the body to its last resting place.

———⋗◈⋖———

Shortly after Mayer Lehman's death, his next-to-youngest son Irving (1876-1945) wrote to his Aunt Esther's husband, Isaias Hellman, his mother's brother-in-law and a close member of the family. (Hellman founded the first bank in Los Angeles and later became president of the Wells Fargo–Nevada Bank in San Francisco.)

Elberon, N.J.
June 30, 1897

My dear Uncle—

We received your kind letter yesterday and though with heavy heart I hasten to answer it. I am afraid that in the worry of the last week, no one felt able to write to you more than the bare facts of our beloved father's death. He had absolutely no warning that there was anything serious the matter until about the end. He complained for a few days and particularly on Friday night of pains and though we called in both Dr. Adler and Dr. Kauffman, a specialist, they both assured us it was only colic. . . . on Sunday they decided to call in a surgeon who told us 2 hours later that there was no hope and on Monday he died peacefully and in his sleep. Our only comfort is that he died without pain & unconscious of his approaching end and before sorrow had darkened his almost perfect life. Dear Mama is of course heart broken but bears up bravely for our sake. She is down here with Clara [Limburg, Mayer and Babette's youngest daughter] & will shortly go to the Catskills. She is perfectly composed and well and of course my dear sisters do not leave her, so I am much obliged at your kind offer to have dear Auntie [Esther

Neugass Hellman] come but I feel that she is really not needed now by Mama. Arthur [Irving's older brother] is expected next Friday. I hope you will excuse these distraught lines but I hardly feel able to write.

Your loving nephew, Irving

———◆———

Mayer's youngest son, Herbert (1878-1963), dictated an oral history late in life in which he remembered his father taking him and his brothers out for a ride every morning after breakfast.

My father loved driving and he'd take us kids out. We'd have breakfast pretty early, at half past seven. My father stabled the horses at McGrath's between 59th and 60th Streets. They would be brought over to 5 East 62nd Street, and my father would take one of his sons each morning to drive with him. We had what was called a T-Cart, a very heavy vehicle with a driver's seat, another seat next to the driver, and a seat in back where two or three people could sit.

Father got a lot of pleasure out of driving this thing. He would drop us off at school, turn over the horses to the groom from the stable and then go downtown. We never called him Dad or Father. We called him "Papa" and we called mother "Mama." Always.

———◆———

Shortly after Herbert entered Williams College, Mayer wrote his youngest son the following letter of practical advice.

September 27, 1895

My dear Herbert,

I wanted to write you a long letter to give you my advice and ideas about different things; however, dear Arthur has more experience and promised me to do it instead; only one thing I urge you to do: use your time advantageously, the four years pass quickly and don't come back. Don't do anything of which you have to be ashamed. Should you, however, with or without your fault, get into trouble, call on me as your best intimate friend and don't hide anything from me. We have great hopes for your advancement and won't spare anything to promote your career. Do your part towards it. Write often. You are in good company who, like you, don't do anything wrong. Stay away from chaps who have less good manners. I'm feeling quite well again. Lots of love from dear Mother.

Your faithful father Mayer

Dear Arthur is sending you a check. I'm going to give you $1,000. Should you need more next year I shall increase it somewhat.

Babette Neugass Lehman, remembered by her youngest son, Governor Herbert Lehman, "as near a matriarch as anyone I've ever known." (Herbert H. Lehman Suite & Papers, Columbia University)

Babette Neugass Lehman

1838–1919

⪡══◆══⪢

New York Times, August 26, 1919

Lehman. On Monday, Aug. 25, at Port Chester, N.Y., Babette Lehman, widow of Mayer Lehman, in her 83d year. Funeral services will be held at the chapel of Salem Fields on Wednesday morning, Aug. 27, at 11 o'clock. Kindly omit flowers.

In letters written to her youngest son, Herbert, at Williams College, Babette Neugass Lehman excelled as a dispenser of motherly advice.

New York, October, 1897
My dear Herbert,
I hope you're wearing your heavy underwear, don't be careless about your shoes, and take care that you won't catch cold. . . .

New York, October 11, 1897
My dear good Herbert,
. . . it's still too early for goose chiblings. They'll only be available next month. I can send you plenty of sugar cookies, and let me know what else. . . . we still miss you. . . . Time hangs heavy on my hands until you come.

New York, March 26, 1899
My dear good Herbert,
How I would love to convey to you verbally my very heartfelt congratulations upon your 21st birthday and give you a warm kiss. It does not need your birthday for me to wish you everything good imaginable because I do this every day. If God grants a favorable hearing to all my wishes, you dear Herbert will lead a joyful and happy life to a ripe old age. But there is much which we ourselves can and must contribute towards it and if dear Herbert you ask yourself in your deeds and actions, would my good father approve or advise this and then act accordingly, you will undoubtedly be lucky and blessed. How often we made plans for you. May God fulfill them. . . .

Would have liked to have sent you a box, dear Herbert. But one can't get half a goose any more and due to Pesech Easter I couldn't pack along a sugar cake.

———◆———

HERBERT H. LEHMAN (1878–1963), *youngest son of Mayer and Babette Lehman* – I remember my mother as a much more positive character than my father. She was very kindly but very firm. All the disciplining of the children was left to

Babette Neugass Lehman in New York City early in her career as a German Jewish matriarch. (Henry Morgenthau III)

my mother. My father hated like the deuce to punish, or even to scold us too hard. My mother was a disciplinarian, but always absolutely fair with the children as well as the household. I used to writhe at the scolding my mother gave to a maid who had been delinquent, but I don't think anyone ever left my mother.

I don't think my father ever took an important step in business without consultation with my mother. She had a very, very keen and practical mind, and she was very, very much a factor in the family life, during and after my father's lifetime. She was as near a matriarch as anyone I've ever known. I don't think a day passed that every member of the family failed to call on my mother, until her death in 1919. Her daughters went driving with her daily in the park. We boys used to stop in late in the afternoon from business and tell her all our troubles. I don't know of any case where a woman was so definitely the head of the family as was my mother. And that went right down not only to her children but also to her grandchildren and great-grandchildren.[1]

HELEN LEHMAN BUTTENWIESER (1905–1989), *granddaughter of Mayer and Babette Lehman; daughter of Arthur and Adele Lehman* – My grandmother was really like a little tyrant. My father was required to visit her every day. If it was snowing terribly, he would have to call and ask to be excused. I think my father liked her, but nobody else did. She was actually a likeable person, just a little bit snappy. She used to spend a few weeks in the summer with us, and we didn't like it because she wouldn't let us embroider on Saturday. Since we weren't religious, it seemed pretty silly. But I don't remember not liking her; she just bossed everybody around. She used to give us peppermints when we visited her. We had to go every Sunday, and then we got our peppermint.[2]

—⊰◆⊱—

FRANCES LEHMAN LOEB (1906–1996), *granddaughter of Mayer and Babette Lehman; daughter of Arthur and Adele Lehman* – Grandma Lewisohn was a shadowy figure to me who died before I was ten. I knew my Grandmother Lehman much better. She lived quite near us in an apartment house on the corner of 58th Street and Seventh Avenue. My Uncle Sig and my Aunt Harriet had their home in the same apartment house, as did their sons Allan and Harold and their families.

Every Sunday morning when I was a little girl and we were in town, we would walk over and visit with Grandma Lehman. She was in her late seventies, but she dressed as if she were ninety, always in black. Her hair was thin and gray and wound up in the back. She wore a little purple pin similar to what you would use to attach an orchid to your shoulder. At the dining room table, Grandma Lehman used the pin to attach a napkin to her blouse. She was quite short, and she was not pretty, but to me she had a sweet face.

Grandma Lehman was a demanding matriarch. Each of her children visited her every day, including Daddy, who went straight from his office to tell her everything that had happened at Lehman Brothers. By the time he got home, he didn't want to talk about business anymore.

Grandma Lehman came to visit us in Elberon every summer for about three weeks. Mother hated it. In the first place, Grandma always moved all the furniture around. In the second place, she'd complain terribly about how Mother was bringing up both Dorothy and Helen.[3]

⟡

HENRY MORGENTHAU III, *great-grandson of Mayer and Babette Lehman; grandnephew of Clara Lehman Limburg* – Clara was the first one in the family to have a Christmas tree. Grandma Lehman would visit various members of the family on a Sunday, and they were all scared to death as to what she would say when she saw the tree because they never had a Christmas tree in the family. So she came in, she looked at it, and exclaimed, "Oh, isn't it lovely." Everyone breathed a sigh of relief, and from then on her children always had Christmas trees.

⟡

JUNE ROSSBACH BINGHAM BIRGE, *great-granddaughter of Mayer and Babette Lehman; granddaughter*

Babette Neugass Lehman, both loved and feared by her family, New York, c. 1900.
(Herbert H. Lehman Suite & Papers, Columbia University)

of Clara Lehman Limburg – Babette was dead before I was born, but still alive when my second brother, Dick Rossbach, appeared. Grandma Lehman came to pay the requisite new-baby call on my mother, took one look at a sickly little boy, and announced, "That one will never make it." This kind of brutal honesty was typical of Jewish matriarchs, as I was reminded of last week when I ran into ninety-four-year-old Kitty Carlisle Hart on Fifth Avenue. We stopped to chat. "Your glasses are dirty," she said. "Your teeth are clean, but your glasses are dirty." I don't think she knew why I burst out laughing, but there, in front of me, was an embodiment of my mother, Mabel Rossbach, my grandmother Clara Limburg, and my great-grandmother Babette Lehman.

<hr />

1. Herbert H. Lehman Suite & Papers. Columbia University.

2. Archives of Henry Morgenthau III.

3. John Langeloth Loeb and Frances Lehman Loeb, with Kenneth Libo. *All in a Lifetime: A Personal Memoir.* New York: John L. Loeb Jr., 1996.

CHAPTER TWO

Sigmund M. Lehman & Harriet M. Lehman Lehman

MAYER AND BABETTE'S OLDEST CHILD Sigmund was born in Montgomery, Alabama, in 1859. Nine years later Mayer and Babette moved with their family to New York. A graduate of Cornell University, Sig—as he was called—subsequently married his first cousin Harriet, the daughter of Emanuel, Mayer's sole partner at Lehman Brothers for over a generation. Sig remained active in the firm until his retirement in 1908.

Sig and Harriet spent much of the rest of their lives either in their sumptuous West 58th Street residence, at their weekend home in Tarrytown, New York, or on regular family visits to Bavaria with stop-offs in London and Paris (where Sig died in 1930). They also spent a great deal of time at Runnymede, a family camp bordering Quebec where Sig enjoyed fishing, and Kildare in the Adirondacks, a camp owned by Harriet and her sister Evelyn, which they bought in the late 19th century.

Sig and Harriet's older son Harold married into the socially prominent Seligman family, whose patriarch Joe Seligman was asked by President Ulysses S. Grant to be his treasury secretary, an offer that he declined. Sig and Harriet's grandchild Orin, born to their son Allan and his wife Evelyn Schiffer, is the last of Mayer and Babette's male descendants to bear the Lehman family name. The name, however, is carried on through the male descendants of Emanuel, Mayer's brother. They include Robert Lehman's son Robin and his three sons Philip, Jason, and Rolf.

Sigmund Lehman & Harriet Lehman Lehman

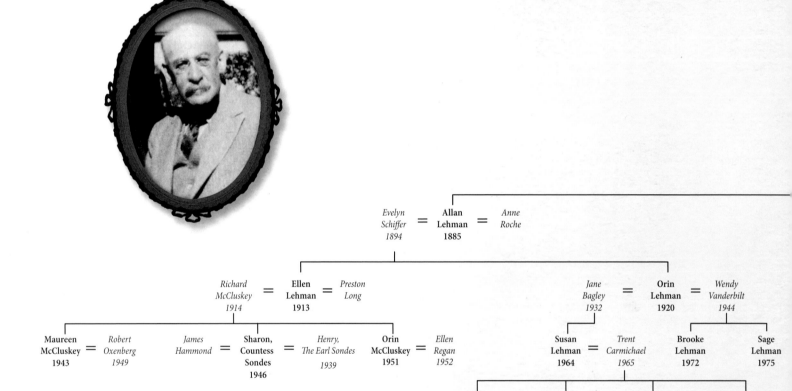

Evelyn Schiffer 1894 = **Allan Lehman** 1885 = *Anne Roche*

Richard McCluskey 1914 = **Ellen Lehman** 1913 = *Preston Long*

Jane Bagley 1932 = **Orin Lehman** 1920 = *Wendy Vanderbilt* 1944

Maureen McCluskey 1943 = *Robert Oxenberg* 1949

James Hammond = **Sharon, Countess Sondes** 1946 = *Henry, The Earl Sondes* 1939

Orin McCluskey 1951 = *Ellen Regan* 1952

Susan Lehman 1964 = *Trent Carmichael* 1965

Brooke Lehman 1972

Sage Lehman 1975

Avery Carmichael 1995

Haley Carmichael 1996

Ryan Carmichael 1999

Whitney Carmichael 2002

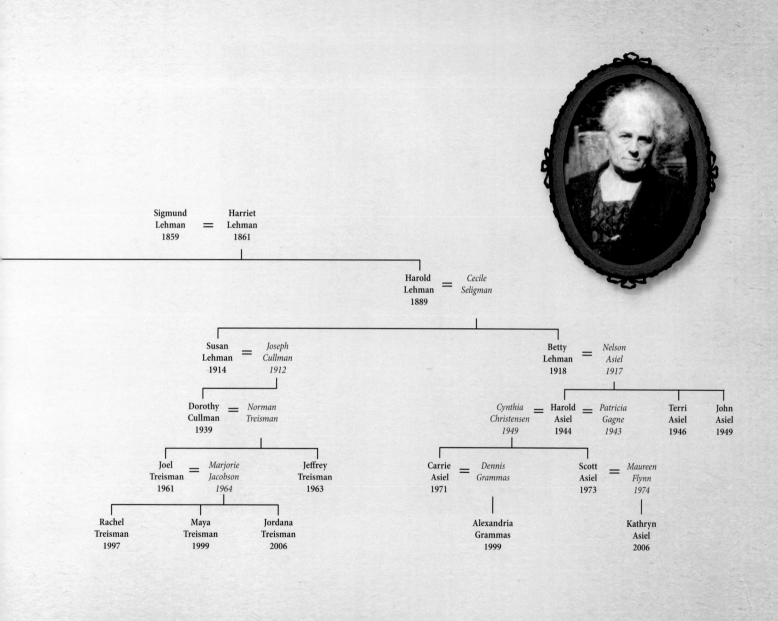

Sigmund
Lehman
1859
=
Harriet
Lehman
1861

Harold
Lehman
1889
=
*Cecile
Seligman*

Susan
Lehman
1914
=
*Joseph
Cullman
1912*

Betty
Lehman
1918
=
*Nelson
Asiel
1917*

Dorothy
Cullman
1939
=
*Norman
Treisman*

*Cynthia
Christensen
1949*
=
Harold
Asiel
1944
=
*Patricia
Gagne
1943*

Terri
Asiel
1946

John
Asiel
1949

Joel
Treisman
1961
=
*Marjorie
Jacobson
1964*

Jeffrey
Treisman
1963

Carrie
Asiel
1971
=
*Dennis
Grammas*

Scott
Asiel
1973
=
*Maureen
Flynn
1974*

Rachel
Treisman
1997

Maya
Treisman
1999

Jordana
Treisman
2006

Alexandria
Grammas
1999

Kathryn
Asiel
2006

Sigmund M. Lehman, Mayer and Babette's eldest child, retired from Lehman Brothers in 1908 and devoted the rest of his life to leisurely pursuits. (Dorothy Treisman; Joel Treisman)

Sigmund M. Lehman

1859–1930

———⊰◆⊱———

New York Times, April 8, 1930

S.M. LEHMAN DIES SUDDENLY IN PARIS

Retired International Banker and Brother of Lieutenant Governor Was 71.

A GRADUATE OF CORNELL

Entered Family Business in 1879 and Remained Until 1908—Traveled Much Since Then.

Special Cable to THE NEW YORK TIMES.

PARIS, April 7.—Sigmund M. Lehman, retired New York banker, who arrived at the Hotel Ritz here with his wife from Cannes four days ago, died suddenly of heart disease this morning. He was 71 years old.

Mr. and Mrs. Lehman had intended to sail for New York from Cherbourg on Wednesday. Their son [Harold] who was in Berlin, was promptly notified this morning by his mother of his father's death and he arrived in Paris late tonight.

The body will be taken to America for burial, probably on a boat leaving on Wednesday.

Special to The New York Times.

ALBANY, April 7. Lieut. Gov. Herbert H. Lehman received word today of the death of his brother, S.M. Lehman, in Paris. Mr. Lehman was a member of the firm of Lehman Brothers, international bankers, for about thirty years. He retired in 1908 and has spent much time traveling since then.

Besides the Lieutenant Governor, he is survived by his widow, two sons, two brothers, Judge Irving Lehman of the Court of Appeals and Arthur Lehman of the firm of Lehman Brothers, and three sisters.

Mr. Lehman was graduated from Cornell University in the class of 1878 and later went into the firm of Lehman Brothers, which was founded by his father and uncle.

Sigmund M. Lehman was born in Montgomery, Ala., but was brought up in New York as a child and received his early education in this city. After his graduation from Cornell he went to Germany, where he studied for a year before entering business. He was one of the earliest members of the New York Stock Exchange. He was also one of the founders and a director of Montefiore Hospital.

Mr. and Mrs. Lehman left their New York home, 270 Park Avenue, in February for Europe. Mr. Lehman's death was unexpected, his son, Harold, said yesterday, as last communications reported that he was enjoying good health.

New York Times, November 3, 1931
[condensed and abridged]

Sigmund M. Lehman left an estate appraised yesterday at $4,088,060. Mr. Lehman gave a life interest in his real estate to his wife Harriet M. Lehman of the Hotel Sherry Netherlands. The real estate included the country place in South Broadway, Tarrytown, and a half interest in the Kildare Club at Piercefield, St. Lawrence County.

Mr. Lehman left $100,000 to the executors to be distributed to charities at their discretion. His sons, Allan S. and Harold M. Lehman, each received a life interest of $1,139,717 in the residue. Mr. Lehman gave $100,000 for life to four grandchildren. The estate owes $20,000 to Kensico Cemetery for a plot and $33,540 for a mausoleum.

———◦◆◦———

One Hundred Years of Lehman Brothers
Privately printed by Lehman Brothers, 1950.
[condensed and abridged]

Sigmund M. Lehman, the first-born child of Mayer and Babette, joined Lehman Brothers in 1878, on leaving Cornell. His first salary on record was the then princely sum of $25 a week. Four years later, on September 1, 1882, he was made a partner, with a 5 per cent share in earnings as a starter. A seat on the New York Stock Exchange was bought in Sigmund's name in 1887. His cousin Philip, Emanuel's only son, began at $20 a week in 1882, the year Sigmund was made a partner. In 1885, the year Philip was made a partner, the New York earnings were split as follows. The founding partners took 65 per cent. Henry's son, Meyer H., and Sigmund received 12 per cent and Philip 10 per cent. Arthur became a partner in 1898 and Herbert in 1908, the year Sig retired.

To avoid distortion of the historical panorama, it should be borne in mind that

"Here are my grandfather and grandmother, Sig and Harriet Lehman, sitting in a boat at Runnymede Lodge in New Brunswick, where my grandfather apparently enjoyed fishing in a tie." —Orin Lehman (Orin Lehman)

The lodge at Runnymede. (Orin Lehman)

"Sig and Harriet relaxing with my father, Allan, at Runnymede Lodge." —Orin Lehman (Orin Lehman)

Lehman Brothers in 1908 devoted most of its time to the commodities markets. As late as 1911, when Herbert made a business tour of England and the Continent, his visits to investment bank correspondents in London and Paris were incidental and secondary. His main assignment was to mend commodities fences.

Philip and Sigmund Lehman's participation in the launching of the Electric Vehicle Company in 1897 was indicative of the firm's interest in new advances in technology. They, with John Jacob Astor, P.A.B. Widener and others, became directors of the company which, in the initial fifteen years of the automotive pioneering boom, collected a royalty from all manufacturers until Henry Ford put an end to their monopoly.

Sigmund retired in 1908. In 1918 the firm consisted of Philip, Arthur, Herbert, and Sigmund's sons, Harold and Allan. Besides the family partners, there was a staff of approximately twelve, its small size due to Goldman, Sachs & Co. shouldering most of the mechanical and sales aspects of the securities issues from 1906 to 1916, when, together with Lehman Brothers, they underwrote and publicly issued securities for seventeen companies.

Harriet Lehman and her daughter-in-law, Cecile Seligman Lehman. Harriet, the daughter of Emanuel Lehman, married Sigmund, the son of her father's brother Mayer. The marriage of first cousins was not unusual at the time. (Dorothy Treisman; Joel Treisman)

Harriet M. Lehman Lehman

1861–1944

———◆———

New York Times, July 13, 1944

MRS. SIGMUND LEHMAN, WIDOW OF BANKER, 83

Special to The New York Times.

Tarrytown, N.Y., July 13.—Mrs. Harriet M. Lehman of 461 South Broadway, widow of Sigmund Lehman, once a member of the New York banking firm of Lehman Brothers and a brother of former Gov. Herbert H. Lehman and Chief Justice Irving Lehman of the Court of Appeals, died today in the Tarrytown Hospital. Her age was 83.

Mrs. Lehman was a daughter of Emanuel Lehman, a founder of Lehman Brothers, and Mrs. Pauline Sondheim Lehman. She was born in Germany during a visit there of her mother, a United States citizen, and was also a first cousin of Governor Lehman and of her husband, through her father, whose brother, Mayer, was the Governor's father.

She had lived chiefly in Tarrytown for the last twenty-eight years, and had a city home at the Sherry-Netherlands Hotel, New York.

Sigmund Lehman died in Paris in 1930, leaving a gross estate of more than $4,000,000.

Surviving are a son, Allan S. Lehman of Tarrytown, a brother, Philip Lehman of New York, four grandchildren and three great-grandchildren.

A funeral service will be held at her residence here at 11 A.M. on Sunday.

———◇———

WILLIAM MAYER, *grandson of Harriet Lehman's sister, Evelyn Lehman Ehrich* – I have vivid recollections of Aunt Harriet, the sister of my grandmother Evelyn Ehrich and co-owner with her of Kildare [the family camp in the Adirondacks]. I believe it was bought around 1896. She wasn't there that often, so it was a great event when she came to Kildare with a huge steamer trunk. You got the feeling (which was wrong) that she would be around for a long time. She had very strong glasses—at least her eyes were bigger than any I had ever seen. She had a spoiled lapdog called Sunny. Unlike most dogs, Sunny ate only the very top cuts of meat. I was quite sure that the sirloin was pushed aside in favor of tenderloin.

Aunt Harriet came to dinner wearing a very large emerald ring, representing to me as a child a kind of royal quality I thought Aunt Harriet had. She seemed less of a matriarch than my grandmother. She loved to gamble, which to me brought to mind images of slot machines in Arizona. Her suite at Kildare is still associated with her name—a bay window and

Sig and Harriet in August 1925. (Dorothy Treisman; Joel Treisman)

handsome bedroom for her, with a small adjoining one for her attendant, Miss Borman. Harriet seemed more like a guest than a host at Kildare, although she was co-owner.

There was a very long dining room table, which could accommodate as many as thirty guests. Aunt Harriet would sit at one end and her sister Evelyn at the other end. When they had a conversation, often involving rivalries, I've been told, all table talk ceased as everyone looked down at his or her plate. They both had a fierce love of the place; however, in retrospect, it seems slightly incongruous to me that Aunt Harriet parked herself in the midst of a dense wilderness every summer; but she did, and her descendants are still doing the same.

Kildare

———

Kildare was originally formed in 1892 as a hunting and fishing club by William Seward Webb and Frederick W. Vanderbilt, along with several others, before it was sold a few years later to Harriet Lehman Lehman and her sister, Evelyn Lehman Ehrich. Harriet and Evelyn were the daughters of Emanuel Lehman, and Harriet had married her first cousin Sigmund Lehman. Kildare became a major focus and center of enjoyment for the entire Mayer and Emanuel clan and their descendants. Its 10,000-acre spread was remarkable enough to have commanded three pages in Harvey Kaiser's classic Great Camps of the Adirondacks, *first published in 1982.*

———

PETER FRIEDMAN, *grandson of Evelyn Lehman Ehrich; son of Ralph and Ruth Friedman* – My grandmother Evelyn Lehman Ehrich and her sister

Harriet Lehman Lehman were joint owners of Kildare, a family camp in the Adirondacks that, according to an exchange of letters in the 1890s between my grandfather and a lawyer representing the owners, they bought from the Vanderbilts. My parents went up there every summer. The families of Emanuel and Mayer were not there together as a rule, but took turns. When my mother first brought my father to Kildare before they were married, she said, "It's a little bigger than I think it ought to be, but I think you'll like it."

The big building was referred to as the Clubhouse. The original building had burned down in 1906 or so and was rebuilt a few years later somewhat along the same lines—logs with bark outside and a shingle roof. There are three fireplaces—one in the dining room; one in the living room, called the Billiard Room; and one in the Red Room, called that because of its décor. Kildare was originally a fishing and hunting club. The mounted fish in the Red Room came from Jordan Lake, right outside the house, or from a nearby creek called the

Jordan River. Some were brought back from Canada or Florida by Allan Lehman [Sigmund and Harriet's son], Jules Ehrich [husband of Harriet's sister Evelyn], or Joe Cullman [husband of Sigmund and Harriet's granddaughter Sue Lehman] and their friends.

There were at various times cottages for different branches of the family, like the Cullman-Asiel cottage and the Mayer cottage. In the overflow of the summer they would set up tents on a wooden base. The camp had a barn that housed the horses and a hayloft. There was also a cowshed and a workshop. I can recall helping to milk a cow. There was a chicken coop, where we could gather eggs, and an icehouse filled with ice cut from the lake. Water was pumped from the lake for bathing and dishwashing. For drinking, water was hauled up in buckets from a natural spring, with a small house built around it.

The staff consisted of a superintendent, his wife, and their relatives. They led hunting and fishing parties and lived in a separate building called the Guides' House. Some of them were also excellent mechanics and plumbers. One of the early superintendents, John Watson, once lost a toe while chopping something with an axe. "Well, there warn't much meat on it," was his response, according to what I was told.

I remember a tradition of making ice cream on Sunday in a big churn packed with rock salt, which I helped to turn. Other activities included swimming, canoeing on the lake, picnics—an old tradition that went way back—and tennis. My father enjoyed bird-watching with his friends. They would do a "masquerade night" sometimes. Charades were very big, as was singing informally. There was an out-of-tune piano off to the side as well as a player piano with music rolls.

Ferdie the Hermit lived in a shack he had built on nearby land, owned by the Ovalwood Dish Company, on which he had established title by adverse possession ("squatters rights"). The story is that he was from Denmark or Sweden and had become a hermit after a disappointed love affair. He wasn't a hermit on parade. He was a genuine hermit, so we didn't see much of him.

He sometimes brought us some trout, which he claimed to have caught on state land, rather than on our land. He did the carving over the dining room fireplace containing an adaptation of the first stanza of a poem by Sir Walter Scott, beginning "Merrie it is in the good green wood . . . ." The rest of the poem is hanging on a plaque on one wall of the dining room. Once a week we brought Ferdie's mail and some groceries to him from Tupper Lake; we left them for him in a box he had set up where the trail to his cabin met the Kildare road.

The picnics were a big thing at Kildare. They were held at a place called Pirate's Point, across the lake, which you could get to by canoe or walk around to it. There was always the same set menu from generation to generation. The superintendent did the grilling, aided by some of the male staff. Steak would be grilled and corn on the cob put into embers of the fire. There were home-fried potatoes and home-fried onions. The first course was always sardines on toast, and pancakes were the dessert. They made their own maple sugar and maple

The main house at Kildare, with a porch overlooking the lake. (Dorothy Treisman; Joel Treisman)

Aerial shot of Kildare. (Dorothy Treisman; Joel Treisman)

The porch of the main house, a venue of many pleasant Adirondack activities. (Dorothy Treisman; Joel Treisman)

An interior shot, showing the main dining area and one of the home's three fireplaces. (Dorothy Treisman; Joel Treisman)

syrup. As a kid I remember having dark maple sugar on cereal. Today I can't find it anywhere but one place in Quebec.

———◆———

JOHN L. LOEB JR., *grandnephew of Sigmund and Harriet Lehman; grandson of Arthur and Adele Lehman* – Kildare is still owned by the family. On the Harriet Lehman side, one of the primary owners is Dorothy Treisman, the only daughter of Joe Cullman and Sue Lehman, one of two daughters of Harriet's younger son Harold. The Asiels also have an interest through Sue's younger sister Betty. As for Evelyn's side, her daughter Ruth married Ralph Friedman and their children are still involved with Kildare. Coincidentally, our caretaker Don Sanford, at the Loeb camp at Gull Bay on Saranac Lake, was brought up at Kildare.

CHAPTER THREE

Hattie Lehman Goodhart & Philip J. Goodhart

~~~

THE YEAR PHILIP J. GOODHART MARRIED Mayer and Babette's oldest daughter Hattie was 1882. It was also the year P. J. established the Wall Street firm of P. J. Goodhart & Co. As his father-in-law Mayer prospered on Wall Street, so did P. J., who for three decades was a member of the New York Stock Exchange. The son of a Cincinnati grain dealer, P. J.

shared a common background with his father-in-law who started out in the cotton business. Both were dedicated philanthropists, with Mount Sinai Hospital and Temple Emanu-El benefiting most from their generosity.

As for Hattie, she was a model of social propriety who prided herself in distinguishing "people we visit" from "people we wouldn't visit." Hattie had reason to take special pride in her progeny. Her daughter Helen married Frank Altschul, a senior partner of Lazard Frères, whose sister Edith would marry Hattie's younger brother Herbert. Her son Arthur, who settled in England and married into a good English family when he wed Cecily Carter, was a distinguished professor of jurisprudence at Cambridge University and became the first American to serve as head of an Oxford college.

Arthur and Cecily produced three sons: Sir Philip Goodhart, a Conservative member of the British

Parliament; the future Lord William Howard Goodhart, a member of the House of Lords; and Professor Charles Goodhart of the London School of Economics, who has served on the Interest Rate Committee of the Bank of England.

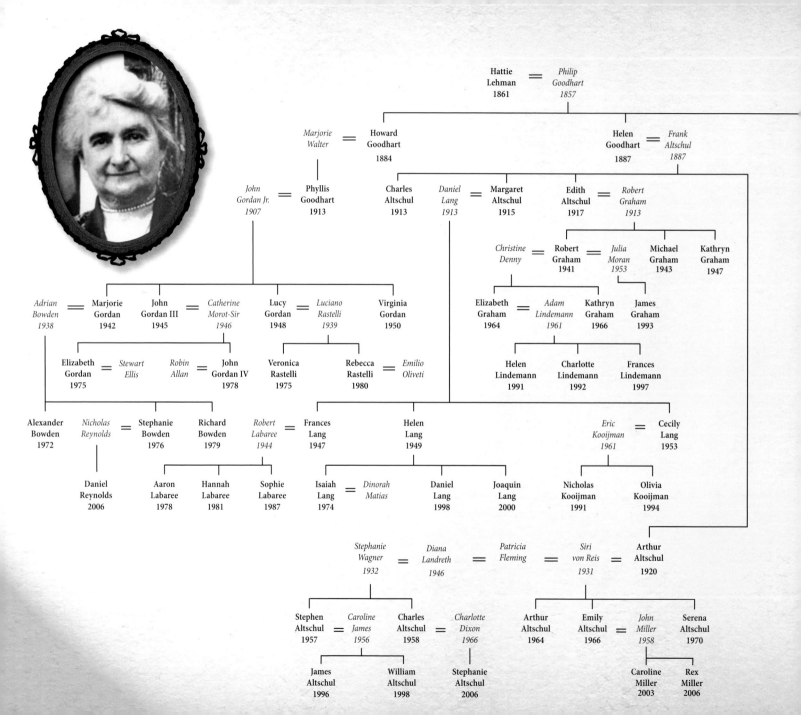

Hattie Lehman 1861 = *Philip Goodhart* 1857

Marjorie Walter = **Howard Goodhart** 1884 **Helen Goodhart** 1887 = *Frank Altschul* 1887

John Gordan Jr. 1907 = **Phyllis Goodhart** 1913   **Charles Altschul** 1913   *Daniel Lang* 1913 = **Margaret Altschul** 1915   **Edith Altschul** 1917 = *Robert Graham* 1913

Christine Denny = **Robert Graham** 1941 = *Julia Moran* 1953   **Michael Graham** 1943   **Kathryn Graham** 1947

Adrian Bowden 1938 = **Marjorie Gordan** 1942   **John Gordan III** 1945 = *Catherine Morot-Sir* 1946   **Lucy Gordan** 1948 = *Luciano Rastelli* 1939   **Virginia Gordan** 1950   **Elizabeth Graham** 1964 = *Adam Lindemann* 1961   **Kathryn Graham** 1966   **James Graham** 1993

Elizabeth Gordan 1975 = *Stewart Ellis*   *Robin Allan* = **John Gordan IV** 1978   **Veronica Rastelli** 1975   **Rebecca Rastelli** 1980 = *Emilio Oliveti*   **Helen Lindemann** 1991   **Charlotte Lindemann** 1992   **Frances Lindemann** 1997

Alexander Bowden 1972   *Nicholas Reynolds* = **Stephanie Bowden** 1976   **Richard Bowden** 1979   *Robert Labaree* 1944 = **Frances Lang** 1947   **Helen Lang** 1949   *Eric Kooijman* 1961 = **Cecily Lang** 1953

Daniel Reynolds 2006   **Aaron Labaree** 1978   **Hannah Labaree** 1981   **Sophie Labaree** 1987   **Isaiah Lang** 1974 = *Dinorah Matias*   **Daniel Lang** 1998   **Joaquin Lang** 2000   **Nicholas Kooijman** 1991   **Olivia Kooijman** 1994

Stephanie Wagner 1932 = *Diana Landreth* 1946 = *Patricia Fleming* = *Siri von Reis* 1931 = **Arthur Altschul** 1920

Stephen Altschul 1957 = *Caroline James* 1956   **Charles Altschul** 1958 = *Charlotte Dixon* 1966   **Arthur Altschul** 1964   **Emily Altschul** 1966 = *John Miller* 1958   **Serena Altschul** 1970

James Altschul 1996   **William Altschul** 1998   **Stephanie Altschul** 2006   **Caroline Miller** 2003   **Rex Miller** 2006

Hattie Lehman Goodhart & Philip J. Goodhart

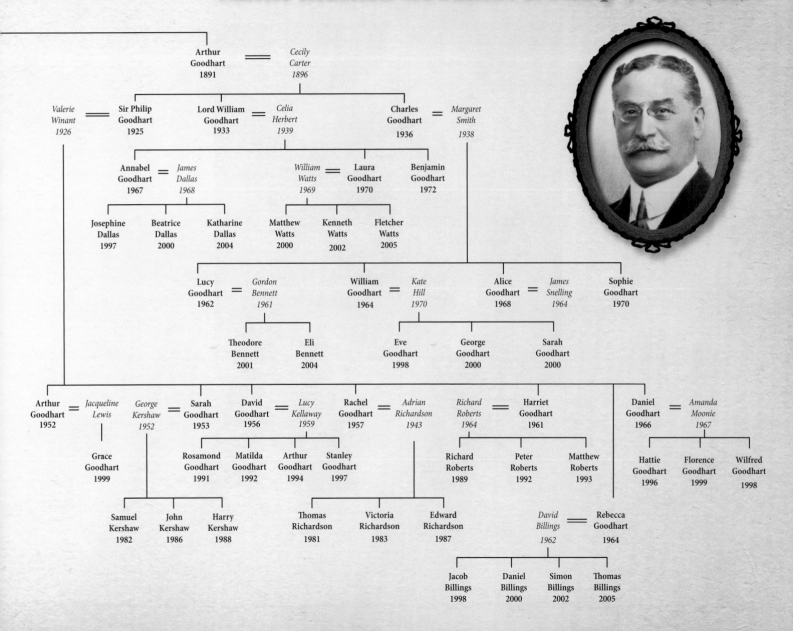

Arthur Goodhart 1891 = Cecily Carter 1896

Valerie Winant 1926 = Sir Philip Goodhart 1925 | Lord William Goodhart 1933 = Celia Herbert 1939 | Charles Goodhart 1936 = Margaret Smith 1938

Annabel Goodhart 1967 = James Dallas 1968 | William Watts 1969 = Laura Goodhart 1970 | Benjamin Goodhart 1972

Josephine Dallas 1997 | Beatrice Dallas 2000 | Katharine Dallas 2004 | Matthew Watts 2000 | Kenneth Watts 2002 | Fletcher Watts 2005

Lucy Goodhart 1962 = Gordon Bennett 1961 | William Goodhart 1964 = Kate Hill 1970 | Alice Goodhart 1968 = James Snelling 1964 | Sophie Goodhart 1970

Theodore Bennett 2001 | Eli Bennett 2004 | Eve Goodhart 1998 | George Goodhart 2000 | Sarah Goodhart 2000

Arthur Goodhart 1952 = Jacqueline Lewis | George Kershaw 1952 = Sarah Goodhart 1953 | David Goodhart 1956 = Lucy Kellaway 1959 | Rachel Goodhart 1957 = Adrian Richardson 1943 | Richard Roberts 1964 = Harriet Goodhart 1961 | Daniel Goodhart 1966 = Amanda Moonie 1967

Grace Goodhart 1999 | Rosamond Goodhart 1991 | Matilda Goodhart 1992 | Arthur Goodhart 1994 | Stanley Goodhart 1997 | Richard Roberts 1989 | Peter Roberts 1992 | Matthew Roberts 1993 | Hattie Goodhart 1996 | Florence Goodhart 1999 | Wilfred Goodhart 1998

Samuel Kershaw 1982 | John Kershaw 1986 | Harry Kershaw 1988 | Thomas Richardson 1981 | Victoria Richardson 1983 | Edward Richardson 1987 | David Billings 1962 = Rebecca Goodhart 1964

Jacob Billings 1998 | Daniel Billings 2000 | Simon Billings 2002 | Thomas Billings 2005

Hattie Lehman Goodhart, known in "Our Crowd" circles for distinguishing "people we visit" from "people we wouldn't visit." (John D. Gordan III)

Hattie Lehman Goodhart

1861–1948

———◆———

New York Times, July 14, 1948

MRS. GOODHART,
SISTER OF EX-GOV. LEHMAN, 88

Mrs. Hattie Goodhart, a sister of former Gov. Herbert Lehman, died yesterday at her home, 550 Park Avenue, after a long illness at the age of 88. She was the widow of Philip J. Goodhart, a broker and philanthropist, who died four years ago.

Mrs. Goodhart was born in Montgomery, Ala., and came to New York when she was 8 years old. . . . In 1928 Mrs. Goodhart was elected a trustee of the Home for Aged and Infirm Hebrews at 120 West 105th Street.

Surviving besides the former Governor and her son, Howard, who resides in New York, are a daughter, Mrs. Frank Altschul of

Stamford, Conn.; another son, Prof. Arthur Goodhart of Oxford University, seven grandchildren, and seven great-grandchildren

A private funeral service will be held today with burial in Salem Fields Cemetery, Brooklyn.

———◦———

STEPHEN BIRMINGHAM, *author of "Our Crowd":* The Great Jewish Families of New York, *from the book's opening paragraph* — By the late 1930s the world of Mrs. Philip J. Goodhart had become one of clearly defined, fixed and immutable values. It was a world of heavily encrusted calling cards and invitations—to teas, coming-out parties, weddings—but all within the group, among the people Mrs. Goodhart visited, a city within a city. There were two kinds of people— "people we visit" and "people we wouldn't visit." When a new name came into the conversation, Mrs. Goodhart would want to know, "Is it someone we would visit? Would visit?" She had an odd little habit of repeating phrases. . . . She and her friends did not make a point of being Jewish. When a Rorschach test was performed on Granny Goodhart after dinner one night, it turned out Granny was an anti-Semite. Still, as one of the grandes dames of German Jewish society, Granny was admired by her friends. To her grandchildren she was a round little person smelling of wool and Evening in Paris who greeted them at the door [like her mother, Babette] with out-stretched arms and peppermint candies clutched in both hands.

———◦———

SIR PHILIP GOODHART, *grandson of Philip and Hattie Goodhart; eldest son of Arthur and Cecily Goodhart* — In the early 1900s my grandfather Philip was walking home from the office one day when he saw an attractive painting in a gallery window. He went inside and bought six paintings by a relatively unknown French painter called Renoir.

Hattie with her great-grandchildren Marjorie
Gordan Bowden and John D. Gordan III, c. 1947.
(John D. Gordan III)

Young Hattie holding baby Howard Goodhart, c. 1885.
(John D. Gordan III)

My grandmother sent the whole lot back the day after they were delivered because she thought they were indecent!

———◦◦◦———

ROBERT M. MORGENTHAU, *grandson of Hattie's younger sister, Settie Fatman; younger son of Elinor and Henry Morgenthau Jr.* – The Lehman women, particularly Hattie, were strong-minded women. They were very ladylike, but they knew exactly what they wanted to do. After the war [World War II] my mother said, "You have to call on Aunt Hattie. Bring your wife with you." So I called to have tea with Aunt Hattie, who was very formal. As we were having tea, Peggy, the widow of Peter Lehman [Herbert and Edith Lehman's adopted son who died in World War II], came into the foyer, and Hattie said to me in a loud voice, "Bobby, who is that?" so that Peggy could hear. I told her who it was, and she didn't invite her in because she had come without being invited.

———◦◦◦———

LORD WILLIAM HOWARD GOODHART, *grandson of Hattie and Philip Goodhart; middle son of Arthur and Cecily Goodhart* – My father, Arthur Lehman Goodhart, was brought up in a brownstone on 81st Street just to the west of Central Park. Hattie's sister Settie and her family lived in the house next door. The two houses were linked by a passage in which was placed the telephone. In those early days the telephone served both houses.

Hattie was the opposite of her husband—small, fierce, dominant, and not much given to jokes. I can remember she used to terrify me as a small child. Later I got to know my grandmother quite well.

My father was the youngest of her three children, and the family view is that one of the main motives for his deciding to make his career in England was to put the Atlantic between him and his mother. She was certainly a dominating figure. Shortly after my parents, Arthur and Cecily, had married and set up house in Cambridge, Hattie and Philip came over to be with them. Hattie insisted on visit-

Interior view of the West 81st Street residence of Hattie and Philip Goodhart. Hattie's sister Settie Lehman Fatman and her family lived next door. (Henry Morgenthau III)

ing all the food shops that my mother was using (this was, of course, long before supermarkets) and on her return told my mother that they were all unhygienic and ordered her to take her business elsewhere. Fortunately, Hattie didn't stay long enough to discover that all the other shops in Cambridge were just as bad.

I can't remember when I was introduced to Hattie and Philip, but it must have been when I was very small, as they came over to England to visit my parents for a month every summer. The first memory I can associate with them was in 1938 (when I was five years old) when it looked as if war was imminent. It was decided then that my grandparents should take my brothers and me back to the United States (with our nanny). I remember spending a night with them at the Ritz in London on our way to catch the *Queen Mary*. We arrived in New York just as the great 1938 hurricane was beginning.

We stayed on in the United States through the winter and returned to England in the spring of 1939. Hattie and Philip did not come over that year. In late August, when the threat of war was about to turn into reality, my brothers and I were shipped off to New York again.

As both our parents remained in England, responsibility for us was divided between my grandparents and their daughter, Helen Altschul. For the next four years, life for my younger brother, Charles, and me fell into a regular pattern (my brother Philip was seven years older than I and was independent of us). We were dispatched to Tucson, Arizona, for the months of October to April—me to a boarding school, Charles with our nanny to the Arizona Inn. We then spent May in New York with our grandparents in their apartment at 550 Park Avenue—a building that is still standing, though now looking rather ancient. I remember the apartment as large and dark, with heavy furniture.

June and September we spent with the Altschuls at Overbrook, their house near Stamford. In July and August Hattie and Philip took us somewhere cooler—in 1940 and 1941 to a house they rented at Cotuit on Cape Cod,

P. J. and Hattie taking it easy, c. 1940. (John D. Gordan III)

and in 1942 and 1943 (perhaps fearing that Cape Cod might be attacked by German submarines) to a cottage forming part of the Whiteface Inn complex on Lake Placid. So for three months a year we saw a great deal of Hattie and Philip. The pattern ended when my grandfather died, in the spring of 1944.

Hattie and Philip were loyal members of Temple Emanu-El and used to walk over to it every Saturday. As my brothers and I were being brought up as Christians (our mother was a devout Anglican), we never went there. As would be expected of members of Temple Emanu-El, the dietary laws were not observed. Food at 550 was good and plentiful, though it didn't match the spectacularly high standards of the Altschuls.

Gentleness was certainly no part of Hattie's character; she was small, determined, and very firm. She was not a person to whom warmth came naturally. She did, however, try—and to a large extent succeed—in being kind to me. (I'm not so sure about kindness to Charles, who was younger and more boisterous.) I remember her teaching me to play gin rummy, and (improbably) she taught me a very good way of shuffling cards, which I still use.

Following my grandfather's death we saw much less of her. After we returned to England in 1945, I saw her only in the summer of 1947, when my parents and Charles and I went to the United States. By that time she was failing and was spending a good deal of time with the Altschuls.

One last story about her comes from the time Helen was hosting a meeting of a women's organization at Overbrook. Frank Altschul gave them all large amounts of an innocent-tasting but lethal cocktail. When Hattie came down from her rest, she found the guests in a stupor, and said, "Helen, dear, your friends seem to be very tired today."

Philip J. Goodhart, Wall Street entrepreneur in his prime, c. 1935.
(Herbert H. Lehman Suite & Papers, Columbia University)

Philip J. Goodhart

1857–1944

—⊷◆⊷—

New York Times, April 27, 1944

PHILIP J. GOODHART,
RETIRED BROKER, 88

Member of Stock Exchange for 31 Years Dies—
A Trustee of Mount Sinai Hospital

Philip J. Goodhart, former stock broker, who for many years was active in Jewish welfare work, died early yesterday morning at his home, 550 Park Avenue, after a brief illness. His age was 88.

Co-founder with his brother, Albert E. Goodhart, of the firm of P. J. Goodhart & Co. in 1882, Mr. Goodhart was a member of the New York Stock Exchange from 1878 to 1909. He also served as a director of the United States Pipe and Foundry Company from 1899 to 1928 and as a member of the company's executive committee for five years.

Born in Cincinnati, Mr. Goodhart attended schools there and was associated with his father in a grain-dealing establishment. He dropped these connections and came to New York at the age of 18 to enter the brokerage business. In 1933, when his Stock Exchange firm was dissolved, he retired. Recently he had maintained offices at 654 Madison Avenue to handle his private affairs.

One of his greatest philanthropic interests was the Mount Sinai Hospital, of which he was a trustee from 1907 until 1933, when he was made honorary trustee. . . . Another activity to which he devoted much of his energies was the Temple Emanu-El, Fifth Avenue and Sixty-fifth Street. Joining the congregation in 1897, he was named a trustee in 1919. When plans were being formulated for construction of the present edifice he was an active member of the building committee.

A Republican, he was known to have enjoyed telling his children that as a boy of 8 he watched a parade honoring Abraham Lincoln during the President's second campaign.

In 1882 Mr. Goodhart married Hattie Lehman, sister of former Gov. Herbert Lehman and of Chief Judge Irving Lehman of the New York State Court of Appeals. Besides his widow, he leaves two sons, Howard Goodhart and Prof. Arthur Goodhart of Oxford University, England; a daughter, Mrs. Frank Altschul; seven grandchildren and three great-grandchildren.

A funeral service will be held tomorrow at 11 A.M. in the Temple Emanu-El. Burial will be private in Salem Fields Cemetery, Brooklyn.

PHYLLIS GOODHART GORDAN, *granddaughter of Philip and Hattie Goodhart; daughter of Howard and Marjorie Goodhart* – Grampa Goodhart's parents had come from Germany, and his father had started out as a peddler, traveling with a wagon in southern Ohio and northern Kentucky. Granny at one

"Hattie and Philip Goodhart on either side of their daughter-in-law Cecily, holding their grandson Charles (b. 1936) and Charles's elder brother Philip (b. 1925), with their father, Arthur, seated on the grass. The picture was taken at Boar's Hill outside Oxford, where Arthur taught for many years."
—John D. Gordan III (John D. Gordan III)

"P. J. Goodhart with his son Howard L. and his grandson William Howard Goodhart, future lord, QC."—John D. Gordan III (John D. Gordan III)

time was engaged to three men at once—Grampa, Mr. Edgar Stern of New Orleans, and another man whose name I may never have known. Grampa was very clever; he took a trip to Europe, and Granny realized she missed him much more than she enjoyed seeing the other men, so she married him.

It seems to me that the women were awfully full of domestic details—counting the teaspoons and that kind of thing. Grampa Goodhart certainly had more intellectual curiosity than Granny and gave much more intellectual leadership to the family, even though he had never been to college, and neither had Granny.[1]

———◆———

LORD WILLIAM HOWARD GOODHART, *grandson of Philip and Hattie Goodhart; son of Arthur and Cecily Goodhart* – Grandpa Philip I remember as a kind and gentle man with a large, white moustache. He was already in his eighties at

this time. I was struck by the fact that he went to a barber every day to be shaved—well after most men had switched to safety razors. He enjoyed telling jokes. His favorite was about a man who lived at the far end of Long Island, where he could hear the sea and see the Sound. It impressed me at the time.

———◆———

JOHN D. GORDAN III, *great-grandson of Philip and Hattie Goodhart; grandson of Marjorie and Howard Goodhart; son of Phyllis and John D. Gordan Jr.* – Arthur Altschul Sr., the son of Helen Goodhart Altschul, used to tell the story of P. J. Goodhart, when he was discussing investments with him, saying: "I'm in this for the long term." Arthur always found that very attractive because P. J. was then a very old man but his horizons continued to be lengthy ones.

———◆———

1. Archives of Henry Morgenthau III.

CHAPTER FOUR

Settie Lehman Fatman & Morris Fatman

———◆———

LIKE HER OLDER SISTER HATTIE and her younger sister Clara, Settie was fully cognizant of being Lehman
geboren (born). It put her in a very special category in
the New York City German Jewish world of "Our
Crowd." It meant that she was a member of a family
with an outstanding reputation in both business and
philanthropy. Not only was Settie a daughter of Mayer

Lehman of Lehman Brothers; she was also the daughter of a major contributor to Mount Sinai Hospital and Temple Emanu-El, with a family residence right off Fifth Avenue.

As was proper for a *wohlgeboren*, or well-born, Lehman, Settie married Morris Fatman, owner of the highly profitable Raritan Woolen Mills of Raritan, New Jersey. Both of Morris and Settie's daughters led interesting lives. Margaret, who sang at the Metropolitan Opera, was the wife of a Smith College music professor, Werner Josten. Elinor, among the first Jewish girls to attend Vassar College, married Henry Morgenthau Jr. (later FDR's secretary of the treasury); their son is Manhattan District Attorney Robert M. Morgenthau.

Settie Lehman & Morris Fatman

Werner Josten 1885 = Margaret Fatman 1888

Peter Josten 1922

Eileen Josten 1925 = Charles Lowe 1921

Sarah Lowe 1956 = Elisabeth Smith 1956

Elizabeth Lowe 1958

Josten Lowe 1959 = Jane Ceraso 1959

Susannah Lowe 1960 = Devin Hess 1955

Simon Lowe 2000

Jessica Lowe 1991

Rory Lowe 1995

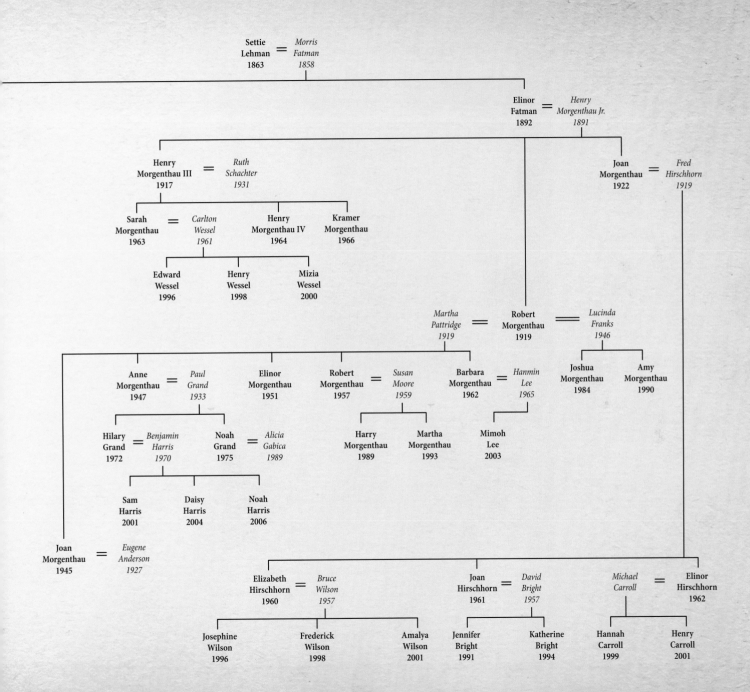

Settie Lehman Fatman, remembered as much for her quick temper as for her peace offerings of chocolate leaves and other delicacies, c. 1920. (Henry Morgenthau III)

Settie Lehman Fatman

1863–1936

New York Times, February 20, 1936

MRS. FATMAN DIES;
GOVERNOR'S SISTER

Widow of President of the Raritan (N.J.) Woolen Mills Succumbs at Home Here.

THE FUNERAL TOMORROW

State Senate Passes Resolution of Condolence—Adjourns in Respect to Her Memory.

Settie Lehman Fatman, a sister of Governor Herbert H. Lehman and widow of Morris Fatman, died early yesterday morning at her residence in the Savoy-Plaza, Fifth Avenue at Fifty-ninth Street.

Mrs. Fatman, who would have been 73 years old on July 26, had been an invalid for several years.

She was born in Montgomery, Ala., a daughter of Mayer Lehman and the former Babette Newgass [sic]. Her father was the founder of the banking firm of Lehman Brothers and one of the founders of the Cotton Exchange.

Mrs. Fatman did not take part in public affairs. She was a member of Congregation Emanu-El, 1 East 65th Street, and of its women's auxiliary. Her husband, who was the president of the Raritan Woolen Mills of Raritan, N.J., died in Atlantic City on Sept. 26, 1930, and the widow had been in poor health since then. Governor Lehman, youngest of three surviving brothers, spent some time at Mrs. Fatman's summer home at Loon Lake last August.

The other brothers are Arthur Lehman of Lehman Brothers, and Judge Irving Lehman of the Court of Appeals. Also surviving are two daughters, Mrs. Werner Josten of Northampton, Mass., wife of the composer, and Mrs. Henry Morgenthau Jr. of Washington, D.C. Both were with her when she died.

One sister, Mrs. Philip J. Goodhart of 550 Park Avenue, and five grandchildren also survive. Another sister, Mrs. Clara L. Limburg, died on Dec. 30, 1932, two days before Governor Lehman took office.

A private funeral service will be held tomorrow morning at the home of Judge Lehman, 37 West Sixty-ninth Street. Burial will be in Salem Fields Cemetery, Cypress Hills.

New York Times, February 22, 1936

MRS. FATMAN, SISTER OF GOVERNOR, BURIED

Mrs. Franklin D. Roosevelt
Among Friends at the Funeral Service.

A private funeral service at which Mrs. Franklin D. Roosevelt was one of the friends present was held yesterday morning for Mrs. Settie Lehman Fatman, a sister of Governor Herbert H. Lehman and widow of Morris Fatman, at the home of Judge Irving Lehman of the Court of Appeals, another brother, at 37 West Sixty-ninth Street. Mrs. Fatman, who had been an invalid for several years, died on Wednesday morning in her apartment at the Savoy-Plaza. Her age was 72.

The Rev. B. Benedict Glazer of Temple Emanu-El officiated. In a eulogy, he said:

"We remember the combination of strength and modesty that marked her approach to the counsels and issues of life and her generous concern for the needy, the ailing and the friendless, to whom she came in a spirit of consecrated personal service, but most of all at this moment we remember her boundless love.

"Her life was rich, complete and blessed. May its lessons be etched upon the hearts of those who loved her as an abiding tribute to her memory, as a source of inspiration and strength."

During the service there were three piano and violin selections, Handel's Larghetto, "The Angels' Serenade" by Braga, which was sung by Rita Sebastian, and Handel's Largo.

Besides Governor Lehman and Judge Lehman, surviving relatives present included a third brother, Arthur Lehman of the banking firm of Lehman Brothers; two daughters, Mrs. Henry Morgenthau Jr., who was accompanied by her husband, the Secretary of the Treasury, and Mrs. Werner Josten of Northampton, Mass., wife of the composer; and a sister, Mrs. Philip J. Goodhart of this city.

Burial took place in Salem Fields Cemetery, Cypress Hills.

—◦◦◦—

HENRY MORGENTHAU III, *Grandson of Settie and Morris Fatman; son of Elinor and Henry Morgenthau Jr. –* Settie had the Lehman look that endowed men and women alike with the appearance of an angry squirrel: paunchy gray cheeks, deep-set eyes, and dark, bushy eyebrows that joined in a perpetual scowl. What Settie lacked in natural beauty she made up for by her sense of style. She wore well-cut high-neck dresses, mostly black, with a grosgrain choker ornamented with pearls and diamonds

Like so many "Our Crowd" women of her generation, Settie viewed a good marriage as a primary family goal. But once coupled, the two partners were expected to run on entirely separate tracks. A man headed for advancement in his career; a woman's place was in the home—when she went out in the world, it was to play a clearly defined supporting role. One measure of a husband's worth was the extent to which he relieved his wife of all household labor. The ultimate achievement was an idle woman who would venture forth with her husband, laden with expensive jewelry and heavy furs, advertising his success. Without a qualm Settie wedged herself into this mold earnestly. She was, after all, a *geboren* Lehman; what more could one aspire to?

Her serious demeanor was perfectly suited to one of her favorite activities: the recounting of what she called her "rows"—disputes, generally with tradespeople though sometimes with family and friends. Settie would relive these battles while presiding over her tea table, her passionate anger exploding from time to time at some innocent guest who had the nerve to show that she was something less than a totally sympathetic ally.

Young Settie Lehman in Saratoga Springs, New York, watering hole for the rich and famous, c. 1880. (Henry Morgenthau III)

Moments later, the temper storm spent, Settie would make a peace offering. "Have another chocolate leaf," she would suggest, while passing a plate of almond wafers coated with chocolate, made to resemble oversized oak leaves. They were expensive delicacies delivered as a standing order along with chocolate éclairs and cream puffs from Dean's Pastry Shop. Settie's teas were served in a second-floor parlor extending across the entire front of her 23 West 81st Street brownstone. A bay window facing south overlooked the small park behind the Museum of Natural History. The parlor was crammed full of comfy overstuffed furniture upholstered in rich brown and gray velvet. A big carved oak desk supported an array of silver- and leather-framed family photographs. The brass in the house was polished regularly, as was the silver. A mysterious man appeared once a week to wind and regulate all the chiming clocks. On the dark green damask-covered walls above the oak-paneled wainscoting were oil paintings of the Barbizon School—French land-scapes embedded in heavy gilt frames under a glaze of yellowed varnish.

In one corner there was an oil portrait of a Jewish patriarch with a full gray beard and piercing black eyes that seemed to follow you and demand attention. "Who is that old man?" I got up enough nerve to ask on one occasion. Grandma was hard of hearing, reputedly a hereditary Lehman trait. She wore a hearing aid that was wired into a black box designed like a handbag. It squealed back at my question when I got too close. "He's an Old Testament prophet," she answered. Hanging on the back of the door next to him was a silk Muslim prayer rug.

Along one wall were several mahogany bookcases with glass doors protecting sets of English, American, and German authors. In handsome leather bindings were the complete works of Shakespeare, Walter Scott, Mark Twain, Edgar Allan Poe and, in German, Schiller, Lessing, Heine, and Henrik Ibsen (translated from the Norwegian). In a separate two-tier case in soft black leather gold-embossed binding was the great eleventh 1910-1911 edition of the *Encyclopaedia Britannica*.

Grandma had a lot to do with providing my mother [Elinor, wife of Secretary of the Treasury Henry Morgenthau Jr.] with servants. She had a Swedish cook who would often cook for us. She instructed two sisters my mother had hired from Scotland as to how to set a table and wear a uniform. Gretchen, who had entered Grandma Fatman's household as my mother's wet nurse, stayed on and became her cook after Mother married.

I remember my mother talking about her mother being brought up in Montgomery and being reunited with her black nursemaid in New York and throwing her arms around her, hugging and kissing her. It was of great interest to my mother that this could happen.

Grandma was very generous, something we grandchildren took for granted. At the end of summer, when she returned from Europe, where she went mainly to shop, she lavished extravagant presents on us. One of her specialties was large Egyptian cotton pocket handkerchiefs embroidered with elaborate monograms. As they seemed too good to use, I stored them away. Some remain to this day in mint condition.

Settie's generosity frequently extended beyond the family. She was known to set forth in her chauffeur-driven Pierce-Arrow limousine, arriving at the home of a sick friend with her favorite remedies: roast squab and a container of chicken soup. One day at noon during the Depression, according to my cousin Frances Lehman Loeb, Settie left her apartment at the Savoy-Plaza Hotel, where she had moved as a widow. Outside on the street corner she noticed a woman selling apples from a small stand. Settie bought one for five cents. Asking when the woman was going to lunch, the woman replied that she had neither time nor money for lunch, whereupon Settie gave her a dollar for lunch while she minded the apple stand for an hour or so. Later that day word went out on the telephone that "poor Settie seems to think she has lost all her money and is out on the street corner selling apples."

PETER JOSTEN, *grandson of Settie and Morris Fatman; son of Margaret and Werner Josten* – I really don't remember anything particularly about Settie except what my mother, her elder daughter, may have told me. I think of her as a very small person; I can't remember any physical contact. She did have a set of emeralds and rubies and diamonds. My mother inherited them all and then passed them on to my sister. It was probably the style for all the Lehman ladies. They were very strong-willed, all of them and very supportive. They worked with their husbands as a team and would push them sometimes.

When my mother went to Paris to study voice, Settie insisted that she write a letter home every day. The letters had to go by steamship, so there were probably a whole group of them going at once. It must have been 1912 or so. In any case she went there and stayed at a pension where my father was staying. They became engaged in 1914; my father returned to Germany when the war broke out. After the war they married. It was the first time in my father's family that anyone had married a Jew

and probably the first time in my mother's family that anyone had married a Christian. There was no opposition whatsoever as far as I know.

I think my mother's family welcomed my father because he had a wonderful personality. His father—my grandfather—was a banker in Elberfeld in the Ruhr. My father, after engaging in banking in England for several years, was allowed to pursue his real interest in music and therefore had moved to Paris. My mother was studying voice with Yvette Guilbert. So she writes a letter home saying that she had met a very nice man, Werner Josten, at the pension where she was staying, and in return she got a letter from Settie saying, "I am shocked that you met a man in Paris."

Settie and Morris met my father's family around the time the war broke out. My parents were already engaged. The Fatmans were in Germany a month or six weeks before they could get a boat back home.

My father, who was the assistant conductor of the Munich opera after World War I, fought in the German army while Mother sang at the Metropolitan Opera, but instead of using the name "Fatman" she changed it to "Farman." My grandmother would get very, very annoyed when people would say, "Mrs. Farman, your daughter sings so beautifully." My father was the second German resident to come over here after the war; they got married almost immediately. I was born in 1922, shortly after my father was appointed a professor of music at Smith College.

We came down to Settie's for Christmas in 1934 or '35. Mrs. Barclay, Settie's nurse, went down to get a present for me at Schwartz, which was just around the corner on 58th Street. It was labeled "Made in Bavaria." Mrs. Barclay didn't realize that was like "Made in Germany." Of course we couldn't keep it, so, much to my regret, the present went back.

They all collected impressionist and post-impressionist pictures in those days. I remember the story of Dorothy Bernhard [Arthur and Adele Lehman's eldest daughter] calling my parents and asking them to come over to see the new Van Gogh she had just gotten and my father saying, "That's the picture that belonged to my sister Hannah that we got engaged under in 1914 in Munich." I don't know where the picture is now. It was at the Metropolitan, but they sold it.

One of my last memories of Settie is in her bedroom, asking Herbert Lehman (who was already governor) if it was extravagant of her to make telephone calls to my mother in Northampton and her younger daughter Ellie Morgenthau in Washington every morning. I remember Herbert's saying, "No, don't worry about it."

⟫◆⟪

JOAN MORGENTHAU HIRSCHHORN, *granddaughter of Settie and Morris Fatman; daughter of Elinor and Henry Morgenthau Jr.* – Grandma Fatman really didn't want my mother Ellie going away to college. Mother was adamant: She was going to go. And she went—to Vassar. Because Grandma loved her daughter, she nonetheless used to send her all these nice clothes from Paris when she was overseas. To wear clothes like that at Vassar would have appeared ostentatious, to say the least. Mother was so embarrassed that she put them all in boxes under her bed.

GABRIELLE FORBUSH (1890–?), *Elinor Fatman Morgenthau's Vassar classmate and lifelong friend* – Mother thought that I had lost my faith at Vassar, and Mrs. Fatman said Ellie would never go to the temple. They were two mothers mourning over their young. . . . Dear old Mrs. Fatman had never had anyone in her family go to college, so she thought of it like a swell finishing school. She outfitted Ellie with all these lovely clothes. And, you know, Ellie was rather indifferent to clothes. Dear Mrs. Fatman would telegraph Ellie—we didn't have phones in the hall—to remember so and so's birthday and send him a congratulatory telegram. We took things casually, but Mrs. Fatman saw to it that Ellie did everything she should do. . . . Her father had a great sense of humor. Dear Mrs. Fatman was a little delinquent there.

Ellie's husband, Henry Morgenthau Jr., sometimes teased Mrs. Fatman gently without her realizing it. "I like to go to the theater with a man," she once assured my husband, Arthur, "and I was always a great flirt." So, Arthur obliged her and flirted with her beautifully, and she would rise to it, you know.[1]

———◆———

ROBERT M. MORGENTHAU, *grandson of Settie and Morris Fatman; son of Elinor and Henry Morgenthau Jr.* – I used to stay with Settie when I came back from school and my parents were in Washington. She always wanted to get me off to the train an hour ahead of time, so I used to hide from her. Once she found me and was very angry I hadn't left already.

It was a very closely knit family. When my grandmother moved over to the East Side from the West Side, various members of the family used to call on her for tea in the afternoon. And when Wall Street was closed, all of the brothers and nephews would come by to see her. When she was dying a slow death of cancer, every family member would come up almost every day at the close of work.

———◆———

1. Archives of Henry Morgenthau III.

Morris Fatman, c. 1920, president of New Jersey's Raritan Woolen Mills, a major supplier of blankets to the American army during World War I.

Morris Fatman

1858–1930

New York Times, September 27, 1930

MORRIS FATMAN DIES IN 73D YEAR

Brother-in-law of Lieut. Gov. Lehman Succumbs at Atlantic City.

HAD BEEN ILL TWO YEARS

President of New Jersey Mills Was Father of Mrs. Werner Josten and Mrs. Henry Morgenthau Jr.

Special to The New York Times.

ATLANTIC CITY, N.J., Sept. 26.—Morris Fatman, prominent New York woolen manufacturer and brother-in-law of Lieut. Gov. Herbert Lehman and father-in-law of Henry Morgenthau Jr., died at the Ambassador Hotel today. He was 72 years old.

Mr. Fatman had been president of the Raritan Woolen Mills of Raritan, N.J. He had been ailing for more than two years and came here early in June in an effort to regain his health. He seemed to be on the road to recovery and his sudden death came as a shock to his business acquaintances and friends.

Dr. Weiner, in New York City, his personal physician, attributed Mr. Fatman's death to a general breakdown.

Besides his widow, he is survived by two daughters, Mrs. Werner Josten, wife of the American composer of Northampton, Mass., and Mrs. Morgenthau.

Lieut. Gov. Lehman had intended to address the meeting of one of the Democratic clubs at Port Chester, N.Y., last night, but he sent a letter to Major William A. Darcy of the club saying that he would be unable to be present owing to the death of his brother-in-law, Morris Fatman. He wrote in part: "We had a very close association of nearly forty-five years, and I know that those to whom I am to speak will appreciate that his death has left me in no fit condition to make an address tonight. Also, I must hurry to be with my sister."

Funeral services for Mr. Fatman will be held at 11 o'clock Sunday morning in the chapel of Temple Emanu-El, Sixty-fifth Street and Fifth Avenue.

<hr>

PETER JOSTEN, *grandson of Settie and Morris Fatman; son of Werner and Margaret Fatman Josten* – All I know about my grandfather Morris is that he made his money as head of the Raritan Woolen Mills in Raritan, New Jersey, which manufactured "shoddy," a felt-like woolen cloth. According to what I've been told, he was a major supplier of blankets to the American army during World War I.

JOAN MORGENTHAU HIRSCHHORN, *grand-daughter of Settie and Morris Fatman; daughter of Elinor and Henry Morgenthau Jr.* – I don't know much about Grandpa Fatman, but I do remember hearing from my mother that his bachelor brother Solly Fatman offered both her and Aunt Peggy [Margaret Fatman Josten] $10,000 if either would name a male offspring Solomon after himself, and Aaron after Solly and Morris's father. Both declined. Peter Werner Josten was named for his father. Henry Morgenthau III was named for his father, and Robert Morris Morgenthau, following a family tradition, was given his grandfather's first name as his middle name.

———— ❖ ————

ROBERT M. MORGENTHAU, *grandson of Settie and Morris Fatman; son of Elinor and Henry Morgenthau Jr.* – When my mother was supporting Woodrow Wilson in 1912, my grandfather said to her, "I did not send you to Vassar to become a Democrat." He fit the description "dyed-in-the-wool Republican."

My grandfather's father, Aaron Fatman and his older brother Joseph, who was the first treasurer of The Jews' Hospital in New York—which later became Mount Sinai—were in the leaf tobacco business on the Green River in Ohio and Kentucky during the Civil War when they were served with General Order No. 11 stating that no Jews or peddlers were allowed in a vast military area called "the Department of the Tennessee" by order of General Grant. They were given twenty-four hours to get out. This created a storm of controversy. The lawyer representing them in this matter was none other than Samuel J. Tilden, who in 1876 ran against Rutherford B. Hayes for president—and lost.

This was a very important moment in Jewish American history. When Lincoln learned of it, without hesitation he instructed General Henry Halleck to cancel the infamous order. Ironically, President Grant emerged as a model of solicitude in behalf of Jews living both at home and abroad.

Morris Fatman at Luna Park, Coney Island, with his daughter Elinor (second from the right)
and three of her friends from Vassar College, c. 1910. (Henry Morgenthau III)

Grandpa Fatman used to ask me if I was the strongest boy in my class at the Lincoln School. In fact, I was. One time I was using an American flag as a cane, and that infuriated him. He said you never put the American flag on the ground.

—⊰◈⊱—

HENRY MORGENTHAU III, *grandson of Settie and Morris Fatman; son of Elinor and Henry Morgenthau Jr.* – I knew Morris Fatman very well. As his oldest grandson, he wanted to take me to baseball games or the circus, but I wasn't interested—he did get me a baseball autographed by Babe Ruth, which I treasured.

He loved his food and was always overweight. He went to a gym called McGovern's. I remember his taking me there. He didn't do any exercises. He got into a sweatbox. When he got out, he weighed less; but then he drank a glass or two of water, and it all came right back. This routine of overeating and going in a sweatbox affected his heart. He died at a relatively early age. What he did was go to Atlantic City, New Jersey, with his doctor. People often took their doctors with them at that time. Unfortunately Dr. Weiner wasn't a very good doctor, and Morris died.

As head of the Raritan Woolen Mills on the Raritan River in New Jersey, Morris did well in business, but he was not in the top financial echelons of the Lehmans, the Lewisohns, and the Blumenthals. Nonetheless, he was a close friend of the Blumenthals, including George. Owner of a prestigious art collection, Blumenthal was the first Jewish chairman of the board of the Metropolitan Museum of Art. His mansion on Park Avenue is now the UN Russian Consulate. Blumenthal started in the button business. Later, George became New York partner of Lazard Frères. My grandfather tried to emulate George Blumenthal in collecting art, but of course he couldn't begin to compete. He bought rather second-rate Renaissance art. Howard Goodhart's daughter, Phyllis Goodhart Gordan, told me he really didn't get very good things.

The Fatmans were always trying to keep up with the Blumenthals. They would go to

Morris and Settie strolling arm in arm, c. 1925.
(Henry Morgenthau III)

Paris every summer. They didn't stay at the Ritz—it was too expensive—but at the Hôtel Vendôme, which looks very much like the nearby Ritz. Settie would send us picture postcards of the hotel with the windows of their rooms circled in ink.

———⟨◇⟩———

LOUISE BLUMENTHAL SULZBERGER (1898– 2001), *daughter of Morris Fatman's close friend Hugo Blumenthal* – My father, Hugo Blumenthal, and his brother Gus were very intimate. The only person they let into this group was Morris Fatman. They told one another everything— about business and not about business. Morris Fatman was a darling man. I remember the day he died: my father heard about it on the phone and burst into tears because they were absolutely devoted. They sometimes walked around the city at night together, the three of them. They called my father and Uncle Gus "the Smith Brothers" after the cough drops because they were so inseparable. I have a picture somewhere of my father, Morris Fatman, and my Uncle Gus Blumenthal walking in Europe, each with a cane, each with a stiff collar, each with a tie on. They all went to the Harmonie Club on Saturday afternoons. They never missed playing poker, and they played for high stakes.[1]

———⟨◇⟩———

1. Archives of Henry Morgenthau III.

CHAPTER FIVE

Clara Lehman Limburg & Richard Limburg

———◆———

CLARA, THE YOUNGEST DAUGHTER of Mayer and Babette, was the first of their children to be born in New York City. Six years later Mayer built a five-floor brownstone residence at 5 East 62nd Street where Clara resided with her three younger brothers Arthur, Irving, and Herbert until her marriage to Richard Limburg, a member of the New York Stock Exchange and a popular figure in Wall Street circles.

Clara had no formal education beyond governesses and private tutors. Nor, as far as is known, did Richard have a college degree. Their two sons, Percy and Alan, however, graduated from Yale and became successful stockbrokers. Their daughter Mabel was a fashion plate in her day. All married into "Our Crowd" families and enjoyed lives of wealth and privilege. Also like her sisters, Clara spent her widowed years in a fashionable residence hotel in Manhattan with a private chauffeur and a lady's maid never far behind. Like them, Clara considered herself a *wohlgeborene* Lehman and behaved accordingly. She is remembered as much for her whalebone corsets in later life as for once having been a beautiful young thing in the eyes of her baby brothers Irving, the future head of New York State's Appellate Court, and Herbert, the future governor of New York.

Clara Lehman Limburg & Richard Limburg

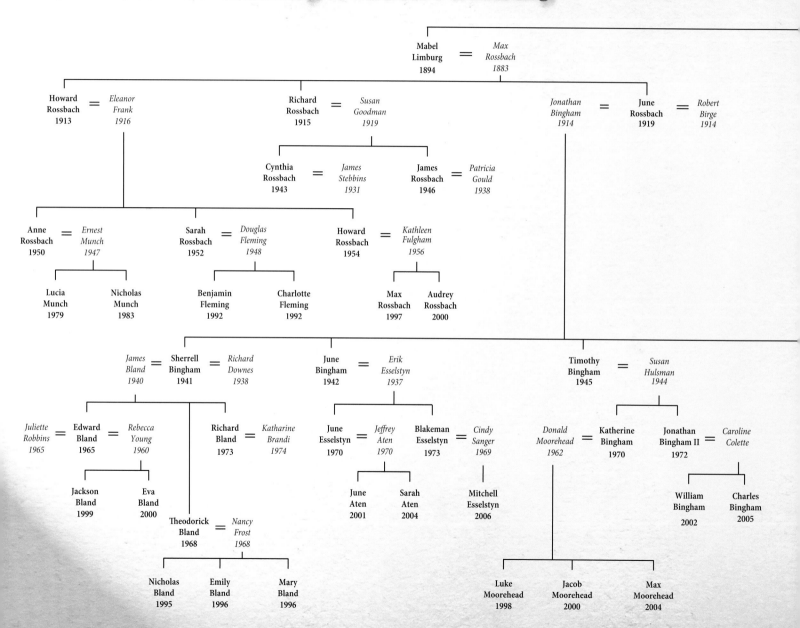

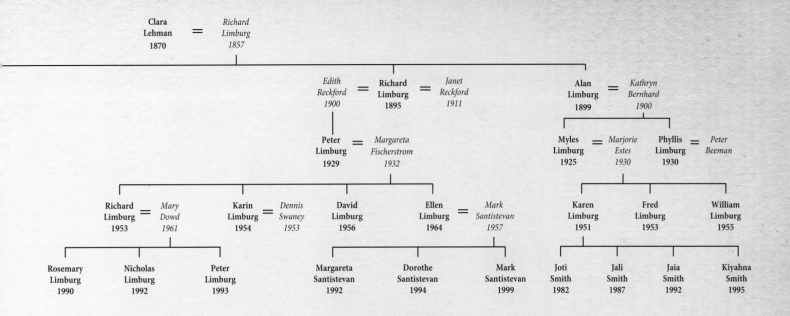

Clara
Lehman
1870
=
*Richard
Limburg
1857*

*Edith
Reckford
1900* = **Richard
Limburg
1895** = *Janet
Reckford
1911*

**Alan
Limburg
1899** = *Kathryn
Bernhard
1900*

**Peter
Limburg
1929** = *Margareta
Fischerstrom
1932*

**Myles
Limburg
1925** = *Marjorie
Estes
1930* **Phyllis
Limburg
1930** = *Peter
Beeman*

**Richard
Limburg
1953** = *Mary
Dowd
1961*
**Karin
Limburg
1954** = *Dennis
Swaney
1953*
**David
Limburg
1956**
**Ellen
Limburg
1964** = *Mark
Santistevan
1957*

**Karen
Limburg
1951**
**Fred
Limburg
1953**
**William
Limburg
1955**

**Rosemary
Limburg
1990**
**Nicholas
Limburg
1992**
**Peter
Limburg
1993**

**Margareta
Santistevan
1992**
**Dorothe
Santistevan
1994**
**Mark
Santistevan
1999**

**Joti
Smith
1982**
**Jali
Smith
1987**
**Jaia
Smith
1992**
**Kiyahna
Smith
1995**

*Robert
Hall* = **Claudia
Bingham
1947** = *Thomas
Meyers
1939*

**Harbhajan
Hall
1968**

**Gurubhajan
Khalsa
1973**
**Satbhajan
Khalsa
1976**

**Sunderta
Khalsa
1997**

*Clara Lehman Limburg, youngest of the three Lehman girls, known as much for being the family beauty in her youth as for her whalebone corsets later in life. (*New York Times*)*

Clara Lehman Limburg

1870–1932

New York Times, December 31, 1932

MRS. CLARA L. LIMBURG, LEHMAN'S SISTER, DIES

Daughter of the Founder of Lehman Brothers and Widow of Richard Limburg.

Mrs. Clara L. Limburg, a sister of Governor-elect Herbert H. Lehman, died yesterday in Mount Sinai Hospital after a brief illness. She was the widow of Richard Limburg, who was a member of the firm of Ladenburg, Thalmann & Co. and a governor of the Stock Exchange.

Surviving are Mrs. Limburg's brothers and sisters, Governor-elect Lehman, Arthur Lehman, Judge Irving Lehman of the Court of Appeals, Mrs. Philip Goodhart, and Mrs. Morris Fatman. She also leaves three children, Mrs. Max Rossbach, Richard P. Limburg, Alan M. Limburg, and six grandchildren.

Mrs. Limburg was the daughter of Mayer Lehman, founder of Lehman Brothers and one of the founders of the Cotton Exchange.

For many years she had quietly carried on philanthropic activities from her home in the Hotel Ambassador, Park Avenue and Fifty-first Street.

She was taken from the hospital to the home of her brother, Judge Lehman, at 37 West Sixty-ninth Street. Funeral services will be held tomorrow afternoon at 2 o'clock in Temple Emanu-El. Dr. H. G. Enelow will officiate. Burial will be in Salem Fields Cemetery.

New York Times, December 31, 1932

LEHMAN TAKES OATH PRIVATELY TONIGHT IN CEREMONY HERE

Plans Changed by Death of His Sister– Brother Will Swear Him into Office.

ALBANY PROGRAM STANDS

Inaugural Not Affected but Governor-Elect Cancels His Social Engagements.

ROOSEVELT LUNCHEON OFF

President-elect and His Wife to Attend Ball–Smith to Speak at State Exercises Monday.

Governor-elect Herbert H. Lehman arrived in New York last night from Albany, and will take the oath of office as Governor in a private inaugural ceremony somewhere in this city before midnight tonight. He will be sworn in by his brother, Judge Irving Lehman of the State Court of Appeals, who has administered the official oath to the Governor-elect on the two occasions when he has taken office as Lieutenant Governor.

The State administration passes into Mr. Lehman's hands at the stroke of midnight tonight from those of President-elect Roosevelt. Normally, the private inauguration would have taken place in Albany, but a change of plan was made because of the death here yesterday of Governor-elect Lehman's sister Mrs. Clara L. Limburg.

There will be no change in the formal inauguration ceremonies, which will take place as scheduled at the State Capitol in Albany on Monday. The official inauguration will be of the most severe simplicity this year, according to plans that had already been made.

Social Engagements Off.

Governor-elect Lehman canceled yesterday plans for the participation of Mrs. Lehman and himself in all the social events that usually accompany the inauguration of a new Governor. Soon after the report of Mrs. Limburg's death reached Albany, Governor Roosevelt announced that the usual luncheon and reception at the Executive Mansion, following the inaugural ceremony on Monday, had been called off.

It was also announced that the Governor-elect would not attend the dinner to be given by Governor and Mrs. Roosevelt at the Executive Mansion in Albany tonight to the members of the Governor's Cabinet. The inaugural ball which will be held tonight in Albany also will go on without the incoming Governor occupying his box. Governor Roosevelt and Mrs. Roosevelt, however, will go and remain for about an hour. . . .

Roosevelt Sets Precedent.

It will be the first time on record in this State that a President-elect has done honor to his successor in the Governorship at an inaugural ceremony.... former Governor Alfred E. Smith, will be present at the inaugural ceremony for Governor-elect Lehman, for whom he holds a warm attachment, and will deliver an address on the occasion....

Secretary of State Flynn will administer the oath of office at the formal inaugural on Monday.

———⟩⟨———

PETER LIMBURG, *grandson of Richard and Clara Limburg; son of Edith and Richard Percy Limburg* – According to my parents, Granny Limburg was an imperious and demanding person with a fierce temper. One of her demands was that her children call upon her every Sunday afternoon, at which occasions Granny always served caviar. When Granny was displeased, which I gather happened pretty often, her nostrils would dilate. I recall her as a fearsome old woman in black hovering over my baby carriage and saying things like, "Oh, isn't he precious?" I don't recall Granny ever speaking directly to me. My main recollection is of a photo of a white-haired woman with lovely features. It stood elegantly framed on top of my parents' grand piano. I think she was the family beauty, as was her daughter Aunt Mabel. Regarding the grand

piano, it was given to my mother by her grandfather Adolph Lewisohn, who one year determined that all his grandchildren should have this emblem of culture. Neither of my parents ever played it.

Granny and Grandpa Limburg visited Europe often, as wealthy people did in those days. In 1912 they had booked return passage on the maiden voyage of the *Titanic* with their three children: Aunt Mabel, my father (who was then attending a boarding school in Switzerland), and Uncle Alan. However, Aunt Mabel came down with chickenpox in Paris, and they missed the boat, no doubt to their immediate chagrin but subsequent great relief.

Granny had a 16-cylinder Cadillac limousine—black, of course. I remember seeing it once in the driveway when she came up for a

Young Clara Lehman in New York, c. 1886. She got better looking as she aged.
(Herbert H. Lehman Suite & Papers, Columbia University)

visit. After she died, my father took it over for a while, until it became too expensive to maintain during the Depression.

When my father was just starting out as a stockbroker, he bought Granny some shares of IBM. I still have a substantial chunk of what began as a speculative investment for my grandmother. Thank you, Granny.

——❖——

JUNE ROSSBACH BINGHAM BIRGE, *granddaughter of Richard and Clara Limburg; daughter of Max and Mabel Rossbach* – In the thirteen years I knew my Granny, she only once said something nice to me, which was, "Sometimes you're quite a nice child." I was overwhelmed. Granny's main occupation was criticizing other people, mostly family members. Every day Granny was "insulted" by one or more of them, and complained bitterly.

When Granny was a girl, rumor had it she was a beauty. One of the young men who came to tea at the Lehman house at 5 East 62nd Street was a Southern lawyer, Edward White, who had known Mayer Lehman before the family moved from Montgomery to New York. But Mr. White was a gentile, and when he became serious about Granny, he was sent away. He later became chief justice of the U.S. Supreme Court.

By the time I knew her, Granny was a formidable lady with steel gray hair, steel gray eyes, and a portly figure with no indentation at the waist. She had been married to my grandfather, Richard P. Limburg, a broker who was reportedly very popular on the Stock Exchange and one of its earliest post–Civil War Jewish governors.

Clara, as a mother, was very typical of her time. She played favorites, preferring the boys, especially Alan, her baby. I don't think he ever entirely grew up. As an undergraduate at Yale, he paid a small, very black child to accompany him to the Bowl, parading a sign reading, "It's mine [the black child], all mine."

Clara did not permit her daughter, Mabel, to go to Vassar, which Mabel's first cousin Ellie Fatman Morgenthau was attending, nor to Barnard, where Mabel's other first cousin,

Helen Goodhart Altschul, and her future aunt Adele Lewisohn had gone. She was not even permitted extension courses at Columbia. She was a great beauty, so maybe it was feared she might attract the wrong kind of man at college. In any event, at age eighteen Mabel married my father, Max J. H. Rossbach, whose family was in hides and skins on Gold Street. She had two sons before she was twenty-one. After her wedding Mabel had to visit or phone her mother every day.

I am sure that when Clara died, Mabel felt a huge sense of relief. Matriarchs bear down on their daughters probably harder than on their sons. And their power was a given, non-negotiable; family was all. One never criticized a parent. It wasn't enough simply to go along with the parents' wishes. One had to do it with good grace.

Because her husband managed to lose a lot of his money and even some of hers, Granny felt herself to be the "poor relation" among the Lehmans, though she was not in the least poor. Perhaps to compensate for the way she felt

about herself, Granny acted the part of the grande dame. By the time I knew her, she was living at the Ambassador Hotel, at Park Avenue and 50th Street, and employed a full-time maid and a full-time chauffeur, who picked her up in her Cadillac to go shopping or calling on relatives and friends.

At home Granny had dressmakers. In those days there were no clothes on the rack. She also had someone come and marcel her hair every few days. Clara treated these people very haughtily. I remember her bawling out her Irish chauffeur for making a wrong turn, and I can still see the red of his rage coming up the back of his neck. He obviously couldn't turn around and say "Stuff it!" because jobs during the Depression were so hard to find.

Granny's life was every bit as restricted as her body was by the huge whalebone corset her maid laced her into every morning. On Thursday her friends Harriet Heimerdinger whom we called "Mrs. Aunt Harriet" and Daisy Straus and a few others would come for tea. All her friends, I now realize, were Jewish. The

Clara Lehman Limburg in formal attire. Clara died in 1932 on the eve of her brother Herbert's inauguration as New York governor. "Our grandmother was every inch the grand dame" —A. Myles Limburg (A. Myles Limburg)

hobbies they shared were bridge and mah jong, shopping, and gossip. Clara also went to the opera every week and to the Philharmonic. She was a chain smoker until her death, at age sixty-two from bladder cancer.

When my parents were off traveling for months at a time, Granny engaged a double room near her apartment for me and my governess. On the governess's day out, Granny took me in her car for tea in one of a chain of Alice Foote MacDougall restaurants. One had a French motif, another was Italian, and a third had a German décor. I enjoyed these outings with Granny because they brought back memories of my visits to Europe during many summers of my childhood and also gave us something to talk about.

In the depths of the Depression, we were at a European spa in Carlsbad and Granny was buying all these beautiful embroidered doilies and spending money like water. Finally, I had a temper tantrum right there on the street: "It's horrible the way you're spending money," I said. And she said, "Don't be such a brat. Think for a minute about the women who have done this incredible embroidery. They need the money." She had a point.

When Mother and I were in Paris, we always stayed with Granny at the Ritz on the Rue Cambon side, which was more elegant, quieter, and quite a bit pricier than rooms facing Place Vendôme.

I was never taken to Temple Emanu-El until Clara's funeral. She died on the 30th of December, when Herbert was governor-elect. I can still remember the excitement over the motorcycle sirens accompanying the big black car of the governor-elect. I enjoyed every minute of it. I loved the organ. It was a marvelous farewell to Clara.

Richard Limburg, member of the New York Stock Exchange and a popular figure in Wall Street circles, c. 1910. (June Rossbach Bingham Birge)

Richard Limburg

1857–1916

New York Times, February 6, 1916

Limburg. On Feb. 5, after a brief illness, Richard Limburg, beloved husband of Clara Lehman, in the 59th year of his age. Funeral services will be held Monday morning, Feb. 7, at the Temple Emanu-El, 5th Av. and 43d St., at 9:15 o'clock. Kindly omit flowers.

PETER LIMBURG, *grandson of Richard and Clara Limburg; son of Edith and Richard Percy Limburg* – My great-grandfather Abraham Limburger came over from Schwabisch Hall in Germany. He was quite rich when he came over. He gave the city park to Schwabisch Hall. A member of Temple Emanu-El, he's buried in Salem Fields. I don't go to Salem Fields because it's a long trip and in a bad neighborhood. I don't recall my parents' going there except for a family member's funeral, so they never set me the example of visiting the family crypt.

The name "Limburger" was changed to "Limburg" before World War I. The story goes that my grandfather liked to take his lunch at Luchow's, a then famous German restaurant on 14th Street. He was a regular patron, and all the waiters knew him by name. One day he ordered a Swiss cheese sandwich. The waiter yelled into the kitchen in his native German, "Schweitzer für Limburger" ("Swiss for Limburger"). The chef, misunderstanding, shouted back, "You know we don't change orders."

This gave Grandpa Limburg the impetus to amputate the final "-er."

Grandpa Limburg was described to me as very jolly and convivial and fond of practical jokes. Once he took a guest fishing off the dock at his camp on Saranac Lake and hired a guide to hide under the dock, dive down, and attach a big dead fish to the guest's line.

Grandpa drank a lot, which may have contributed to his early death. Once, my father told me, he dumped all my grandfather's booze into the lake. According to my late cousin Dick Rossbach, Grandpa Limburg made a couple of disastrous business decisions while tiddly. Still, the family obviously kept plenty of money.

Grandpa Limburg retired from the Stock Exchange at fifty and apparently spent his time drinking and going to ball games. My father always said he died of boredom. I do have the silver loving cup his friends at the Stock Exchange gave him when he retired. Its inscription reads, on one side, "New York Stock Exchange March 3, 1881–January 27, 1910," and on the other, "Dear Old Dick from His Old Fond Friends."

———◆———

MABEL LIMBURG ROSSBACH (1894–1967), *daughter of Richard and Clara Limburg –* While in his teens my father contracted TB and was sent to the Adirondacks to recover. The mountains cast their magic over him, and he vowed when he was grown, to have a camp there. In 1898 he built Rock Ledge on the northeast shore of Lower Saranac Lake. Except for three summers we spent abroad, we occupied it regularly until 1918. It was my favorite place, and the happiest memories of my youth are associated with it. While Rock Ledge was among the early camps, within a few years many friends and relatives also built, and we would drive to Lake Placid or Upper Saranac to visit them. We visited Aunt Adele and Uncle Arthur at Adolph Lewisohn's camp, Prospect Point, and late in September we sometimes went to Kildare, Uncle Sig and Aunt Harriet's fourteen-thousand-acre place near Tupper Lake.

The house at Rock Ledge was architecturally far from attractive. Mother had been the architect, and her esthetic values left a good bit to be desired. It was three stories high, built of logs and shingles. A wide veranda hugged it on three sides, jutting out at odd moments to form rotundas and nooks. This porch was furnished with wicker swings and couches, rocking chairs, rustic chairs, and tables of every shape. From it, gravel paths led to the lake, the boathouse, and the tennis court. We played tennis with our parents but were not supposed to make them run, as they were quite stout. We also had a motorboat, which we raced.[1]

———◆———

JUNE ROSSBACH BINGHAM BIRGE, *granddaughter of Richard and Clara Limburg; daughter of Max and Mabel Rossbach –* When my mother was a little girl, someone asked her, "What does your daddy do?" "He goes downtown and makes money," she replied. Mother's governess told her that this was the wrong way to answer. The next time someone asked her, "What does your

Clara and Richard in Atlantic City, c. 1905. Their pet name for each other was "Pettie."
(Herbert H. Lehman Suite & Papers, Columbia University)

daddy do?" she said, "He goes downtown and does not make money."

Like many people, I never had the pleasure of seeing a grandfather; both of mine were dead before I was born. My paternal one, Joseph Rossbach, died of a kidney ailment that would likely be cured now within days by antibiotics. My maternal one, Richard Limburg, died of sclerosis of the liver. This disease, though sometimes caused by hepatitis, is still associated with too much alcohol.

Dick Limburg had the singular honor of numbering among the members of the governing board of the New York Stock Exchange. On the day of his retirement in 1910 the Stock Exchange, closed for half an hour in his honor. Yet his widow never mentioned him to me. Nor did my mother, except on rare occasions. To have a family member who was an alcoholic was a disgrace. My mother remembered how chagrined her father had been when her mother discovered some of the bottles he had hidden away for secret imbibing and how bitterly she had scolded him. Yet I gathered that Clara and Dick were deeply fond of one another. They called each other "Pettie" and greatly enjoyed each other's company.

— ⇒◆⇐ —

1. Archives of June Rossbach Bingham Birge.

CHAPTER SIX

Arthur Lehman &
Adele Lewisohn Lehman

———◆———

ARTHUR LEHMAN WAS ONE OF THE MOST eligible bachelors of turn-of-the-century New York. A graduate of Harvard, a charter member of the Century Country Club, and the son of Mayer Lehman of Lehman Brothers, Arthur was the epitome of what every New York son of German Jewish origin wanted out of life. Arthur's marriage in 1901 to Adele Lewisohn, daughter of pioneer copper magnate and modern art collector Adolph Lewisohn, and herself a Barnard undergraduate and budding suffragist, was considered the marriage of the year in "Our Crowd" circles.

On a plot of land at 31 West 56th Street given to them by Mr. Lewisohn, Arthur and Adele built a handsome five-story brownstone house, which they furnished with priceless medieval paintings and tapestries. In the twenties they moved to an even more sumptuous residence on East 70th Street (now owned by the Estée Lauder family) and to Ridgeleigh, a Westchester country estate originally owned by the Harriman family.

Arthur and Adele reared three daughters who more than fulfilled their expectations as scions of two illustrious families: Dorothy worked with her uncle, Herbert Lehman, in bringing family members to the United States from Germany during the Nazi period, and became a leader in Jewish communal activities and family philanthropic affairs; Helen, inspired by her uncle Irving Lehman, chief justice of the New York State

Court of Appeals, the highest court in the state, became an outstanding lawyer; Frances (known as "Peter"), the youngest, was an integral part of New York's social scene for over half a century and for 12 years was head of the New York City Commission for the United Nations, Consular Corps & Protocol under the administrations of mayors John Lindsay and Abraham Beame.

Arthur Lehman & Adele Lewisohn Lehman

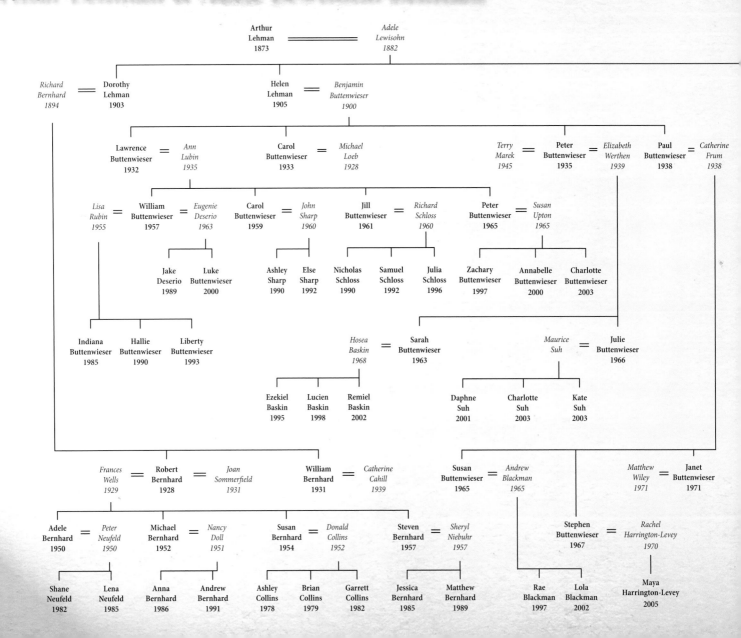

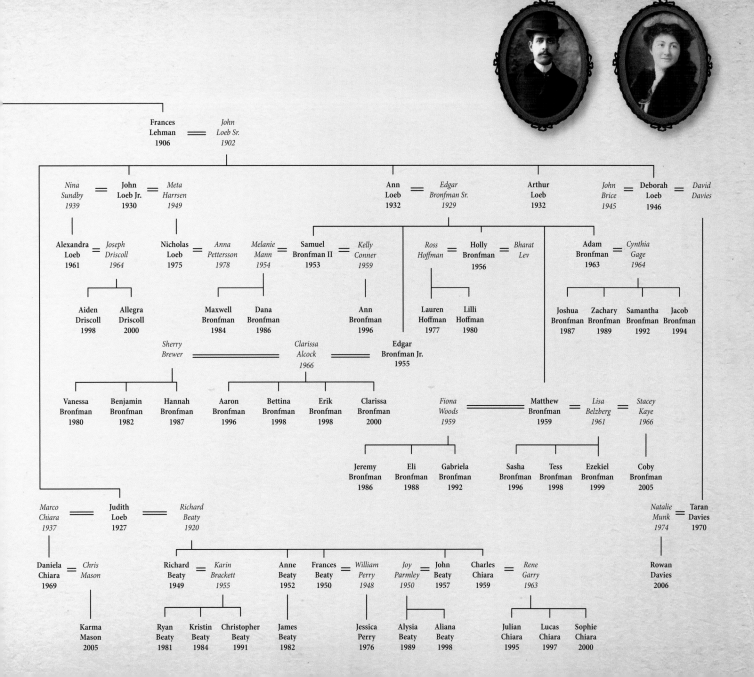

Frances Lehman 1906 = John Loeb Sr. 1902

Nina Sundby 1939 = John Loeb Jr. 1930 = Meta Harrsen 1949

Ann Loeb 1932 = Edgar Bronfman Sr. 1929

Arthur Loeb 1932

John Brice 1945 = Deborah Loeb 1946 = David Davies

Alexandra Loeb 1961 = Joseph Driscoll 1964

Nicholas Loeb 1975 = Anna Pettersson 1978

Melanie Mann 1954 = Samuel Bronfman II 1953 = Kelly Conner 1959

Ross Hoffman = Holly Bronfman 1956 = Bharat Lev

Adam Bronfman 1963 = Cynthia Gage 1964

Aiden Driscoll 1998

Allegra Driscoll 2000

Maxwell Bronfman 1984

Dana Bronfman 1986

Ann Bronfman 1996

Lauren Hoffman 1977

Lilli Hoffman 1980

Joshua Bronfman 1987

Zachary Bronfman 1989

Samantha Bronfman 1992

Jacob Bronfman 1994

Sherry Brewer = Clarissa Alcock 1966 = Edgar Bronfman Jr. 1955

Vanessa Bronfman 1980

Benjamin Bronfman 1982

Hannah Bronfman 1987

Aaron Bronfman 1996

Bettina Bronfman 1998

Erik Bronfman 1998

Clarissa Bronfman 2000

Fiona Woods 1959 = Matthew Bronfman 1959 = Lisa Belzberg 1961 = Stacey Kaye 1966

Jeremy Bronfman 1986

Eli Bronfman 1988

Gabriela Bronfman 1992

Sasha Bronfman 1996

Tess Bronfman 1998

Ezekiel Bronfman 1999

Coby Bronfman 2005

Marco Chiara 1937 = Judith Loeb 1927 = Richard Beaty 1920

Natalie Munk 1974 = Taran Davies 1970

Daniela Chiara 1969 = Chris Mason

Richard Beaty 1949 = Karin Brackett 1955

Anne Beaty 1952

Frances Beaty 1950 = William Perry 1948

Joy Parmley 1950 = John Beaty 1957

Charles Chiara 1959 = Rene Garry 1963

Rowan Davies 2006

Karma Mason 2005

Ryan Beaty 1981

Kristin Beaty 1984

Christopher Beaty 1991

James Beaty 1982

Jessica Perry 1976

Alysia Beaty 1989

Aliana Beaty 1998

Julian Chiara 1995

Lucas Chiara 1997

Sophie Chiara 2000

A dapper Arthur Lehman early in his career at Lehman Brothers, c. 1905. (Century Country Club)

Arthur Lehman

1873–1936

———✦———

New York Times, May 16, 1936

ARTHUR LEHMAN, BANKER, IS DEAD

**Brother of New York Governor
Stricken Suddenly at His Home in This City.**

LEADER IN CHARITY WORK

**Served as a Director of Many Corporations—
Judge Lehman of Court of Appeals a Brother.**

Arthur Lehman, senior member of the banking house of Lehman Brothers, 1 William Street, and a brother of Governor Herbert H. Lehman, died suddenly at 12:15 o'clock this morning at his home, 45 East Seventieth Street, of a pulmonary embolism, which his physician considered the secondary effect of a thrombosis of a leg vein, from which he had been suffering for the last two weeks. He would have been 63 years old on June 1. Until this illness his health had been excellent and he had been going to his office as usual.

The members of Mr. Lehman's immediate family who survive are his widow, the former Adele L. Lewisohn; three daughters, Mrs. Richard Bernhard, Mrs. Benjamin Buttenwieser, and Mrs. John Loeb; a sister, Mrs. Philip Goodhart; [a cousin Philip Lehman of Lehman Brothers; and two brothers], Governor Lehman and Judge Irving Lehman of the Court of Appeals, all of New York. Another sister, Settie Lehman Fatman, died last Feb. 19.

Arthur Lehman was born here on June 1, 1873, the son of Mayer and Babette Newgass [sic] Lehman. He was educated at Dr. Sach[s]'s School and Harvard College, from where he was graduated with an A.B. degree in 1894. Before starting his banking career with Lehman Brothers, he spent a year with a cotton firm in New Orleans and later served an apprenticeship of a year and a half in a New York bank.

Former Head of Jewish Federation

He was director of a score of industrial and banking organizations and aside from his charitable endeavors he was interested and took an active part in educational and communal affairs of the city.

He was at one time president and one of the organizers of the Jewish Federation and the Federation for the Support of Jewish Philanthropic Societies. He was Commissioner of the Department of Public Welfare, having received the appointment from his brother, Governor Lehman.

He also was a member of the board of directors of the Merchants Association of New York, a member of the board of trustees of the New School for Social Research, a trustee of the Museum of the City of New York and a member of the board of trustees of the City Housing Corporation and the Andrew Freedman Home. . . .

He was a member of the City, City Midday, the Broad Street, Harmonie, Lotos, Harvard, Recess, Whist and Century Country Clubs.

Owned Valuable Tapestries

Mr. Lehman was an amateur art collector of note, being interested particularly in fifteenth and sixteenth century tapestries and pictures. One of the outstanding objects of art in his collection was a golden tapestry of the fifteenth century representing "The Holy Family," a rare example of Gothic textile art. It is said to be worth more than $100,000.

Mr. Lehman was an ardent optimist. Even during the blackest days of the depression he persistently held out hope and in many instances contributed valuable aid. Despite his acknowledged approval of many outstanding acts of the current administration at Washington, he was one of those who believed and openly stated that government should aid and not compete with private business.

An indication of his attitude toward the national administration was reflected in a statement made by him early in 1935, when he said: "The enlarged participation on the part of the government in the affairs of business, both in labor relations and trade practices, has probably acted as an unsettling factor. But it is possible to say that on the whole the constructive acts of the government have overbalanced those adverse factors which have resulted from other government actions."

Gave $200,000 to Harvard

In honor of the thirtieth anniversary of his graduation from Harvard, Mr. Lehman gave the university $200,000 for a new administration building. This was one of the many contributions made by him during his lifetime to charitable and educational causes.

When Arthur Lehman went to New Orleans at the outset of his business career he was following in the footsteps of his father, Mayer Lehman, and his uncles, Emanuel and Henry, founders of Lehman Brothers, who were cotton and commission brokers before coming to New York.

In 1925 the seventy-fifth anniversary of the founding of Lehman Brothers was celebrated in New York. At that time it was estimated that the firms it had underwritten had a combined capitalization of $1,250,000,000. Another indication of the extent of Lehman Brothers operations was given four years later when Arthur Lehman was named president of the Lehman Corporation, an investment trust with capital funds of $100,000,000.

During the annual Jewish Charities campaigns, Mr. Lehman invariably had a prominent part either as president, director or one of the principal contributors. In his activities in behalf of the Federation for the Support of Jewish Philanthropic Societies, he headed many bankers' divisions, speaking at bankers' clubs, pleading the cause and in most cases showing the way with his own contributions.

———⟫◆⟪———

New York Times, May 18, 1936

OFFICIALS ATTEND LEHMAN SERVICES

Rites for Banker, a Brother of the Governor, Are Held in Temple Emanu-El.

HIS CHARITY IS PRAISED

Felix M. Warburg in an Address Hails 'His Generosity, His Desire Always to Share.'

Officials of the Federal, State and city governments and leaders in banking and allied fields of business and in organized charity and philanthropic work attended the funeral service yesterday for Arthur Lehman, banker and brother of Governor Lehman, at Temple Emanu-El, Fifth Avenue and Sixty-fifth Street.

The service was conducted jointly by Rabbi Jonah B. Wise of the Central Synagogue and Rabbi B. Benedict Glazer of Temple Emanu-El. The Rev. Dr. Nathan Krass, rabbi emeritus of Temple Emanu-El, shared the pulpit.

The bronze coffin rested beneath a blanket of orchids in front of the pulpit. Other floral tributes filled both sides of the chancel.

Members of the Lehman family attending were Mrs. Arthur Lehman, the widow; Governor Lehman, Mrs. Lehman and their daughter Hilda Jane; Mrs. Richard Bernhard, Mrs. Benjamin Buttenwieser and Mrs. John Loeb, daughters; Mrs. Philip Goodhart, a sister, and Philip Lehman [Arthur's cousin and a senior partner of Lehman Brothers]; and Judge Lehman of the Court of Appeals, a brother.

The service began with organ music, followed by a prayer and the reading of the Twenty-third Psalm by Rabbi Glazer. The Congregation Emanu-El choir sang "O for the Wings of a Dove," and this was followed by a eulogy paid by Dr. Wise.

"Arthur Lehman came of a distinguished family noted for its ability to see the need for service," Dr. Wise said. "He maintained the high standard of his family. He had an understanding of his responsibilities as an American. It sprang from his inherited loyalties. To him it was a privilege as an American and a Jew. We have been witnesses to a full and beautiful life."

Felix M. Warburg also eulogized Mr. Lehman, saying:

"He undertook his duties smilingly, giving every one surrounding him generously of that sunshine which was his nature. There was no better American and he was a good Jew. Those who knew him knew that one of his greatest virtues was his generosity, his desire always to share."

Among those in attendance were Postmaster General Farley; Henry Morgenthau Jr., Secretary of the Treasury; Supreme Court

Justice Samuel I. Rosenman; David Adie, State Commissioner of Social Welfare; Victor F. Ridder, former State Senator Nathan Straus and Walter S. Mack Jr.

Others in the assemblage were Samuel D. Leidesdorf, president of the Federation for the Support of Jewish Philanthropic Societies and Jefferson Seligman. . . .

Burial, which was private, was in Salem Fields Cemetery.

***

Arthur Lehman wrote the following letters to his youngest brother, Herbert, when Herbert was a student at Williams College.

New York, Nov. 16, 1895

My dear Herbert [then a freshman at Williams College] . . .

I have been going out very little of late, there being really no affairs to go to. Joe Dreyfus gave a 21st birthday celebration about ten days ago at which I once more became an embryo of Chauncey Depew giving an after dinner speech at which I acquitted myself fairly well. The audience didn't fall asleep at any rate. . . .

The next event on the calendar is Jesse S[traus]'s wedding Wednesday, on which occasion you know I am to act as usher. [Jesse was the son of Isidor Straus, co-owner with his brother Nathan of Macy's. Arthur and Herbert's middle brother Irving married Nathan's daughter, Sissie Straus.] If there is not too large a crowd present we ought to have a very jolly time.

Nov. 5, 1897

Last night I moved down from 81st St. to 62nd St. [to be with his mother after the death of his father, Mayer Lehman, earlier that year] but as yet am imperfectly installed in my new quarters. I suppose it will take a few days to get fully settled. . . . I see from your letters that you are profiting by the example I gave you while in Williamstown, and are taking more exercise than you had previously done. I do not think that it will hurt you any to continue this right through the year.

Jan. 20, 1898

Today is Clara's birthday and the whole family will be at the house for dinner.

May 31, 1898

Clara left for Elberon this morning, and I suppose that for the rest of the week our house will seem very empty without her and the children. . . . Hattie and Settie have practically decided to rent the Ehrich Cottage at Saranac. This, you know, is right adjoining the property on which Clara is now building, and will make it very pleasant for all concerned.

June 4, 1898

I don't know whether Irving has written you that he received notice yesterday regarding his examinations, to the effect that he had passed in them all. It goes without saying that this was just what we had expected.

Nov. 13, 1898

Presumably you have already heard that Clara moves away from us about the 15th of December, so that when you take your Christmas holidays you will find the house much more quiet than you have during the past year or so. We are all more than sorry, as you can well imagine, to have her go, and I am afraid it will be dreadfully lonely for Mama, but under the circumstances I suppose it is the best thing to do, particularly as sooner or later we would have to come to it anyhow. It is too bad, however, that she did not decide to remain for this winter, for next year with you in New York the house would not have seemed quite so empty as I am afraid it will be now with only three occupants. Clara has rented the same house which she had a few years ago, 11 East 64th Street, but has taken it only until the first of May, she and Dick still adhering to their original intention to move then to some out-of-town place near New York. It remains to be seen whether they will find any house to suit them, and whether they will eventually carry out their idea.

For the most part, during the past few weeks I have been away from Saturday afternoon until Sunday evening at the [Century] Country Club, as I am now making the best of the present opportunities. . . . The Country Club is a great success, judging from the attendance they have had on Sundays and holidays. On Election Day I think there were something like 85 people there, out of a total membership in the neighborhood of 135. Irving joined me last week at my suggestion. . . . I myself am just as enthusiastic as ever about golf, but am sorry to say that as

yet my game does not show very much improvement.

I have been going quite a good deal lately to a number of dinners, chiefly those which were given in honor of the various engaged couples. Madeleine Beer and Sidney Borg are to be married on Thanksgiving Day morning, and I am to be one of his ushers. They will have a small ceremony at the house, and then a large breakfast, to which I believe five hundred people have been invited at Delmonico's. Next Friday evening is to be the ushers' dinner, and I believe that, contrary to the usual custom, he has invited young ladies for that occasion.

Hattie has been unwell for the last week or ten days, and although there is nothing seriously the matter with her, she, as usual, has been very much worried, and imagined that she had all sorts of ailments. She is feeling much better now and will be up and about again in a couple of days. . . .

Did you hear that Leonard H. made the D.K.E. fraternity at Yale? He had evidently expected to do so, and from what I hear, had the choice of two or three societies. Otherwise I know of nothing of interest.

———⋄———

FRANCES LEHMAN LOEB (1906–1996), *youngest daughter of Arthur and Adele Lehman* – Daddy was born in New York and was educated at Dr. Sachs's School and Harvard College. As a child, I didn't know Daddy. I didn't think of him. He was just a man with a moustache who had a jovial voice and was very busy at Lehman Brothers. Daddy played golf very badly and bridge very well. He was kind and never got excited. He just became very cross if things didn't go his way. As a child that's all I really knew about him. . . .

Around 1920 Daddy began to look for property in Westchester. In 1923 he bought Ridgeleigh, a seventy-eight acre estate adjoining Whitelaw Reid's property. E. H. Harriman's first cousin Oliver and his family occupied Ridgeleigh before us. Legend has it that Mrs. Harriman's lover was Jay Gould and that he

really paid for Ridgeleigh. At any rate the Harrimans lived there for twenty-five years and raised three or four children. The house was redbrick "bastard Georgian," which my father proceeded to make more bastardly by adding sleeping porches on the second floor. The architect Julian Levi made additional changes. Sam Marks of Chicago helped mother decorate. Two rooms and a bathroom were given up to make one huge living room. The paneling there and in the library came from rooms in old English houses. Ridgeleigh could not have been more beautiful. The terraces, the gardens, the greenhouses, and all the wonderful plants were Mother's ideas. Very soon we took up residence in 1923. Ridgeleigh became our favorite home. It was the magnet that drew my generation and the next together. [1]

———⋄———

WILLIAM L. BERNHARD, *grandson of Arthur and Adele Lehman; son of Richard and Dorothy Bernhard* – Unfortunately, I do not remember my grandfather really at all. There were a lot of pictures,

An aerial view of Ridgeleigh, including its extensive gardens, as it was c. 1940. The estate is now owned by Arthur and Adele Lehman's grandson John L. Loeb Jr. (John L. Loeb Jr.)

and there was a painting of him at Ridgeleigh in what was called the telephone room which fascinated us because his eyes would follow you wherever you were in the room. He always had a white carnation in his lapel, and I seem to remember a cigar, but whether that's true memory or not, I don't know. Cigars always have a little ring around them, and we used to like to play with them. I do remember that.

––––◦–◦–◦––––

JUDITH LOEB CHIARA, *granddaughter of Arthur and Adele Lehman; eldest child of John L. and Frances Loeb –* Grandpa would take me on his lap. He would ask me things I don't remember, but I was very comfy with him. He would give me the ring from his cigar. One time I was playing at the pool, and I was teaching all the children how to jump in backwards. Johnny [Judith's younger brother] hit his chin at the edge of the pool, and he had to have three stitches. Everybody was furious with me. I remember running to my grandparents, and my grandpa took me in

his lap and was very comforting, saying it wasn't my fault.

––––◦–◦–◦––––

JOHN L. LOEB JR., *grandson of Arthur and Adele Lehman; elder son of John L. and Frances Loeb –* My memories of my grandfather are accompanied by a sense of great warmth and acceptance. Every Sunday I would run across the lawn from our house to my grandparents'. Grandpa would be having breakfast on the terrace, which I look out on now. I would sit with him, and he would give me toast with honey on it. I think of my grandfather often because I am very lucky to be living at Ridgeleigh, the estate he purchased in the 1920s and where I grew up as a child.

Arthur Lehman and my father (Arthur's son-in-law) never really hit it off. My father did not endear himself to his in-laws. For instance, in 1932—three years after the crash of 1929 when Mother was pregnant with twins—Father said at a lunch with Arthur and Adele Lehman, "You know, Arthur, I married your daughter for her looks and her money, and now she has lost both." I suppose he meant to be funny, but I don't know whether they took it that way.

June Rossbach Bingham Birge, *granddaughter of Arthur Lehman's older sister Clara Lehman Limburg; daughter of Max and Mabel Limburg Rossbach –* Uncle Arthur was at our White Plains house for lunch when I was about four. After the meal he went out on the sun porch and pulled a sausage-like brown item from his pocket, cut off one end, put the item in his mouth, and set fire to the cut end. As he puffed smoke like a dragon, I asked what it was. "A cigar; want to try it?" I nodded, and he put it in my mouth and told me to breathe in. I did so and choked and gasped and handed it back. He laughed, but I didn't think it was funny—and have hated the smell of cigars ever since.

Lawrence B. Buttenwieser, *grandson of Arthur and Adele Lewisohn Lehman; eldest son of Benjamin Joseph and Helen Lehman Buttenwieser –* Based on what I have been told about my grandfather, Arthur Lehman, it would be hard for me to believe that he was not the top dog of any enterprise in which he was involved after the age of twenty. He must have been the man who ran Lehman Brothers, certainly from World War I on. He could not have breathed in an organization where he was not at the very top.

Soon after my parents married in 1929, Arthur offered my father, Benjamin J. Buttenwieser, $10,000 to change his last name to Lehman, an offer that, obviously, Ben declined.

Of Arthur's descendants, only Bobby Bernhard, Johnny Loeb, and I have strong interests in Judaism and Jewish history.

Arthur Lehman Loeb, *grandson of Arthur and Adele Lehman; younger son of John L. and Frances Loeb –* There was a discussion among members of the family one evening. The question was: If you could come back to earth after death, who would you like to be? Some wanted to be a

Arthur and Adele Lehman when Arthur was senior partner of Lehman Brothers and Adele was an important figure in Jewish philanthropy, c. 1930. (John L. Loeb Jr.)

great figure, such as a political leader, a general, an artist, a writer, a poet. According to family lore, my grandfather said, "I would love to come back to earth again as Arthur Lehman."

Somewhere in Europe, Grandma Adele and Arthur Lehman were not receiving proper service at a hotel. My grandmother said to my grandfather, "Please go down and tell the concierge who we are so we can get better service." My grandfather was quite willing to do this. "Of course," he said, and started down to see the concierge before coming back and saying quizzically to his wife, "Who *are* we?"

The third story is about Judy [Arthur Loeb's older sister] and Grandpa Lehman. They were walking through the rose garden at Ridgeleigh, and Grandpa commented, "Aren't those roses beautiful?" Judy, never lacking an ability to speak out, said, "Grandpa, it's not those roses, but *them* roses," obviously learning her grammar from the Irish help.

＊＊＊

ROBERT BERNHARD, *grandson of Arthur and Adele Lehman; older son of Richard and Dorothy Bernhard* – When I was at Lehman Brothers in the 1950s, they didn't refer back to "when the family ran it." I rarely, if ever, heard my grandfather Arthur's name. I don't think Bobby Lehman [Emanuel Lehman's grandson, Philip's son, and senior partner of Lehman Brothers after the death of Philip] ever really accepted his cousin, my grandfather.

Bobby's grudge against my grandfather goes back to 1928, when FDR asked Herbert to be his lieutenant governor. Clearly Herbert had to get out of Lehman Brothers. In resigning as an "x" percentage partner, he was given "x" percentage of the value of the firm in cash without any entanglements, though they could have paid him off with shares they owned in private companies—Helena Rubinstein, for example. If Philip had really objected to it, it wouldn't have gone that way because Philip was the senior partner.

Then the '29 Crash came along, and the firm had a liquidity problem in running the

Arthur wearing his signature boutonniere. Portrait by Daniel Greene. (John L. Loeb Jr.)

business. What Bobby Lehman did was to blame Arthur for risking the firm to pay off his brother, even though Arthur could not have foreseen the Crash. Then Bobby wanted to bring on board John Hertz of Hertz-Rent-a-Car as a partner. To say the least, Bobby was a very difficult person. Over Arthur's objections, Bobby and Philip brought Hertz in. It alienated my grandfather—that I know. My grandfather died fairly shortly thereafter in May of 1936.

He had a blood clot in his leg, and it traveled to his heart. He died much too early, but that was the way it was in those days.

Bobby Lehman used to have people visit the house of his father, Philip. It had all these great pictures in it. My grandmother Adele, before she died, wanted to see them. I went to Bobby and said, "My grandmother isn't well. She's never been in the house. Would you invite her?" He wouldn't do it. He still bore the grudge.

Adele Lewisohn Lehman around the turn of the century, when she was active in the women's suffrage movement. (John L. Loeb Jr.)

Adele Lewisohn Lehman

1882–1965

New York Times, August 12, 1965

MRS. ARTHUR LEHMAN DIES AT 83;
A LEADER IN PHILANTHROPIC WORK

Widow of Investment Banker
Was Honorary Chairman of Jewish Federation

PURCHASE, N.Y., Aug. 11—Mrs. Arthur Lehman, widow of the investment banker and a leader in New York philanthropic and cultural circles for more than half a century, died of a cerebral hemorrhage this morning at her estate, Ridgeleigh, on Anderson Hill Road. She was 83 years old.

Mrs. Lehman, the former Adele Lewisohn, was for many years honorary chairman of the Federation of Jewish Philanthropies. She was a board member of the New York Service for the

Orthopedically Handicapped and founder, in 1954, and a board member of the Arthur Lehman Counselling Service.

A funeral service will be held at 11 A.M. Friday at Temple Emanu-El, Fifth Avenue and 65th Street, New York. Burial will be private.

Had Active Roles in Agencies

Mrs. Lehman inherited her interest in charitable activities and in welfare work from her father, the late Adolph Lewisohn, a leader in prison reform and in many other areas. Like her father, she was not only a substantial donor—among his gifts was Lewisohn Stadium—and an active fund-raiser, but she took responsibility for the administration of charitable agencies, serving as an officer or board member of many.

She was born in New York on May 17, 1882. Her mother was the former Emma Cahn. She was educated at the Annie Brown School and attended Barnard College. In 1901, at 19, she was married to Arthur Lehman, brother of Herbert H. Lehman, the late Governor and Senator, and of Irving Lehman, former judge of the State Court of Appeals.

Arthur Lehman became a senior member of the investment banking firm of Lehman Brothers at 1 William Street. He too was interested in charitable activities, and he was a founder of the Federation of Jewish Philanthropies.

Mrs. Lehman devoted the early years of her marriage to her daughters, Dorothy, Helen and Frances. Afterward she gave much of her time to less fortunate children. Though a shy, reserved woman, she was active in the day-to-day concerns of the Service for the Orthopedically Handicapped and its predecessor agency and of other institutions.

The Lehmans first lived at 31 West 56th Street. Later they moved to 45 East 70th Street, where, over the years, Mrs. Lehman entertained frequently for the philanthropic, civic and cultural causes with which she was associated.

At the town house Mrs. Lehman and her husband assembled notable collections of tapestries, rugs, paintings from the 15th century to the 20th and other art objects.

Until World War II, Mrs. Lehman was also active in sports. She played championship tennis from the turn of the century until after the First World War, mostly at Long Branch but also at Elberon and Deal, N.J. She won 38 cups in championship play. As a golfer she competed in local metropolitan team matches in Westchester.

Mrs. Lehman's husband died in 1936. Her father died two years later.

Served Voters' League

In the 1940's Mrs. Lehman was active in the League of Women Voters, serving as a vice president in 1945. For several decades she was also active in musical circles. She was a member of the auxiliary board of the Philharmonic-Symphony Society of New York for many years and in 1947 was elected to the society's board of directors.

The same year she took up painting, doing floral, still life and landscape pictures.

Mrs. Lehman made a gift to Barnard College in 1957 that made possible Adele Lehman Hall, a building which also houses Barnard's Wollman Library. It was the college's first major addition since 1926.

Mrs. Lehman is survived by her 3 daughters, Mrs. Richard J. Bernhard, Mrs. Benjamin J. Buttenwieser and Mrs. John L. Loeb, all of New York; 10 grandchildren and 21 great-grandchildren.

FRANCES LEHMAN LOEB (1906–1995), *youngest daughter of Arthur and Adele Lehman* – Mother was the middle child. She had two older sisters, Florence and Clara, and two younger brothers, Sam and Julius. Mother went to a rather stylish school in New York called Miss Annie Brown's. She enjoyed going to school. Although I never thought of Mother being intellectual, she was very forward looking and an early believer in women's suffrage. She was allowed to go to college, although her parents did not particularly approve of it. She entered Barnard College in 1900. Many years later I helped establish Adele Lehman Hall at Barnard. Mother left in 1901 to marry Daddy over the objections of Grandma Lewisohn, who apparently thought she was more important than the Lehmans.

After they returned from their honeymoon, they began building their house at 31 West 56th Street on a plot of ground given to them by Grandpa Lewisohn. At that time women in a delicate condition were not allowed out once they couldn't wear corsets. Because Mother became very fat every time she was pregnant, she had to stay indoors for almost six months of every pregnancy. Being a natural athlete, she found these restrictions very difficult.

When I came into this world on the third floor of the 56th Street house on September 25, 1906, Grandma [Babette] Lehman was waiting most anxiously in the sitting room below for a son to bear the family name. When Daddy told Grandma Lehman I was a girl, all she said was, "Oh, isn't that too bad."

My mother was a suffragette, she went to college, but her independence ended with all that. She didn't take a strong stand at the dinner table. She had a few close friends, but most of them were the wives of my father's friends. My father had a roving eye. That was typical of the men of the generation. I'm sure Mother was less than pleased, but she never said boo.[2]

———>◦◦◦<———

JUDITH LOEB CHIARA, *granddaughter of Arthur and Adele Lehman; eldest child of John L. and Frances Loeb* – Grandma was one of the truly good people I

Adele as a young woman, c. 1900. "She was just this wonderful presence,"
granddaughter Judith Loeb Chiara recalls. (John L. Loeb Jr.)

ever knew. You were in the presence of a real lady; therefore, it behooved you to be nice. She studied, she painted, she cared. She was always available, always had a willing ear.

Every Sunday for lunch as long as I can remember we went over to Grandma's. It was at the pool, and it was a buffet, and the children were free. We could do whatever we wanted. Nobody cared where we went, what we ate—if we screamed, we were told to go away. We could swim when we wanted to. I wanted to go every Sunday to Grandma's for lunch because it was freedom.

Before I grew up, she was just this wonderful presence. After I had my first child, Richie, I spent my first summer at her house, where everyone treated everyone else so nicely. That's when I saw the amount of work she really had to do to run Ridgeleigh and make it appear effortless. She had ten in help, and she organized everything. That was a big job, and in the city, too, and Florida—what everybody ate, what to order, who would sit where. People don't often realize that even if you have money,

if you do it beautifully, it takes a lot of work on your part.

⟹◆⟸

JOHN L. LOEB JR., *grandson of Arthur and Adele Lehman; eldest son of John L. and Frances Loeb –* My grandmother Adele Lewisohn Lehman lived much longer than my grandfather, and so I remember her more clearly, but I never really had a close relationship with her. She was almost like the Queen of England—very regal, very quiet; listening, rarely saying anything, but always a strong presence. Grandma was concerned very much with the flowers and the greenhouses and that everything be perfect when it came to flowers. I remember her painting a great deal as she grew older.

Everybody I met considered her to be a most important person. Whenever I went anywhere, even as a child, when it was learned that I was related to Mrs. Arthur Lehman, it seemed to immediately enhance my relationship with the person I was talking to. Every time my father invited somebody important out to

Purchase for the weekend, perhaps trying to close an important business deal, he would always take them over to Grandma's for lunch, tea, or cocktails as a way of emphasizing how important he was because of his mother-in-law, Mrs. Lehman.

When Adele died, the flag at the Century Country Club was lowered to half-mast. She had been, at that time, the only woman member of an all-male club. I believe even widows lost their memberships when their husbands died, and they could no longer be members by themselves.

In retrospect, Grandmother Adele was rather remote. We didn't have what you might call a personal relationship. I do remember confiding to her once that I didn't have any-one to take to the New Year's Eve party she held every year, because I wasn't going steady at the time. Her reply was: "Not to worry. Only the help go steady." I don't remember any other exchange of a personal nature that passed between us. Yet I think she loved having us kids around, because I remember she was not happy when my parents built their own

swimming pool and we didn't come around to use hers as often.

During the summer at Ridgeleigh there were always six or seven cousins of all ages liv-ing at my grandmother's. We spent the hot, heavy days half-naked, roaming like bandits on our bicycles over the back roads and forest paths or playing Fox and Hounds for hours in the pool. We learned every hiding place, every stump, every fallen tree and thicket on Ridgeleigh. In winter, when we couldn't go sleigh-riding because the runners would stick, we would take out our pans and trays and spin crazily down the hill

Adele was unlike my Granny Loeb, who had an enormous warmth about her and talked with me about my future. She even predicted that I would one day be an ambassador! Granny Loeb, like Aunt Settie Lehman, was born in Montgomery, Alabama; spoke with a heavy Southern accent; and followed Southern tradi-tions. She always called Grandpa Loeb "Mr. Loeb" except when she was peeved with him. Then she called him "Carl." She called all her

Adele with her father, Adolph Lewisohn, and her daughter Dorothy (standing), in the library of the Lewisohn home on Fifth Avenue, c. 1937. (John L. Loeb Jr.)

grandchildren "beaus" and "belles" and made a big fuss over us, which Adele never did.

Perhaps one of the reasons I remember so little of talking with Adele about anything personal was that there were so many other people around, such as Aunt Helen and Uncle Ben Buttenwieser and my Buttenwieser cousins Larry, Carol, Paul, and Peter and of course my Bernhard cousins Billy and Bobby and their parents, my Aunt Dorothy and Uncle Dick. Also, during World War II the Bernhards were sheltering two British children, Sandy and Susan Courage (as in "Courage Ale & Beer"). It was always an extremely busy place. The children usually did not eat with the adults, except perhaps Sunday lunches, where conversation never became personal.

One of the main social events of our lives was Grandma Lehman's New Year's Eve parties at her 70th Street home. She had taken those parties on from her father, Adolph Lewisohn, whose New Year's parties were legendary. To be invited to Mrs. Lehman's for New Year's Eve was very prestigious, and a lot of the older men like my father would come in white tie. Grandma was always seated on a chair in the library near a Romney painting. People didn't really bow or kneel, but they managed to give the impression that they were. When my grandparents got married, Adele's father, Adolph Lewisohn, offered the newlyweds either a Romney or a Gauguin from his art collection. Alas, my grandfather picked the Romney, whose value went steadily downhill.

When I started to go to WASP parties, I was looked down on because I was not in the Social Register. So I began looking through the book, and much to my surprise I found my Grandma Lehman in it. Nobody in the family had the chutzpah to ask her, "How did you get into the Social Register and none of the rest of us?" I did some research and found out that her father was in the original Social Register, which I believe had its origins as a handbook sponsored by local carriage trade stores! No members of the Lehman family, including my mother and aunts, were in it. As a young man I assumed the reason was they had married beneath them. Today, I and my children, Nicholas and Alexandra, are in the book, but I don't believe anyone else in the family is.

My mother's sister, Helen Buttenwieser, who was a lawyer, was the executor of my grandmother's estate when she died in 1965. Grandma's 70th Street townhouse (which she and my Grandfather Arthur Lehman had built) was still almost fully furnished when Aunt Helen had it put on the market. My father wanted to buy it, but my mother didn't. She liked their apartment on Park Avenue, and she also didn't want to live in her mother's house. By that time I had my brownstone townhouse on East 61st Street, but I would love to have bought it anyway. Before I was aware that it was up for sale, it had been sold.

The house and furnishings went to Estée Lauder for only $500,000, because at that point McMansions weren't "in." Aunt Helen was very pleased that her mother's 70th Street residence with all of its furnishings including the renowned tapestry collection and all the antique furniture had been taken off her list of responsibilities. Today the house and furnishings would probably be worth something like $50,000,000.

Estée never wanted any member of our family to enter the house again. As chance would have it, fifteen years after Grandma Lehman's house was sold, my cousin Billy Bernhard and I were invited to a charity event held at the house. Upon entering the premises, we marveled—not a thing had been changed! All the family furnishings were still in place. It looked just like the Lehman house we grew up in—tapestries and all.

⟫•◊•⟪

ANN LOEB BRONFMAN, *granddaughter of Arthur and Adele Lehman; daughter of John L. and Frances Loeb* – Grandma's New Year's parties at her home on 70th Street were great fun. When you walked in, there was a small ballroom quite a way in front of you, down some steps. There was a men's cloak closet on one side and a women's on the other. And then this beautiful staircase.

Adele would be up there sitting in some chair waiting to be said "hello" to. She always seemed very pleased to see you. She'd tell us to have a good time. Grown-ups were on the second floor, and we'd go back downstairs, where there was dancing with a live orchestra.

One New Year's Eve Mother was pregnant with Debby and in tears because she couldn't get into one of her original evening dresses. So she wore the dress, not fastened all the way up in the back, topped with a Chinese jacket, and you couldn't tell anything. I remember a friend of mine—a very good dancer named Donald Eisman—asked my mother to dance. And Mother said, "Well, I can't do that because I'm pregnant." He was really stunned—Mother was nearly forty, though she didn't look it.

Everyone at Ridgeleigh loved Adele—from Garbett, the chauffeur, who taught us how to drive, to Arthur Griffiths, the butler, who was terribly proper, and wore a uniform, and stood up very straight. He was a wonderful, educated, intelligent man who later became my father's assistant at Loeb, Rhoades. I still miss him. And Katie, Grandma's maid, who was wonderful. Katie would lay out Grandma's clothes gently and say, "Isn't this beautiful."

And there was Margaret the cook, who cooked on a stove fueled by wood. Grandma eventually got her an electric stove, but she still used the wood stove. The toast tasted so good. And she cooked all these things from Grandma's garden. It wasn't like today, when you can get asparagus twelve months out of the year. They raised their own corn, peas, and carrots. And potatoes. She kept chickens during the war in coops across the pond. We had our own eggs, and we ate our own chickens.

———✦———

PETER LIMBURG, *grandson of Richard and Clara Limburg; son of Richard Percy and Edith Limburg* – My parents were in awe of my mother's Aunt Adele. They always told me I had to be on my best behavior and watch what I did when we were visiting Aunt Adele. Here's another word to describe Aunt Adele, which may help explain why my parents were in awe of her—imperious.

———⟾◆⟸———

PETER L. BUTTENWIESER, *grandson of Arthur and Adele Lehman; middle son of Benjamin and Helen Buttenwieser* – My grandmother Adele was a lovely old-style woman, progressive in her thoughts but old-fashioned in her way of life. If you went there for dinner, it was a fairly formal affair. I remember learning from her how to use silverware. For a little boy to sit down at a table that had maybe three forks and three knives and a spoon here and a bowl there, it was a lot to learn. She never admonished you. She did it in a very approving, easy sort of way—when you stand up from the table, when you sit down, how to stand in a crowd—I am eternally grateful, as there is no other way to learn such things.

After I went away to the Putney School at a very young age, she would go to the local gourmet store—there were far fewer in those days—and pick out things she knew I loved and have them shipped off to school. She could have told the help to do it, but she didn't. Now that's a very hands-on thing to do.

There were ground rules at her house, one of which was that there would be no arguments in her presence. You went somewhere else to do that. In her world she was treated like a little bit of royalty. Definitely, the world came to her. Was she imperious? To some she may have appeared so, but in actual fact she was a marshmallow.

———⟾◆⟸———

PAUL A. BUTTENWIESER, *grandson of Arthur and Adele Lehman; youngest son of Benjamin and Helen Buttenwieser* – My grandmother Adele Lehman was a great music lover. She was a trustee of the New York Philharmonic, and she had a box every other Thursday night. In addition, she had a Monday night subscription at the Metropolitan Opera. And on Saturdays she would invariably listen to the opera on the radio. I have memories of going to Ridgeleigh in the spring on weekends and listening to the opera together. At the time I was an aspiring serious musician.

One time I arrived home from boarding school for a vacation, and there was a Philharmonic concert, to which naturally I was invited. I was tired, or I wanted to do something else and I declined the invitation. When I saw Adele the next day, she said, "Oh we missed you last night!" And I felt awful because that was really what we had together more than anything, and it gave her pleasure to have me at concerts with her.

One of my most cherished memories of spending time with her was one summer after I graduated from high school. At the time my grandmother was traveling in Europe with Edna Hellman and Mr. and Mrs. Oscar Strasser. Wherever Adele went, there would be a car and a chauffeur and a maid. The maid for Adele, as Edna put it, "maided me as well." If they stayed in a city for any length of time, there would be a courier or factotum kind of person to get tickets, make arrangements.

I have wonderful memories of going to Tanglewood with her. We would be driven up by Lind, her Swedish chauffeur. The car, of course, was very comfortable. We would "stop" at the Curtis Inn and go to the Friday night, Saturday night, and Sunday afternoon concerts—just the two of us. I don't care what we would hear—it could be Beethoven—and she would say, "That was charming." I used to tease her about that. I don't think she was strongly moved by music. I think she did listen, but I don't think she responded in a deep way.

I remember going with her as a boy to art galleries of the caliber of Wildenstein's and Duveen's, which was a tremendous experience, to see all that kowtowing as they would bring things out, though there was nothing hoity-toity about Adele. She subscribed to the *Christian Science Monitor*, a "high-minded" newspaper like the *Manchester Guardian*. Her New Year's party invitations simply read "Mrs. Arthur Lehman, at home December 31st from 10 o'clock." She was not haughty. Actually, she had what I always thought of as a slight Brooklyn accent. Adele was completely unaffected. To me she came across as the most unambiguously adored person in my life.

LAWRENCE B. BUTTENWIESER, *grandson of Arthur and Adele Lehman; eldest son of Benjamin and Helen Buttenwieser* – My grandmother, Adele, lived two lives. She first lived the life you would have expected of someone who was Adele Lewisohn. A favored child, she goes to college, and gets married, and lives very comfortably. She and her husband, Arthur, have a house in Elberon, New Jersey. She and Arthur also have a townhouse on 56th Street, and then in the early twenties a friend of theirs builds eight houses on 70th and 71st Streets between Park and Madison, and Arthur takes one for himself and Adele and another one for his oldest daughter, Dorothy. David Sarnoff and Maurice Wertheim are among their neighbors.

Then in 1936 Arthur dies of a pulmonary thrombosis, and Adele's life changes drastically. Instead of merely being the wife of a rich man, she becomes her own person. Never thereafter does she have what you would call a date. She gets escorted to dinner, the theater, or concerts by male friends, but there is not a hint of romance, despite the fact that she is quite hand- some and rich and doesn't have children under- foot. I would have thought she'd have men buzzing around her; I never saw one.

Adele said she didn't want any. She had a totally different life. Though terribly shy, she became a public speaker. She had to because she became president of the New York League of Women Voters. She founded a camp for the orthopedically handicapped in New Jersey because she has a mildly orthopedically handi- capped grandson. She created a social agency called The Purple Box that had a benefit every spring at her home. She became an influential member of the board of the New York Philharmonic.

Art was very important in her life, and the key figure in her acquisitions was James Rorimer, curator of medieval art at the Met. James was glad to advise her on tapestries because the expectation was that they would wind up at the Met. Most did not. Those that did not were sold to Estée Lauder when Estée purchased the house on 70th Street following Adele's death.

After Ann Lubin and I were engaged, we were invited by Adele to her very nice, very comfortable Palm Beach house on Jungle Road. The house had a lovely patio, where she did most of her painting in the wintertime. She was a lightly talented amateur, and painting gave her great pleasure. She had a passion for flowers. When I was eight or ten I was to get 25 cents if she pointed to a flower and I could identify it.

Adele lived right across the street from the Century Country Club and was always in charge of the grounds, as she would lend her gardener to take care of the grounds around the clubhouse. It was a no-brainer for the officials at Century—she supplied both the labor and the materials.

For lunch, which was at a quarter to one, Adele would serve chicken sandwiches with the crusts cut off or tomato sandwiches done with a cookie cutter so they were round and without crusts. She had a quite grand establishment—a butler and maids. They adored her, though one of the butlers had to be fired because he was taking kickbacks from a vendor. It caused great excitement. Adele probably asked her daughter Dorothy to do the firing.

One has to take account of the general style of the day to understand how my mother and her sisters were brought up. The girls did not see their father more than a half-hour a day on weekdays until they were in their teens. Their upbringing, I imagine, was totally supervised by their mother. Arthur may have had some input in major decisions—whether to send a daughter to this school or that school—but I don't think very much beyond that. Adele didn't send them to any old school. She wanted to be sure they could go as far as their intellects and ambitions took them. She was the stimulus.

None of Adele's three daughters could have begun to write a Mommie Dearest story. She always put her children's interests ahead of her own. My Aunt Dorothy [Bernhard] had a permanent home in my grandmother's house in Purchase. She and Adele would be together every weekend and every summer. My Aunt "Peter" [Frances Lehman Loeb] and

Adele with her three married daughters, (from left) Frances ("Peter") Loeb, Dorothy Bernhard, and Helen Buttenwieser.
They were her three greatest achievements. (American Jewish Historical Society)

my Uncle John lived literally in the shadow of Adele's house. And my mother, Helen, was devoted to Adele. I cannot recall any concern in the family that Adele had done something harmful or unkind.

Adele was not harsh, strict, or demanding. She had wonderful relationships with her three daughters—who were quite different— but, then, Adele had wonderful relationships with everybody. She was without ego, which proved very helpful with three quite strong-willed daughters with more than enough ego for the entire family. She was a wonderful listener. You didn't visit her to receive the wisdom of a grandmother. You were there to tell her what you were doing, what interested you. She listened very skillfully, and you never quite realized it. She was not an observant Jew. I can't ever remember her going to services other than marriages or funerals or my bar mitzvah at Shearith Israel, to which she went gladly.

—❖—

ROBERT BERNHARD, *grandson of Arthur and Adele Lehman; elder child of Richard and Dorothy Bernhard* – Philanthropy was my Grandmother and Grandfather Adele and Arthur Lehman's religion. I can count the times on one finger that I attended services at Temple Emanu-El as a child. Like her mother, my mother [Dorothy Lehman Bernhard] found her spiritual fulfillment in philanthropy.

—❖—

MARJORIE LEWISOHN (1918–2006), *daughter of Adele Lewisohn Lehman's brother Sam* – Aunt Adele was lovely—very refined, upper class. She was always beautifully groomed. She had wonderful servants, all of whom were Irish and delightful. They were always very good to me in Palm Beach—unpack your suitcase and bring you breakfast in bed. Adele always had a lot of guests. I know Billy Bernhard was absolutely captivated by his grandma. We used to visit her in Palm Beach at the same time. She always had a group of "Our Crowd" there that included Adele's close friend Edna Hellman and my

Uncle Franz Lewisohn, who adored her and influenced me to become a doctor. She wasn't terribly outgoing. She was kind of quiet, but she had a quiet fortitude and a sense of humor. She liked people, and they all loved her. She adored all her children and grandchildren, me, and some other nieces and nephews. She was a great hostess. Even if some people didn't get along with other people, she got along with them all.

———⋙◆⋘———

JOAN MORGENTHAU HIRSCHHORN, *granddaughter of Adele's brother- and sister-in-law Morris and Settie Fatman* – Aunt Adele came up with Dorothy Lehman Bernhard to see our new house in Old Greenwich. I hadn't furnished the house, but I did hang a reproduction of a Cézanne still life, which I had acquired at the Met Museum's gift shop during a Cézanne retrospective. Aunt Adele exclaimed that the original was one of her favorites in her own collection.

———⋙◆⋘———

ROBERT BERNHARD, *grandson of Arthur and Adele Lehman; elder child of Richard and Dorothy Bernhard* – They were all very strong women—Adele, Dorothy, Helen, Peter [Frances]. They all made their mark. You know about Peter and all she and John [Loeb] did for Harvard, Vassar, New York University, New York Hospital, and other institutions. Helen became a lawyer, basically representing children. She even reached the point of arguing before the Supreme Court. My mother, Dorothy, was on the boards of the Federation of Jewish Philanthropies and the American Joint Distribution Committee. What drove her into philanthropy was her mother, who was very much involved on a number of boards. I wouldn't doubt that it was expected that the daughters would follow suit. Philanthropy was their religion. Adele was one of the early and major contributors to Lincoln Center.

We were members of Temple Emanu-El from year one. When Emanuel Lehman moved from Montgomery to New York prior to the Civil War, he was one of its principal supporters. Yet we hardly ever went there. The High

Holy Days would come and go, and if there was a golf game, that was better. I remember going with my mother once for Friday night services because she wanted us to see what it was like. Having said all that, the big rose window at the end of Temple Emanu-El was contributed by the children of Mayer and Babette Lehman.

My grandfather bought my grandmother a rather ornate set of cabochon emeralds—ring, bracelet, necklace, pins—everything. That was virtually the only jewelry my grandmother had. After she died, I collected the emeralds and put them in the Lehman Brothers safe. A week or so later Mother and Helen came down and I laid them out just before Peter stormed into the room and said, "My dears, you're never gonna wear these." She opened her pocketbook—in went the emeralds—she closed her pocketbook, and off she strode. And the two other sisters absolutely broke into tears they were laughing so hard. Afterward Helen said, "She's absolutely right."

———⊰◆⊱———

WILLIAM L. BERNHARD, *grandson of Arthur and Adele Lehman; younger son of Richard and Dorothy Bernhard* – You know the end of the story. At some point I said to Peter when she was wearing the emeralds, "They look good on you," and she said, "These are not the emeralds. I sold them. These are fake. But nobody will know the difference. Knowing me, they will think I am wearing the real thing."

My grandmother used to have friends and family to dinner. One night at Ridgeleigh there was a big table of fifteen or eighteen people, and the Loebs had brought along John's friend and business partner, Palmer Dixon, and his beautiful wife, Joan, who had been an actress. John went to Harvard with Palmer and knew him as a Harvard tennis champion. They were a very handsome couple, as were the Loebs. Palmer was sitting on my grandmother's left, John to the right, and my father at the end of the table— because we lived there in the summer. There was some discussion of a family connection and Palmer, who was the epitome of a WASP gentleman said, "Oh, you mean that's your *mish-*

pocheh" ["kinfolk" in Hebrew]. The response was total silence.

My grandmother was extremely affectionate and warm and took a real interest in me, as she did in all her grandchildren. I was with her a lot. We lived at Ridgeleigh in the summers, and I visited her in Palm Beach. My mother was not keen on Palm Beach at all. She wasn't a resort person, and Palm Beach was divided along religious lines. My mother found it not her cup of tea.

My father and I, however, loved it. We all got up, had breakfast, and sometime in the morning would go to the beach. In those days there were these wonderful Phipps Pools in the middle of town. We would ride or bike there. They were open to the public for a fee—big, beautiful pools, Olympic size, with access to the beach. There were dressing rooms on the ground floor. And then you could go upstairs to a solarium, where the older men would lie in the sun and play cards and talk. Friends and family would congregate, but not exclusively, as WASPS did at the Bath and Tennis Club and the Everglades Club.

The Everglades had a small golf course right in the center of Palm Beach built on landfill areas susceptible to flooding. At some point an eighteen-hole golf course was commissioned to be built a little farther away. Called the Palm Beach Country Club, it was definitely open to Jews and pretty much exclusively to them. Grandma was asked to be one of the founding members, which she was. It was very convenient because of her membership, for whoever was a guest of Adele's, and she and my father loved to play as well.

Robert Young (the railroad tycoon) happened to live nearer to the Palm Beach Country Club than to the Everglades, and he wanted to join because it was closer and the golf course was bigger. So he did. Among his guests every winter were the Duke and Duchess of Windsor. So in the midst of this Jewish enclave, there was Robert Young playing golf with the Duke of Windsor. I think the rest of Palm Beach was quite fussed that the Duke of Windsor would go to that club, but it was convenient, and it was a better course.

I was walking with my grandmother in New York between 70th and 71st streets and Park, and I said something about an upcoming divorce of people we knew in the area. Divorce in those days was practically unknown, at least in this group. She said to me, "You know, you never know what goes on between a couple unless you're under the bed." For my grandmother, it was a very surprising thing to say—but she was wonderfully down-to-earth.

She loved the rose garden at Ridgeleigh and gardens in general. She met regularly with the superintendent on most days when she was in Westchester, an excellent man named Mr. Leach. She would often walk around with a trowel and gloves and scissors to cut the roses and other flowers. To some extent she did the flower arrangements, though she had people who were very good at that.

Garbett was her chauffeur. He taught my cousins, my brother, and me how to drive. Garbett was a very charismatic figure for kids, and we were often at the garage. He was a tough character. He wouldn't put up with any nonsense. There were quite a lot of cars. He took care of them all. And he'd take us to White Plains to get ice cream. He'd take us to the movies. He was always part of the action. The Loebs [John and Frances] lived next door, right on the same property, just below Grandma's house. If anyone got out of hand, he would love to say, "This is Lehmans, you know. Not Loebs."

<hr/>

ARTHUR LEHMAN LOEB, *grandson of Arthur and Adele Lehman; younger son of John L. and Frances Loeb* – I didn't know my grandfather after whom I am named. I was only four—actually three-and-a-half—when he died in 1936, and I have no memories of him, but I was very close to my grandmother. During the summer we lived at Ridgeleigh, her property in Purchase, New York. She was very supportive. She made each of her grandchildren think that he or she was her favorite grandchild. I remember once she came to see me act in a play at the Harvey School when I

Three generations of Lehmans, (left to right): Adele's granddaughter Judy Loeb Beaty holding her firstborn, Richie,
Judy's mother (Adele's youngest daughter, Frances), and Adele herself. Richie was born in 1949. (John L. Loeb Jr.)

was eleven. Many years later she told me how terrible it was, but at the time she said it was the greatest.

She was highly cultivated. Her house on 70th Street in New York City was full of medieval tapestries and 17th-century Dutch paintings. She had made a real effort to learn all about her art. She was also a very good reader. She would read the *New York Times* book review every week, cover-to-cover, and was always reading the latest novel or the latest biography. She also loved classical music and went to the Philharmonic every week.

She was a passionate sportswoman as well. She had been a very good tennis player in her youth, and by the time I knew her, she had become a very good golfer. It was only when she had to give up golf because of a heart attack that she took up painting. I liked one of her paintings so much that I asked my parents—who inherited it—to leave it to me, which they did.

———⟨◆⟩———

1. John Langeloth Loeb and Frances Lehman Loeb, with Kenneth Libo. *All in a Lifetime: A Personal Memoir.* New York: John L. Loeb, 1996.
2. Ibid.

CHAPTER SEVEN

Irving Lehman &
Sissie Straus Lehman

—◆—

IRVING LEHMAN'S MARRIAGE TO SISSIE STRAUS in
1901 constituted the merging of two great New York
German Jewish families—the Lehmans of Lehman
Brothers and the Strauses of Macy's. Irving was a
graduate of Columbia, Sissie of Barnard. One hundred and thirty guests seated under tents enjoyed an
elaborate wedding feast catered by Delmonico's

before the couple left for a round-the-world honeymoon. In Constantinople they visited with Henry Morgenthau Sr., American ambassador to the Ottoman Empire, whose son Henry Morgenthau Jr. (later FDR's secretary of the Treasury) would marry Elinor Fatman, the daughter of Irving's sister Settie.

Having no children of their own, Sissie and Irving took a special interest in their grandnieces and grandnephews, many of whom visited them regularly. The only observant Jew among his siblings, Irving was president of Temple Emanu-El (to which he gave his world-renowned collection of Judaica) and was awarded an honorary degree from the Jewish Theological Seminary. He also served as president of the Jewish Welfare Board and New York City's 92nd Street Y.

Along with Sissie and Irving's grandnieces and grandnephews, Albert Einstein and Supreme Court Justice Benjamin Cardozo were frequent visitors at their country home in Port Chester, where Sissie,

ever fearful of germs, instructed all her guests—
regardless of who they were—to "wash your paws"
before eating.

Irving Lehman & Sissie Straus

Irving

Lehman ══ *Straus*

1876 - 1945 *Sissie*

1879 - 1950

Judge Irving Lehman, c. 1910, considered a liberal, described himself as a libertarian.
He was responsible for helping to shape New York's labor, housing, and transportation policy for many years.
(Herbert H. Lehman Suite & Papers, Columbia University)

Irving Lehman

1876–1945

———◆———

New York Times, September 23, 1945

IRVING LEHMAN, 69, NOTED JURIST, DIES

Chief of the Court of Appeals,
Brother of Ex-Governor—Made Liberal Decisions

Special to THE NEW YORK TIMES.

PORT CHESTER, N.Y., Sept. 22—Chief Judge Irving Lehman of the New York State Court of Appeals died here of a heart ailment at 1:30 o'clock this morning at his home in Ridge Street. He had been a member of the State's judiciary for thirty-seven years. His age was 69.

With him when he died were his wife, Mrs. Sissie Straus Lehman, and his physician, Dr. C. C. Craven of Rye. His heart condition became serious a week ago, but he had been ill since

July 7 when, in strolling on a path at his estate here, he tripped over his pet boxer, Carlo, and broke his ankle in two places.

Long active in the public life of the State and New York City, Judge Lehman's last public appearance was at the city's reception to Gen. Dwight D. Eisenhower last June 19, when he delivered the address of welcome to the military commander.

Besides his widow, he leaves a brother, former Gov. Herbert H. Lehman, director of the United Nations Relief and Rehabilitation Administration, and a sister, Mrs. Philip Goodhart of New York. His New York home was at 119 East Seventy-first Street.

A private funeral service will be held on Monday. Prayers will be offered by the Rev. Dr. Nathan A. Perilman, associate rabbi of Congregation Emanu-El in New York. Burial will be in the family plot in Cypress Hills Cemetery.

Double Honor for Brothers

Judge Lehman was elected Chief Judge of the New York State Court of Appeals in 1939. His younger brother was then serving as Governor. From that date until Governor Lehman resigned in the Fall of 1942 to take a Federal post, New York had brothers at the head of its executive and judicial departments for the first time in its history.

Before he became Chief Judge, Irving Lehman had won the esteem of lawyers, judges and the public by the character of his service. At his first election to the Court of Appeals in 1923 he was the candidate of both the Republican and Democratic parties. He was re-elected in 1937 with bi-partisan endorsement, and when he was elected two years later as Chief Judge in place of Frederick E. Crane, who had retired, he carried the American Labor party's nomination as well as those of the older parties.

His reputation as a jurist rested upon a double foundation: He was known to the general public as a liberal, whose interpretation of the law made it a living force subject to change and development with the appearance of new problems and new outlooks; and he was known to lawyers for an ability to slash through legal verbiage and to get to the heart of complex commercial and financial problems.

Although his mastery of these complex problems escaped general public notice, his decisions in cases involving social and economic problems did not. An opinion by him written in 1928, almost a decade before the right of collective bargaining came to have general statutory recognition, won wide attention. It called for voiding an injunction obtained by the Interborough Rapid Transit Company in a dispute with its employees. The reasoning set forth in the opinion was largely responsible for shaping New York's labor policy for many years.

Denied Trolley-Fare Rise

Judge Lehman also wrote the prevailing opinion for the Court of Appeals in 1930 denying surface transportation lines in New York an increased fare. . . .

In the case of Carmen Barber, a member of the Jehovah's Witnesses, writing the unanimous opinion of the court, Judge Lehman held that the State was not bound by a contrary decision of the United States Supreme Court limiting scope of guarantees of religious freedom in the Federal Constitution. Reversing the defendant's conviction for distributing and attempting to sell religious materials without a license, he declared:

"In determining the scope and effect of guarantees of fundamental rights of the individual in the Constitution of the State of New York," Judge Lehman noted, "this court is bound to exercise its independent judgment."

In a speech in 1925 before the Association of the Bar of the City of New York he outlined the philosophy that guided him as a jurist.

"As a judge," he said, "I can conceive of no human justice which is not founded on system; I can conceive of no justice except justice according to law. But law is not so removed from human affairs that its application to a particular case can fail totally to take into consideration the merits of that case as distinguished from other cases."

Father Came From Bavaria

Judge Lehman was born in New York on Jan. 28, 1876. His parents were Mayer and Babette Newgass [sic] Lehman. His father, who had left Bavaria in 1848 and settled in Montgomery, Ala., where he established a cotton business, had come to New York in 1864 as an Alabama Commissioner to supervise the welfare of Confederate prisoners held here, and had remained here to live after his official business had ended.

Irving Lehman was graduated from Columbia University with an A.B. degree in 1896. A year later he obtained a Master's degree there and at the end of the second year his law degree. In his final year at the law school he won a prize in constitutional law. Columbia, in 1927, St. Lawrence University, in 1936, and Syracuse University, in 1943, conferred on him the degree of LL.D. The Jewish Theological Seminary honored him with an L.H.D. in 1936.

Before his first election to the State Supreme Court in 1908 he served as a member of the law firm of Marshall, Moran, Williams & McVicker and later with Worcester, Williams & Lehman.

All his life Judge Lehman was active in Jewish philanthropic work and in the improvement of Jewish educational institutions. From 1921 to 1940 he served as president of the board of trustees of the Jewish Welfare Board, parent organization of 328 Jewish Centers and Young Men's Hebrew Associations and a member agency of the United Service Organizations. Afterward he was honorary president.

President of Y.M.H.A. Here

For eight years he was president of the Young Men's Hebrew Association at Ninety-second Street and Lexington Avenue. He also served as a member of the executive committee of the American Jewish Committee, as honorary secretary of the Jewish Theological Seminary, and for years as president of Temple Emanu-El, a post to which he was elected shortly after the death of Louis Marshall.

He was keenly interested in preparation for the bar and was a member of the board of visitors of the Columbia Law School.

Judge Lehman also manifested a keen interest in the work of the Henry Street Settlement, having served as a volunteer social worker between the time he was graduated from college and his first election to the bench in 1908.

In 1901 he married Miss Sissie Straus, daughter of the late Nathan Straus, merchant and philanthropist. Mrs. Lehman also was actively interested in welfare movements. . . .

———◆———

New York Times, June 27, 1901

A Day's Weddings

Lehman-Straus

Irving Lehman, third son of the late Meyer [sic] Lehman, and Miss Sissie Straus, only daughter of Mr. and Mrs. Nathan Straus, were married at the residence of Mr. Straus, 27 West Seventy-second Street, at 6:30 o'clock last evening. The Rev. Dr. Kauffman Kohler and the Rev. Dr. Gottheil officiated. The ceremony was performed in a bower of foliage arranged in the bay window in the dining room at the rear of the house.

White orchids and roses were scattered through the greens and a large bell of white orchids was suspended over the heads of the young couple.

The bride, who walked to the bower with the bridegroom, wore a beautiful gown of tucked white chiffon over silk, and a tulle veil. She carried a bouquet of lilies of the valley. Neither Mr. Lehman nor the bride had any attendants. After the ceremony a dinner was served for 130 guests in the large tent that had been raised on the vacant space east of the Straus residence. This enclosed space was so arranged and filled with palms and growing plants as to look like a garden. There were twenty-seven tables in all. The bride's was decorated with an immense centre piece of lilies of the valley and white roses, and that of Mrs. Straus, the bride's mother, had a large mound of pink roses. The other tables had vases of pink or white roses placed on them. Delmonico catered. The house was decorated throughout with asparagus vines and the stairways were con-cealed with pink and red peonies, which were draped thickly over them.

Mr. and Mrs. Lehman will leave today for Vancouver, B.C., and will take a steamer at that port for Japan. They intend being absent four months. Some two years since, when a guest at Constantinople of her uncle, Oscar S. Straus, then Minister to Turkey, Mrs. Lehman was decorated with the order of the Chef Khat by the Sultan.

Among the guests at the wedding were Mr. and Mrs. Oscar S. Straus, Mr. and Mrs. Isidor Straus, Mr. and Mrs. Jesse I. Straus, Emanuel Lehman, Mr. and Mrs. Max Nathan, Mr. and Mrs. S. M. Lehman, Mr. and Mrs. Rothschild, Mr. and Mrs. Philip Lehman, Mr. and Mrs. Goodhart, Mr. and Mrs. Kohns [sic], Mr. and Mrs. Fatman, Mr. and Mrs. E. C. Blum, Dr. Joseph E. Walter, Miss Walter, Miss Lewisohn, Mr. and Mrs. H. J. Bernheim, Mr. and Mrs. Louis Marx, Charles C. Marshall, Mr. and Mrs. T. Ashley Sparks, Mr. and Mrs. Isaac Untermeyer, Mr. and Mrs. Richard Limburger, Frederick

Young Irving Lehman as a Columbia student, c. 1895.
(Herbert H. Lehman Suite & Papers, Columbia University)

Lavanburg, Frederick Stein, Stephen G. Williams, Eugene Meyer, Jr., Howard S. Gans and Mr. and Mrs. A. J. Cammeyer.

<hr />

HERBERT LEHMAN (1878–1963), *younger brother of Irving Lehman* – I doubt that any brothers were closer than Irving and I, as we thought alike on almost every public issue. He'd been on the bench continuously since 1908 and I was extremely proud of my brother's record. I think the Court of Appeals had a record of probity and intellectual honesty and ability second only to the Supreme Court of the United States. He and I used to discuss a great many things. We were always on the same side. We always looked on things pretty much the same way.[1]

<hr />

ROBERT M. MORGENTHAU, *grandson of Irving Lehman's older sister Settie* – When I was six years old, the first seder I ever went to was at Uncle Irving and Aunt Sissie Lehman's. Sissie served the children white grape juice, which I thought was wonderful. Every Wednesday we went to Bible class with Sissie's brother Nathan Straus's children at The Beresford, on 81st Street and Central Park West. The class was conducted by Rabbi Stephen Wise's son, Dr. James Wise. We did it on Wednesday because my parents and all their friends went to their country homes on weekends. I remember shooting paper clips at the girls. I was a little bit of a troublemaker.

Around that time I had two ambitions—to be a fireman or to go to West Point. My mother said, "You know, you really ought to be a lawyer." But my parents didn't lean on me. Uncle Irving also said I should be a lawyer. He was very definite about that.

When I was studying law with Uncle Irving in the summer of 1940, I lived with him and Aunt Sissie in Port Chester, New York. I had just finished my junior year at Amherst College, and he was already the chief judge of the New York Court of Appeals. He wanted to interest me in the law, which I was already interested in. He'd give me various briefs to read—he was very considerate—things that he was working on.

Irving Lehman, rarely without a tie, with his close friend, Supreme Court Justice Benjamin Cardozo. Sissie, Irving's wife, was like a mother to both of them. (Herbert H. Lehman Suite & Papers, Columbia University)

This was at the start of the war and he was vitally interested in what was going on in Europe. He would leave the radio on and his hearing aid off. There was music in the background and he could tell when the music went to the news, so as soon as that would happen he would turn on his hearing aid and turn up the radio and listen.

He was responsible for bringing quite a few Jewish relatives over from Nazi Germany—fifty-five at least—by establishing with Herbert a Lehman family fund, administered by our cousin Dorothy Lehman Bernhard. I remember when I started in the Navy he gave me a Leica camera that one of the people he had brought over had given to him. I didn't want it, but Uncle Irving was proud of the fact it was the only thing of value that particular refugee was able to take out of Germany, so I took it. That Leica went down to the bottom of the Mediterranean when the USS *Lansdale*, on which I served as executive officer and navigator, was torpedoed and sank on April 20, 1944.

I asked him what law school I should go to, and I remember him saying, "If you're in the top third of your class it doesn't matter what law school you go to, as you'll get a good education. If you're in the bottom third, you shouldn't be going to law school. It only makes a difference if you're in the middle third." Then he added, "I think you're going to be in the top third."

When we were working at night, Sissie liked to cook scrambled eggs for Irving. Sissie was wife, mother, and trained nurse to Irving. She really took care of him. She was very worried about what would happen if she died before Irving; so she made a deal with a first cousin of my mother, Edith Haas, an unmarried woman, that if she died first, Edith would come and look after Irving. She was scared to death that there would be a fire and he wouldn't get out. . . . Sissie also looked after Associate Justice of the Supreme Court Benjamin Cardozo, a bachelor with whom Irving had a very close relationship.

I remember Uncle Irving liked good wine, though he was not a heavy drinker. He had a terrific cellar. His two favorite wines were Château d'Yquem sauterne and a white burgundy Montrachet.

LAWRENCE B. BUTTENWIESER, *grandson of Irving Lehman's elder brother Arthur* – Irving was a somewhat austere figure. I cannot recollect him dressed informally. Figuratively, he woke up in the morning and put on a black tie. He was also partially deaf. My father [Benjamin J. Buttenwieser] told me that, at his introduction to the Lehman family at a cacophonous Friday evening gathering, the Lehmans all brought their hearing aids with them, which electronically interfered with each of the other aids. . . .

The most important stimulus in my mother's [Helen L. Buttenwieser's] decision to become a lawyer was her Uncle Irving. Irving and Helen were very close.

———◆———

HENRY MORGENTHAU III, *grandson of Irving Lehman's elder sister Settie* – There was not much humor in the family, certainly not among the women. Irving was an exception. He loved to tell amusing stories putting himself down. One of his favorites was an account of his quick rise in the New York State judiciary sys-tem: "I was a very young lawyer, in practice only a short time, I was deaf, and I was Jewish. None of these helped. But I was married to Nathan Straus's daughter, and Mr. Straus was a friend of Al Smith." Irving also noted that his father-in-law had contributed $50,000 to the Democratic Party. "Irving, we don't say things like that in public," a party boss would say, but to no avail.

Another of Irving's favorites was the one about the man for whom Irving had promised to find a job (from a party boss), but every time the man showed up, Irving would tell him, "Just wait. I haven't forgotten." Finally, after coming back for five years, Irving announced to the supplicant, "Well, I didn't forget my promise. I have arranged to have you appointed an assistant postmaster. 'Sir' the man replied, 'if you don't mind, I would rather just keep my grievance.'"

Irving also liked to tell the story of how when he went on the bench he put his investments into a kind of blind trust in the hands of his brothers. A few years later he asked them how he was doing, and it turned out they had completely forgotten their trust. Actually, Irving said his neglected investments did better on their own than had those of his brothers who were running Lehman Brothers.

My parents, Ellie and Henry [Morgenthau Jr.], were always a bit uncomfortable about Irving being so Jewish. He was the only one who had a mezuzah on the door and conducted Passover seders at home. When my parents got married, he supplied the silver wedding cup, which was passed on to me. I used it at my wedding, as did my daughter, Sarah, at hers.

<hr />

New York Times, December 17, 1929

Judge Lehman Heads Emanu-El
Member of the Court of Appeals,
Is Chosen by Congregation to
Succeed Louis Marshall

Judge Irving Lehman of the State Court of Appeals was elected president of Congregation Emanu-El last night to succeed Louis Marshall who died recently while in Europe. The election took place at the annual meeting of the congregation in the community house of the temple at 1 East Sixty-fifth Street. . . .

New by-laws to govern the combined congregations of Emanu-El and Beth-El were adopted at the meeting. The by-laws provide that the congregation shall be known as " 'Congregation Emanu-El of the City of New York' but that the chapel in the new temple shall be for all time known as 'Beth-El Chapel.' "

Judge Lehman, the new president of the congregation, is widely known as a jurist and is a brother of Herbert H. Lehman, Lieutenant Governor of New York. He is a native of this city and was born on January 28, 1876, the son of Mayer Lehman and Babette Newgass [sic] Lehman.

<hr />

JUNE ROSSBACH BINGHAM BIRGE, *granddaughter of Irving Lehman's elder sister Clara* – Uncle Irving served as a judge from 1909 to 1944, a

*Governor Herbert Lehman (at left) watches on December 31, 1939, as New York State Court of Appeals Chief Judge Frederick E. Crane swears in the governor's brother, Irving Lehman (at right), as the Court of Appeal's new chief judge. (*New York Times*)*

year before his death. One of the things he became famous for was his hearing aid. Experienced prosecutors and defenders got to know the signs of Judge Lehman's getting ready to turn it off, and they would speed up their arguments. A sign that it was actually off was Irving's wonderful beatific smile.

His main passion in the law concerned the Constitution. His other was the common law. Even before becoming a judge (at age 32), Irving felt that lawyers themselves bore a sacred trust:

> In countless offices . . . lawyers . . . are guiding and protecting men, women and children who have sought their help. The trickster . . . the ambulance chaser . . . loom large in the public eye. They are more dramatic in their destructive activities than the lawyers and judges who, day in and day out, build and preserve the common law and the institutions of America. It is upon them that America must rely for the wise solution of many of its perplexing problems.

Uncle Irving worked hard over his decisions, often reading them aloud to Aunt Sissie, who surely knew more legal shoptalk than almost any other layperson and was frank in pointing out to him if some statement was unclear.

In 1939 a challenging and unique situation arose in New York when Chief Judge Crane of the state's highest court, the Court of Appeals, had to resign because he had reached the age of seventy. Uncle Herbert wanted to appoint Irving, who was the senior associate judge, to that position. But some people said that no single family should gain that much power.

New York City mayor Fiorello LaGuardia considered running for chief judge on the Republican or Independent ticket, but LaGuardia's trial balloons failed to fly. The *New York Times* said about Irving, "Of Judge Lehman's eminent qualifications it is almost impertinent to speak." The state and city bar associations endorsed Irving, as did the Republican and American Labor parties as well as the Democrats. LaGuardia was therefore persuaded to withdraw his name, and Irving Lehman was elected.

He had a healthy respect for the legislative and executive branches of government and was often supportive of their activities. This attitude was unusual in his day, though by now it has become commonplace, and it put him at odds with the four conservative justices on the Supreme Court who openly resisted most New Deal laws and thus helped to trigger the court-packing crisis of 1937.

Irving said he was not a "liberal" (which then meant predictable support for everything FDR was proposing) but rather a "libertarian." This means that he believed our constitutional freedoms are inalienable and God-given and therefore must not be messed with by any branch of the government. We would probably call him a "civil libertarian" today. In any event, his decisions are still pored over by law students all over the country.

⟹◆⟸

1. John Langeloth Loeb and Frances Lehman Loeb, with Kenneth Libo. *All in a Lifetime: A Personal Memoir.* New York: John L. Loeb, 1996.

Sissie Straus Lehman, daughter of Nathan Straus of Macy's, graduate of Barnard, and social activist. (Associated Press)

Sissie Straus Lehman

1879–1950

—◆—

New York Times, February 18, 1950

MRS. LEHMAN DIES; JURIST'S WIDOW, 70

Sister-in-Law of Senator Was Daughter of Nathan Straus— Active in Charitable Work

Mrs. Sissie Straus Lehman, widow of Chief Judge Irving Lehman of the New York State Court of Appeals, died yesterday of a heart attack in her home at 119 East Seventy-first Street. Her age was 70.

The only daughter of Nathan Straus, noted merchant and philanthropist, and his wife, Mrs. Lina Gutherz Straus, she joined with them in charitable activities, and helped continue their philanthropies after the death of her mother in 1930 and her father the next January.

Born in this city, Mrs. Lehman attended the Sachs School and was graduated from Barnard College in 1901, when she was married to Judge Lehman, brother of Senator Herbert H. Lehman. She attended the New York School of Social Work from 1912 to 1914, when it was known as the School of Philanthropy.

An ardent supporter of the League of Nations in 1919, Mrs. Lehman also was active in the Democratic party. She was a contributor of campaign funds and was prominent in the Women's Democratic Club of New York. . . .

Mrs. Lehman was president of the New York section of the National Council of Jewish Women in 1922 and 1923 and was also chairman of the section's legislative committee. She was an officer of the Young Women's Hebrew Association and a member of the Ivriah, the women's division of the Jewish Education Association.

An honorary president of Irvington House, a convalescent home for cardiac children, Mrs. Lehman retired from active public life after her husband died of a heart ailment in 1945 at the age of 69. One of her last appearances at a public function was late in 1948 at the opening of a youth center dedicated by Senator Lehman and his wife in memory of their son, Peter, killed in action in 1944 while on duty with the Army Air Force.

Surviving are two brothers, Nathan Straus, president of Station WMCA and former administrator of the United States Housing Authority, and Hugh Grant Straus.

A funeral service will be held Sunday at 10 A.M. in the Beth El Chapel of Temple Emanu-El, Sixty-fifth Street and Fifth Avenue. Dr. Julius Mark, senior rabbi of the temple, will officiate. Burial will be at Salem Fields Cemetery, Brooklyn.

IRVING LEHMAN STRAUS, *nephew of Sissie Straus; son of Nathan Straus Jr.* – My earliest memories stem from being at Aunt Sissie and Uncle Irving's in Port Chester. Aunt Sissie was my father Nathan Straus Jr.'s sister. During the years before my parents created Quarry Lake as their home away from home, we were invited by Sissie to come to her home in Port Chester for summer vacations. Uncle Irving was a distinguished New York State judge, but that didn't mean all that much to us at the time. I can't tell you how many times we were there, but I vividly remember the caretaker and his wife, Max and Eula Stillman, who looked after us when the grown people were away. They lived in a house away from the main house, opposite the stable.

My recollection is that there was a huge lawn going down from the main house toward where Max and Eula lived. When I went back there as a grown-up, I discovered that the lawn I thought was so huge and awe-inspiring was really very small. I also remember a garden in the back of the house with various kinds of hedges. There was a Boy Scout camp next door,

divided from the Lehman property by a brook. The brook had watercress, which my father loved; we used to go down and pick it. This sticks in my mind because my father made a big point of the fact that there was a Boy Scout camp on the other side of the brook, and he wanted watercress to be picked only upstream so we wouldn't get watercress where the boys were brushing their teeth . . . but this all ended when I was twelve or thirteen years old and went away to school.

Sissie was a soft, lovely lady with white hair who was typically old school. Before eating, she used to say, "Wash your paws." She wasn't a mean person, but she had a biting tongue. There's the story of Uncle Irving working and Aunt Sissie sitting outside his office door, allowing no one to go in until he finished work. I don't remember ever seeing it, but I heard of it. She was definitely a "character," in the best sense of the word.

I think people were a little frightened of her. She was very proper, demanding, fastidious in her habits. You couldn't be late by one minute.

When lunch was served at one o'clock, it was served at one o'clock and you were expected to be there. In her own quiet way she was setting a standard that most people couldn't live up to all that well. It was much more of a test to pass with Aunt Sissie than with anyone else.

Einstein was a frequent visitor. Many of the summers we were there, he was there. I remember Aunt Sissie saying, "Einstein is thinking, so you have to be quiet." I had an interest in science and was an avid collector of insects. In an experiment I conducted, I took a female moth, tied it up with a little thread to a tree, and took away a male moth—and it came back to the female moth. I was telling Einstein about it and have a picture of him listening to me or me listening to him. If it wasn't for the picture, I wouldn't remember any of this.

One thing that stands out about Sissie is that the table setting even for lunch was a formal affair, with linen tablecloths and china, finger bowls, different servings for several courses—including squab from their pigeon house—the kind of thing people don't even do for dinner. I remember in New York City at their townhouse very much the same kind of formal luncheon. It was outstanding because people didn't do it even in those days.

How religious she was I don't know, but she sure had strong Jewish convictions. Anybody who wasn't Jewish she called an *oetlaender*. I use the phrase myself on occasion.

———⋈———

EILEEN JOSTEN LOWE, *grandniece of Irving and Sissie Lehman; daughter of Werner and Margaret Josten* – We grew up in Northampton as country bumpkins, so I saw very little of Irving and Sissie. However, I did take private violin lessons from Louis Persinger, a teacher who taught at Juilliard. Once a month, my companion and I would travel from Ethel Walker School in Simsbury, Connecticut, to New York, where we stayed overnight at Irving and Sissie's. They might come in to say hello, but I didn't really see them. I just went to Louis Persinger's house to take my lesson, came back, and was served dinner with my companion in our room.

A precocious Irving Lehman Straus with Albert Einstein, a frequent guest at Sissie's table, as Irving Lehman looks on approvingly. (Herbert H. Lehman Suite & Papers, Columbia University)

HENRY MORGENTHAU III, *grandnephew of Irving and Sissie Lehman; son of Elinor and Henry Morgenthau Jr.* – When I was at prep school at Deerfield Academy, Uncle Irving and Aunt Sissie would come to visit and take me out to dinner. This was a big treat. We would go to the nearby Greenfield Inn. One of the great pleasures was to order from the menu. But Aunt Sissie always ordered everything in advance, as she said it was undignified to order food in public. That was a big disappointment. . . . Sissie was very punctilious, and Irving was her baby. They had no children. Sissie would sit at the table with him, and as each dish would be served, Irving would look up to get Sissie's okay or disapproval.

———◆———

LAWRENCE B. BUTTENWIESER, *grandnephew of Irving and Sissie Lehman; son of Benjamin Joseph and Helen Buttenwieser* – I remember Sissie's wonderfully acerbic tongue. The telephone lines would be busy the next day with a particular zinger of the prior day. My mother was often the target because Irving liked my mother inordinately,

and Sissie was obviously a bit miffed about that. She didn't like Irving to like anybody but herself. Sissie described my mother as "Alice in Wonderland, but superannuated." Somebody once said to Sissie, "Helen is four months pregnant," and Sissie said, "How do you know? Helen always looks four months pregnant." My mother was delighted to repeat these remarks.

———◆———

ROBERT A. BERNHARD, *grandnephew of Irving and Sissie Lehman; son of Richard and Dorothy Bernhard* – Aunt Sissie always gave me the impression that you didn't want to cross her. The person Sissie reminds me of is Sara Delano [Roosevelt]. I can remember this little woman in Campobello and thinking to myself, "This is someone you don't want to fuss around with." I felt the same way about Sissie.

Mother [Dorothy Lehman Bernhard] had some guest from out of town who was commenting on the hugeness of the city, and Mother said, "New York isn't a huge city. It's a conglomeration of many small towns. If we look out this window on 71st Street, I am sure we will see someone I know. So they sat there, and in about ten minutes Mother said, "Do you see that elderly gentleman walking down the street?" "Yes," the woman said. "That's my Uncle Irving," my mother told her, to which she replied, "I'll bet you're going to tell me the little lady ten paces behind him is your aunt." And mother said, "It is."

———◆———

ANN STRAUS GERTLER, *Sissie Straus Lehman's niece* – Maynard and I were married by Uncle Irving on September 20, 1942, at my parents' home in Harrison, New York. Uncle Irving was president of Temple Emanu-El then. Aunt Sissie gave us $1,000 as a wedding present; it was great because we were both students.

My strongest memory is of tea with Aunt Sissie and Uncle Irving. After a suitable interval, Aunt Sissie said to Irving that he should "say a nice word to each of the guests and go upstairs to write decisions" because she did not want him "to be writing decisions after midnight."

In 1938 I was a fellow guest at their Ridge Street home, along with Professor Albert Einstein. The news of Prime Minister Chamberlain's "Peace in Our Times" speech came over the radio. Chamberlain had just come back from Munich. The grown-ups were acutely distressed. In a more amusing vein, I remember when Aunt Sissie sent Professor Einstein to wash his "paws" before coming to luncheon.

———◆———

JUNE ROSSBACH BINGHAM BIRGE, *grandniece of Irving and Sissie Lehman; daughter of Max and Mabel Rossbach* – Like the Sig Lehmans at Kildare, the Irving Lehmans enjoyed fishing every summer. They did not own an Adirondack camp but instead went to Mégantic, a lodge with cabins on the Canadian border. No hot water or luxuries like that, but long, happy days of casting for lake trout, swimming, and paddling about in canoes. Aunt Sissie wore knickers with high socks, and Uncle Irving wore a crumpled Irish tweed hat. Perhaps it was the hat that inspired

A pre-teen Sissie Straus posed as though communing with nature, c. 1890. (Herbert H. Lehman Suite & Papers, Columbia University)

Sissie Straus at the turn of the century. (Herbert H. Lehman Suite & Papers, Columbia University)

him to sing Irish ballads as we trekked single file across the portages between the small lakes while the guides carried our canoes, fishing gear, and picnic lunch. The chief guide was Omar, a man of immense dignity and knowledge about nature. I wondered what he thought of my uncle's slightly off-key musical ebullience.

Aunt Sissie had a beautiful face but a dumpy figure, not fat, just shapeless. But nothing about her was less than perfect in the eyes of Uncle Irving. And the same was true about him from her point of view. He was huge-nosed and prematurely bald, stooped and unathletic, but in her eyes he was *le beau idéal*.

Irving was an idealist without being naïve, a realist without being cynical. Unflinching in facing up to evil, he also never gave up hope. The only one of the seven Lehman siblings to be devout, he shared with his wife everything that mattered. To be around them was a pleasure because they were so happy together. I can still see them swimming the sidestroke, he on the left, she on the right, so that they could face one another.

Aunt Sissie had two brothers, Nathan and Hugh Grant Straus, the latter called "Grant." They were the children of the cofounder of Macy's. Grant was married to the daughter of Leopold Stieglitz, who was the family doctor to the whole Lehman clan. Leopold's brother, Alfred, the photographer, was married to Georgia O'Keeffe, but I never heard them mentioned, either in the Lehmans' townhouse on 71st Street or in their house in Port Chester.

Aunt Sissie tended toward formality. For example, she always referred to "Walter" Disney. When I was a fourteen-year-old at boarding school, Aunt Sissie phoned to make arrangements about my spending spring vacation with them. "By the way," she said, "I have an extra man for you." "Oh, Aunt Sissie!" I said, "Who?" "Albert Einstein." And Aunt Sissie was not the kidding type. The following year, my "extra man" at the Lehmans was Uncle Irving's closest friend, Benjamin Cardozo. An associate justice on the Supreme Court, he was considered one of the great legal thinkers in American history.

My mother, Mabel Limburg Rossbach, and I went to Europe with the Lehmans when I was fifteen. They took along an Irish maid to do their packing and to wash and iron one of Uncle Irving's two seersucker suits each day. By 10 A.M. he always looked as if he had slept in it. One day we drove out to Fiesole to visit Bernard Berenson at his villa, I Tatti. He seemed much like Uncle Irving, famous in his field but not trumpeting his expertise.

Aunt Sissie was adamantly against germs. You had to have just washed your hands before being allowed to partake of a meal. In Europe she wouldn't let us eat salad or any fruit that didn't have a heavy peel; nor could we have milk or cream that hadn't been boiled. One day in Florence, Uncle Irving, as frustrated as I was by Sissie's restrictions, invited me to come for a walk. Off we went down narrow sewage-strewn lanes Aunt Sissie would have put off-limits. We went to where the Florentine people lived, not where the tourists were segregated amid sanitized surroundings. Finally, sin of sins, he bought two gelati from a street vendor. Nothing ever tasted better.

I adored Aunt Sissie. She was like a grandmother who was interested in everything I was doing or thinking. She was very bright and very well read and loved to laugh. She was also direct in expressing approval and disapproval. In 1939 I was semi-engaged to a young man whom Irving and Sissie were visibly not enthralled by. They wanted to know what his plans were for improving the world. In truth, he was far more interested in making money. Not knowing what else to say, I changed the subject to another young man who was planning to devote his whole life to public service. His name was Jonathan Bingham. Six months later our wedding reception was held at the Lehmans' big Elizabethan house on Ridge Street in Port Chester. Jonathan went on to become a highly respected and much admired congressman from the Bronx, serving from 1965 to 1982.

When Irving died, Sissie was devastated. The following summer I took my four small

Sissie and Irving in an informal moment, c. 1940.
(Howard Rossbach)

children to visit her at Lake Placid. She loved seeing the children, but her grief was not to be assuaged. In 1950, when Sissie had a sharp heart attack, Dr. Stieglitz was summoned. "Is it a bad one?" she asked. "Yes, Sissie. I'm sorry to say it is." She turned away from him, smiled blissfully, and closed her eyes. "I'm coming, my darling," she said—and died.

CHAPTER EIGHT

Herbert Lehman & Edith Altschul Lehman

NOT TO BE OUTDONE BY HIS OLDER BROTHERS—Arthur, who married a Lewisohn, and Irving who married a Straus—Herbert married Edith Altschul, whose brother Frank was a senior partner of Lazard Frères. Frank was also the husband of the daughter of Herbert's eldest sister, Hattie—Helen Goodhart. From his boyhood years as a volunteer at Lillian Wald's Henry Street

Settlement House, Herbert dedicated a large part of his life to public service. Advancing from colonel in World War I to lieutenant governor of New York under FDR, then on to the governorship, director of the United Nations Relief and Rehabilitation Administration (UNRRA) during and after World War II, and finally U.S. senator, Herbert—with Edith often at his side—came to represent the nation's conscience during the McCarthy period.

Herbert's impact was acknowledged in various ways: Lehman College is named after him, as was Kfar Lehman, a small village in Israel. As busy as they were in public life, Herbert and Edith were never too busy for their grandchildren, all of whom remember Herbert and Edith with deep and abiding affection.

Herbert Lehman & Edith Altschul Lehman

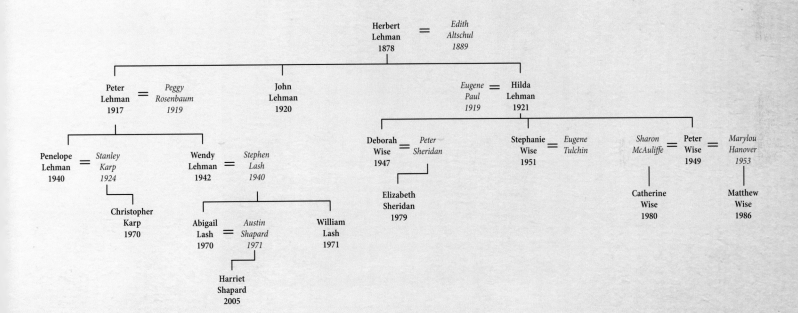

Herbert
Lehman
1878
=
*Edith
Altschul
1889*

Peter
Lehman
1917
=
*Peggy
Rosenbaum
1919*

John
Lehman
1920

*Eugene
Paul
1919*
=
Hilda
Lehman
1921

Penelope
Lehman
1940
=
*Stanley
Karp
1924*

Wendy
Lehman
1942
=
*Stephen
Lash
1940*

Deborah
Wise
1947
=
*Peter
Sheridan*

Stephanie
Wise
1951
=
*Eugene
Tulchin*

*Sharon
McAuliffe*
=
Peter
Wise
1949
=
*Marylou
Hanover
1953*

Christopher
Karp
1970

Abigail
Lash
1970
=
*Austin
Shapard
1971*

William
Lash
1971

Elizabeth
Sheridan
1979

Catherine
Wise
1980

Matthew
Wise
1986

Harriet
Shapard
2005

Senator Herbert Lehman, the conscience of the nation during the McCarthy period, on the steps of the U.S. Capitol. (New York Times)

Herbert Lehman

1878–1963

———❖———

New York Times, December 6, 1963

HERBERT LEHMAN, 85, DIES;
EX-GOVERNOR AND SENATOR

By ROBERT ALDEN

Herbert H. Lehman, a towering figure in the liberal political movement in the United States and a noted philanthropist, died yesterday morning at his home after suffering a heart attack. He was 85 years old.

Mr. Lehman was elected to four consecutive terms as Governor of New York and he served as a United States Senator for eight years. President Franklin D. Roosevelt referred to him as "that good right arm of mine."

Mr. Lehman also was director of the United Nations Relief and Rehabilitation Administration after World War II. The organization aided more than 500 million war victims.

Governor Rockefeller proclaimed a 30-day period of mourning to mark the death of Mr. Lehman. Flags on all state buildings, already flying at half-staff because of the death of President Kennedy, will remain at half-staff until Jan. 5.

Mr. Lehman was stricken as he was about to leave his apartment at 820 Park Avenue to go to Washington to receive the nation's highest peacetime award to a civilian—the Presidential Medal of Freedom. With 30 others, he had been chosen for this honor by President Kennedy. The award was to have been presented by President Johnson at a White House ceremony today.

Yesterday, President Johnson praised Mr. Lehman as a "distinguished leader who ably and effectively served his state and nation."

He said that perhaps the best words that he could use to describe him were contained in the citation that was to have accompanied the award: "Citizen and statesman, he has used wisdom and compassion as the tools of the government and has made politics the highest form of public service."

In preparing for the trip to Washington yesterday, Mr. Lehman, always an early riser, was dressed and packed and had finished breakfast when he was stricken in his bedroom at 9 A.M. He had had no history of heart disease.

Although he had suffered a broken hip in a fall last February, members of his family said that he had been recovering well from that accident and had appeared to be in generally good health.

President Johnson's tribute was one of the first of a multitude of tributes to Mr. Lehman—tributes that cut across partisan politics.

Former Vice President Richard M. Nixon said:

"Senator Lehman was one of the kindest men I have ever known . . . I'm sure that one of the many tributes members of the two parties can pay to him is that he had the quality of never growing old."

Governor Rockefeller said: "He was truly a beloved figure in the affairs of our state and nation, an outstanding Governor and United States Senator, a humanitarian whose works spanned oceans and continents to reach the hearts and raise the hopes of men and women throughout the world."

Mayor Wagner called Mr. Lehman "a father to our whole city and state."

"I have never known a better man, a kindlier man or a more courageous man," the Mayor said.

Mr. Lehman's body will lie at the Universal Funeral Chapel, Lexington Avenue and 52d Street, today and tomorrow. The public will be able to pay their last respects from 1 to 10 P.M. on Friday and from 10 A.M. to 10 P.M. on Saturday.

A funeral service will be conducted at Temple Emanu-El, Fifth Avenue and 65th Street on Sunday at 1 P.M. Burial will be private.

Mr. Lehman's family asked that floral tributes be omitted and donations made instead to charitable works.

Although best known because of his career in public service, Mr. Lehman was a philanthropist whose charitable activities encompassed a broad spectrum of human needs.

A co-founder in 1914 of what later became the American Joint Distribution Committee, Mr. Lehman gave generously and often anonymously to hundreds, perhaps thousands, of charities around the world.

The money involved probably ran into the millions, but even close members of the Lehman family would not venture a guess as to how much. . . .

In 1960, Mr. Lehman and his wife gave $500,000 for establishment of the Children's Zoo in Central Park. The occasion was the couple's golden wedding anniversary.

Editor's note: Besides the front-page coverage of the death of Herbert Lehman (who, even after his subsequent service in the United States Senate, liked to be called Governor Lehman), the New York Times *of December 6th devoted all of page twenty-eight to encapsulate his entire career. Half of page twenty-nine in the same issue quoted tributes from forty famous dignitaries.*

One of the encomiums that would have especially pleased him came from Dore Schary, national chairman of the Anti-Defamation League of B'nai B'rith: "We can never forget his fight for civil liberties, when he stood virtually alone in the Senate against the nightmare of McCarthyism, or his eloquent advocacy of human rights all the years of his life."

DUANE TANANBAUM, *Associate Professor of History, Lehman College* – The influence and the example set by his father, Mayer, are crucial to understanding Herbert Lehman. Mayer indoctrinated his children with the idea that one had a responsibility to be concerned with one's fellow man, that one was not placed on this planet solely for one's own pleasure, but that one had an obligation, a duty to do good works. It is very clear that at an early age Herbert was infused with the sense that he had an obligation to use his position and his wealth to help others.

We see it as early as when he goes down to Lillian Wald's Henry Street Settlement, where he led a boy's club. Later on, as a member of the Henry Street board, he goes through their financial statements, he offers advice. He is very much involved in Henry Street for the rest of his life, as is Edith. In the 1940s they contribute money for a new building named after their son

Pete, who was killed in World War II. It's called Pete's House.

Though much of his philanthropy focused on Jews, Herbert was on the board of the NAACP. What his parents did on behalf of Mount Sinai Hospital, Herbert expanded into his work first with the American Jewish Joint Distribution Committee during and after World War I and then as the head of UNRRA, which was established to help as many people as possible, Jews and non-Jews, who had been liberated but were still displaced and starving during and after World War II.

Herbert Lehman did not go into the family business immediately. Instead, he worked for a textile manufacturer for some years before joining Lehman Brothers in 1908, the year his older brother Sigmund retired.

Mayer Lehman was a committed Democrat who named his son after Hilary Herbert, a former congressman and secretary of the navy in the Cleveland administration. In 1912 Herbert Lehman contributed generously to William Sulzer's gubernatorial campaign, and in 1916 he played an active role in the Wilson campaign by wiring money to California to make sure the ballot boxes weren't stuffed by the Republicans.

After the United States entered World War I, Herbert Lehman worked in the Navy Department with Assistant Secretary of the Navy Franklin D. Roosevelt for several months before obtaining a direct commission as a captain in the army.

When the war ended, Herbert was a colonel handling procurement and transportation on the general staff. He received the Distinguished Service Medal, the highest award for noncombatant service.

Herbert attended Democratic National Committee functions in the 1920s and, through Lillian Wald, Belle Moskowitz, and other liberal Democrats close to Al Smith, became an early and very enthusiastic Al Smith supporter. In 1928 Herbert Lehman contributed generously to Al Smith's presidential campaign. Herbert Lehman remained a lifelong friend of Al Smith, even though he backed Franklin Roosevelt at the 1932 Democratic presidential convention.

Herbert Lehman with FDR, whom he served as New York State lieutenant governor, and Al Smith, whom he supported in his 1928 bid for the presidency. (Penelope Lehman)

In an oral history conducted in 1957, Herbert talked about his views on Zionism at great length. He states very strongly that he "is not now and never was a Zionist." For him Zionism meant the establishment of a political state in Palestine, which was something Lehman never really supported until 1948, when Israel became a reality. While a long-time supporter of Palestine as a refuge for Jews fleeing persecution, Herbert did not believe it should become a political entity, as it raised in him and other "American Jewish Committee" Jews the specter of dual citizenship and a questioning of their loyalty.

Going through the Lehman correspondence, I have been struck by the absence of any mention of Rosh Hashanah, Chanukah, or Passover or any Jewish holidays or celebrations. Yet Judaism was important to Herbert—not in the ritual, the observance of the festivals, going to shul, but in the sense of doing good works. Sometimes he had to be reminded it was Yom Kippur. Nevertheless, for decades he was the leading Jewish spokesperson on practically every political issue involving Jews. There's an article I came across in a 1955 *Look* magazine in which people were asked to name the leading Jews in America. The only name that appeared on everyone's list was Herbert Lehman.

At Herbert's funeral a letter was quoted from a young boy asking whether Lehman's religion had ever been a handicap in his public life, and Lehman very clearly responded: No, being Jewish had neither helped nor hindered his career. Lehman advised the boy that he should never be ashamed of being a Jew. He should never try to hide it, never try to compromise with his convictions. From all my study I would say that's what Herbert Lehman did with his Jewishness. He never tried to hide it or minimize it. In New York politics, he capitalized on it.

—➤•⟷—

JUNE ROSSBACH BINGHAM BIRGE, *granddaughter of Herbert Lehman's elder sister Clara* – Uncle Herbert and Aunt Edith Lehman were very happy, although she was taller than he and could beat him at tennis. When I was a teenager, I mentioned in her presence an expression of the day. The word wimp hadn't yet been invented. You described someone like that as "a Helpless Herbert." "Do me a favor," she said. "Don't use that phrase, especially not around me or Uncle Herbert." I never used it in their presence again.

When I was grown up, I would occasionally join the Lehmans for dinner. Beforehand, Uncle Herbert always enjoyed his martini, or even—like his friend Franklin Roosevelt—his two martinis.

For reasons that wholly escaped me, Herbert had retained his early boyhood crush on his older sister, my grandmother Clara Lehman. He recalled her as a glamorous young lady who was beautiful and popular and kind to her little brothers Irving and Herbert. In fact, on the evening when she announced to her family at dinner that she planned to marry my grandfather Richard Limburg, young Herbert, aged twelve, flung himself from the table, ran to his room, and locked his door. It was probably

the only time in history that any member of the Lehman family didn't finish dessert. Anyway, half a century later, he would look at me over his cocktail and say, "Too bad you don't look more like your grandmother." Since I remembered her only as a fat grumpy old lady, I would smile and nod. It was the only time I was less than honest with Uncle Herbert.

I also remember that he and Aunt Edith would meet up with my grandmother in Monte Carlo every summer or two. They loved to dress up and gamble, as did my mother, but I was always left back at the hotel. You had to be eighteen to be admitted to the casino. In addition to gambling, Uncle Herbert also smoked. He had a library of pipes, and he puffed on cigarettes. Yet despite this habit, he lived to the then astounding age of eighty-five.

Uncle Herbert was sworn in as governor of New York State on December 31, 1932, the day after the death of his older sister Clara. The nation was then in the depths of the Depression. A quarter of the workforce was unemployed, and Americans were literally

*Herbert being sworn in for his second term as lieutenant governor on January 1, 1930,
by his brother, New York State Appeals Court Judge Irving Lehman, while
Governor Franklin D. Roosevelt and Herbert's wife, Edith, look on. (New York Times)*

Herbert Lehman being sworn in as governor on December 31, 1932, by his brother Irving with (left to right) his brother Arthur, his son Peter, his wife Edith, his daughter Hilda Jane, and his younger son John looking on. The oath of office took place in a private ceremony, as the governor's sister Clara Limburg had died the day before. (Camilla Rosenfeld)

starving for food and shivering in the winter storms, against which they had no shelter. Uncle Herbert was able to turn New York into one of the best states of the Union in terms of care for its poor and homeless citizens. Soup kitchens were set up, and shanty towns were permitted to be erected, including one in Central Park. Much of what he thereby learned he applied a decade later, when he was appointed by FDR to head the United Nations Relief and Rehabilitation Administration (UNRRA), which saved millions of lives abroad.

———⊰◈⊱———

ROBERT A. BERNHARD, *grandson of Herbert Lehman's older brother Arthur –* My Uncle Herbert became lieutenant governor when FDR became governor in 1929. I remember, when Herbert was governor, being taken to the opening of Whiteface Park in the Adirondacks in one of a caravan of cars, with a police motorcycle in front and sirens blaring. FDR came up, and they had a big parade. I remember sitting right behind FDR, watching bands going by, when somebody asked me what was the most important thing I saw that day, and I said, "The bandleader!" FDR turned around and said, "He's absolutely right."

At the end of Herbert's life, Bobby Lehman, then the senior partner of Lehman Brothers, made an effort to get friendly by inviting Herbert to lunch, having borne a grudge all these years against Arthur and Herbert. For years Herbert and Bobby never spoke, nor did Bobby have anything to do with my grandmother, because she was Arthur's widow. Yet Bobby was very fond of my mother, Dorothy, Adele's eldest daughter. The reason I believe I was asked to become a trustee of the Robert Lehman Foundation was because of his relationship with my mother.

———⊰◈⊱———

HENRY MORGENTHAU III, *grandson of Herbert Lehman's elder sister Settie –* My mother, Ellie Fatman Morgenthau, as a girl was very close to Herbert. The story is that when Herbert and Edith were first married, they invited my mother and father to the Adirondacks, and it was love at first sight. Later, as they all got involved in politics, there was considerable rivalry between my father, Henry Morgenthau Jr., and Herbert. They tended to distance themselves from each other. It seemed to them that the space for Jews in the political arena was very limited.

When King George VI and Queen Elizabeth of England visited Hyde Park in the summer of 1939, Herbert and Edith were there because Herbert was governor of New York state. My father, then secretary of the Treasury but also a Dutchess County neighbor, was the only cabinet member who was invited, along with his wife and three children. The queen, according to my mother, found it quite interesting that the U.S. secretary of the Treasury and the New York governor were close relatives.

———— ❖ ————

JUDITH LOEB CHIARA, *granddaughter of Herbert Lehman's elder brother Arthur* – Uncle Herbert came into my life after the Lindbergh kidnapping. Because he was governor of New York at the time, my parents were very worried—we lived in the same building. State troopers were always around, so in my mind Uncle Herbert was very important.

I always liked him, and he was always nice to me. When I was going to boarding school, he would send me an orchid for Easter. He was always warm and cozy, but I can't say I really knew him.

There was a comic strip about a politician called "The Shmoo." And I loved the comics. So I'm home reading "The Shmoo" and Uncle Herbert comes to visit Mother to talk about who knows what and have tea in the library. I'm looking at the comics, and I run into the library and say, "Uncle Herbert, do you realize this is you?" I must say Mother glared at me. Poor Uncle Herbert. He didn't want to be called a Shmoo.

Dick Beaty, my first husband, and I rode around in one of those sound trucks in Staten Island calling from bullhorns, "Vote for Herbert Lehman." When he was running for U.S. senator, he was nearly eighty, and he won. Whatever values you ought to have, he had. He really cared about people. They called him a "Parlor Pink," a pejorative at the time, indicating someone just this side of a Communist, which really annoyed me. Just because you're rich doesn't mean you're not allowed to help the poor. It doesn't mean that you have to be poor too.

———⬦———

JOHN L. LOEB JR., *grandson of Herbert Lehman's elder brother Arthur* – My mother, Frances Lehman Loeb, took me at the age of six to Uncle Herbert's inauguration as governor in Albany. I was forever after fascinated with Herbert's career. I wrote papers about him both at Hotchkiss and at Harvard. When we moved from Westchester to a duplex at 820 Park Avenue, we lived in the same building as Uncle Herbert when he was governor. There was a policeman standing outside, always on guard. At that time my family had been threatened, as had other wealthy families after the Lindbergh kidnapping, and every day a police car came to see if everything was okay at our

home on Anderson Hill Road in Purchase. The policeman at 820 Park was for Governor Herbert Lehman, but as a six-year-old, seeing policemen up at Purchase all the time, I just assumed that everyone had their own policemen. When Herbert Lehman and Aunt Edith lived in Washington, while he was serving as a U.S. senator, I had lunch with them a few times at the Wardman Park, where they lived. Herbert was quite short—about five-five— and I am six-four. Once when I went to Washington to see him about something, he came off the Senate floor to greet me. Estes Kefauver, who was my height, came by, and Uncle Herbert very proudly introduced me as his nephew. The two of us towered over him— but Herbert was the giant.

When I was starting out in politics, the Lehman name was so powerful that I toyed with the idea of changing my name to John Lehman Loeb, which irritated my father. My grandfather Arthur Lehman died in 1936, and in effect Herbert Lehman then became the head of the family. To me, he was always a great hero.

Governor and Mrs. Lehman hosting the president and Mrs. Roosevelt for tea at the New York State governor's Executive Mansion in Albany in 1933, shortly after their respective elections. (Associated Press)

Editor's note: The following are excerpts from a series of letters and news articles written from 1936 through 1950. They provide intimate glimpses into the background of Herbert Lehman's life and political career. The letters are from Governor Lehman's archives housed at Columbia University's Herbert H. Lehman Suite & Papers.

Franklin Delano Roosevelt
The White House
March 19, 1936

Dear Henry [Morgenthau Jr., secretary of the Treasury],

I am greatly disturbed by the enclosed from Herbert Lehman. He simply cannot be permitted to withdraw [from running for another term as governor of New York]. You and I know what a mess would be caused by trying to find a successor, quite aside from the fact that the State and its citizens need him as Governor.

⟫◆⟪

Herbert Lehman
Palm Springs, Calif.
March 19, 1936

Dear Irving [Lehman],

I have promised to speak at the fiftieth Anniversary of the Jewish Theological Seminary. I wonder whether you could get someone in New York to prepare an address for me for this occasion? I would like it to deal with the spiritual qualities of Judaism and the necessity of not only interesting our young people but instilling in them a sense of pride for our traditions and history. . . . I want to emphasize the fact, however, that if you cannot find anybody to do it, I would feel terribly badly if you attempted to do it yourself.

⟫◆⟪

Herbert Lehman
[To his wife Edith, Hotel Mark Hopkins, San Francisco]
Albany, August 25, 1937

239

Dearest:

I am sending you these typewritten lines since I am afraid that if I wait until I have time to write you in longhand, I will not get a letter off to you today. . . . There is nothing particularly new here. I had the district attorney and the sheriff of Erie County and the chief of police of one of the towns come down here today to warn them to enforce the law in their jurisdiction with regard to gambling, which apparently has gone on quite openly in some parts of the county, and has caused a good deal of newspaper and other comments. . . . My plans for next week are: Tuesday at Buffalo, where I am attending the Convention of the Veterans of Foreign Wars and reviewing their parade, and on Friday I will have to be at Williamstown to appear at the Institute of Human Relations, and will probably return to Albany from Williamstown the same evening and will go down to New York on Saturday morning.

⇒◇⇐

Dorothy Lehman Bernhard [daughter of Herbert Lehman's elder brother Arthur]
New York City
November 17, 1937
Dear Herbert:
You will remember that a little over a year ago you and Irving asked me to take charge of all the problems that came up concerning the connections of our family in Germany, and their desire to emigrate to this country. The balance of this fund is only a little over $500. I am therefore writing to the family to ask them to replenish this fund with the sum of at least $1000 from each branch of the family, in order to carry on this work.

Fondly,
Dorothy

⇒◇⇐

Herbert Lehman
January 10, 1939
Dear Franklin [Delano Roosevelt]:
As you know, it has always been my brother Irving's ambition to be appointed to the

Governor Lehman and President Roosevelt in a celebratory moment at a Democratic Party convention. (John L. Loeb Jr.)

Supreme Court. I very deeply share in that ambition. When Judge Cardozo passed away I would have spoken to you in the fall with regard to the matter had it not been for the vicious rumors that were spread during the campaign to the effect that the price which was paid for my running again was a promise of Irving's appointment to the Supreme Court—in other words, that a deal had been made between you and me. . . . I realize that there is at present no vacancy but I do want you to know how much it would mean to him and to me to have Irving appointed to the Supreme Court, if and when a vacancy should occur.

Franklin Delano Roosevelt
The White House
January 16, 1939

Dear Herbert:

I believe that Irving is one of the two or three outstanding judicial minds in the country today. Frankly, two thirds of the population of the Nation has no Justice on the Supreme Court. [Nearly all the Supreme Court justices were from the Northeast.] There is my predicament. In any event, there will probably be no further vacancies for some time but I don't need to assure you, not only of my deep personal feeling for Irving, but also in my belief in his outstanding qualifications.

Hans Gerst
Bemberg, Germany
March 11, 1939

My dear Mrs. Dorothy [Lehman Bernhard, head of the Lehman Family Refugee Fund]:

I beg your pardon writing you only just now but we are so busy that I am able only today to send you our best thanks for your cable. We are so delighted about your kindness and your loveliness. Of course we shall keep you informed of all. I suppose you know we must deliver now all our objects of value; it is very hard for Irma to lose all remembrances of the grandparents and parents. But our main aim is always to leave as soon as possible. Give please my love to your whole family. Irma and Ernest send you their best regards and I remain with affectionate greetings, very sincerely and thankfully yours,

Hans

———&—◇—&———

Herbert Lehman
Jasper Park Lodge
Jasper, Alberta, Canada
August 3, 1939

Dear Dorothy [Lehman Bernhard],
I have received your report with regard to refugees. I have read it with the greatest of interest. Frankly, even I did not realize the amount of work you had done or the extent of the obligations which we have assumed. Many thanks, again, for all the trouble you have taken.

———&—◇—&———

Dorothy Lehman Bernhard [daughter of Herbert Lehman's elder brother Arthur]
September 20, 1939

Dear Herbert,
I had some correspondence with Hans [Gerst] before he left Germany. He sent his furniture here which I have had cleaned and stored and insured for him. I had received no word from Hans for two months and could not imagine what had held up his emigration. My first knowledge of their arrival in England came from Sidney Ehrman [a descendent of Isaias and Esther Hellman] in San Francisco.

———&—◇—&———

Carolin Flexner [Herbert Lehman's longtime personal assistant]
He always gave me the leeway I needed to help people. When the refugees came when he was in Albany, I wrote to him or talked to him and said, "Governor, I'm swamped with appeals on refugees. How much time do you want me to give to

them?" "Spend as much time as you can because these people are in trouble and need help." [So] I started working with their families, many of whom were very simple people. Most of them were far, far away on the family tree. I worked with Mrs. Richard Bernhard, who is still in charge of the family fund. She very wisely employed a social worker, who investigated and found out what these people needed. To this day they are still putting money into that family fund to keep up the people who are too old to readjust to the life.

———⊰⋅⊱———

Herbert Lehman

Cable to Herbert Lehman's grandnephew

Robert M. Morgenthau at Amherst College

JAN. 23, 1940: WE HAVE JUST LEARNED OF YOUR ELECTION AS EDITOR IN CHIEF OF THE STUDENT NEWS-PAPER PERIOD EDITH AND THE CHILDREN JOIN ME IN THE HEARTIEST CONGRATULATIONS AND BEST WISHES TO YOU PERIOD WE ARE ALL VERY PROUD OF YOU PERIOD

———⊰⋅⊱———

Herbert Lehman

[Written to his wife Edith while on a trip on behalf of UNRRA]

Algiers

March 18, 1944

Dearest Love:

I feel very sad today because [George] Xanthaky [Executive Vice President, Greek War Relief Association] and General [Edwin S.] Chickering are leaving at noon for Cairo and I am held here. They have not yet put the plaster cast on my leg as they wanted to be sure all the swelling had disappeared. The difficulty will be getting in and out of planes. I hope to get to Cairo in the next few days. Even if I do not I can do a certain amount of work here if the boys keep me in touch with conditions in the Middle East. . . . The hospital is a very nice

244

President Roosevelt congratulates Governor Lehman on his becoming director of the State Department's Office of Relief and Rehabilitation Operations (a predecessor of UNRRA, the United Nations Relief and Rehabilitation Administration) with Edith watching, in December 1942. (Associated Press)

one. There are excellent doctors and most attentive nurses. I couldn't be more comfortable in the Mount Sinai or the New York Hospital. . . . Hilda Jane [Herbert and Edith's adopted daughter] had two days' leave and was with me almost continuously. She really is very sweet and could not be more attentive. . . . I want to give you my absolute assurance (honest) that there is nothing wrong with me except this little fracture of the kneecap. From now on I suppose I shall have to be pretty careful.

—◆—

Jonathan B. Bingham [first husband of Herbert Lehman's grandniece June Rossbach Bingham Birge]
October 22, 1949
To the Editor of the *New York Times*
Day by day your reporters have drawn an indelible picture of John Foster Dulles as a man who will stop at nothing to keep his seat in the Senate. . . . Dulles's insinuations have been unmistakable. Most incredible of

all was this appeal to an upstate crowd: "If you could see the kind of people in New York City making up this bloc that is voting for my opponent, Herbert Lehman, if you could see them with your own eyes, I know that you would be out, every last man and woman of you, on election day." . . .

I have talked to a number of Republicans, some of them personally acquainted with Dulles, who are so shocked by his campaign that they have decided to vote against him.

—◆—

New York Times, November 4, 1950
Senator Herbert H. Lehman disclosed last night at a rally for his re-election that Mrs. Lehman had "for the first time" urged him to campaign for return to office.

—◆—

Frances Lehman Loeb [daughter of Herbert Lehman's elder brother Arthur]
November 14, 1950
Dear Herbert,

We do want to offer you our sincere congratulations on your reelection as Senator. I am a person who lives a lot in the past, and I keep thinking back to Grandma [Babette Neugass Lehman]—what hopes and ambitions she must have had for all her sons—perhaps particularly for her son Herbert —her "mistake," as you once told me you heard her say. As I listened to your last broadcast the other evening and saw before me the steady advance that you had made until now you have reached your full stature of usefulness, power and dignity in this large community, I realized what pride and sense of fulfillment she would have had. This must be your greatest satisfaction, and I for one, am very proud to be related by blood as well as love to her memory and your wonderful reality.

Peter

⇒◆⇐

Herbert Lehman
November 14, 1950
Dear Frances [Lehman Loeb],

Although I spoke with you just before leaving home, I cannot refrain from thanking you for the lovely letter. I want to also take this opportunity of thanking you for your fine work during the campaign. I have heard from all sides how generously and effectively you gave of your time during the busy fall weeks. As Edith and I sit in the Florida sunshine reflecting over the events of the campaign, the one thing that stands out and gives us the greatest joy is the devotion and loyalty of our family and friends, who, as usual gave unstintingly of their time and thought to insuring the success on election day.

⇒◆⇐

WILLIAM MAYER, *great-grandson of Herbert Lehman's uncle Emanuel Lehman* – The world remembers Herbert's concern for the underprivileged; his generous spirit also encompassed his own family. It was Herbert Lehman who made it possible for me to audition my musical trip around the world, *Hello, World!*, for Eleanor Roosevelt.

Herbert Lehman in 1959 during a speech to the townspeople of Kfar Lehman, a small Israeli settlement in western Galilee, which was named for him. (Associated Press)

What I didn't know was that Mrs. Roosevelt was subject to catnaps. She fell asleep in the middle of the rehearsal of the piece, and of course I thought my music had bored her into the snooze. What a relief when I heard from her secretary (who spoke in the same intonations as Mrs. Roosevelt) that she was willing to narrate the work. *Hello, World!* was brought out on an RCA Victor label, and the recording undoubtedly helped propel the work into its many performances, including four seasons with the Philadelphia Orchestra. Herbert made it all happen.

———⊰•⊱———

PAUL A. BUTTENWIESER, *grandson of Herbert Lehman's elder brother Arthur* – I remember seeing McCarthy on the Senate floor saying, "I have here papers showing such and such about Communist spies," and Herbert coming over from his seat and actually standing in front of McCarthy and saying, "Let me see that!" and McCarthy refusing to let him see anything.

JULIUS EDELSTEIN (1912–2005), *Herbert Lehman's special assistant for many years* – As a United States senator, Herbert Lehman was listened to very attentively as the voice—the apostle—of the liberal point of view. On such matters as civil rights and, of course, Israel, his voice was the authoritative one representing the liberal side. He's a man who, when he gets an idea, just feels that it has to be said. . . . He participated in debate as much as any senator I've ever seen. Not that he was a great debater—nobody would ever say that. He was not good at a quick thrust, at repartee, which in this day and age marks the skillful debater. But at critical times he spoke from the heart, and he would command attention on the subject.

———⊰•⊱———

WILLIAM L. BERNHARD, *grandson of Herbert Lehman's elder brother Arthur* – My cousin Larry Buttenwieser and I were in Chicago during both the Republican and Democratic conventions in 1952. We had both gotten minor jobs at the Republican convention through our fathers.

We were very much, as our fathers were, for Eisenhower. There was a week between conventions, and I was staying with Larry at the University of Chicago when the Democrats came to town. Through Herbert we both got jobs as pages on the convention floor. We were so totally for Ike that we felt it didn't make any difference who the Democrats ran—Ike had it. It was quite a convention that, until the end, was up for grabs. In the end Governor Harriman threw his support for Stevenson, who gave one of the great political speeches of all time. Larry and I were Stevenson people from that moment on. And it was entirely due to Herbert, who was the head, I believe, of the New York delegation, that we were there on the floor.

My mother, Dorothy Lehman Bernhard, was close to Herbert. They were very tight. She was often at 820 Park [the Herbert Lehman home in New York City] for lunches and dinners. She frequently went to Albany and Washington, where she worked with him for the Democratic Party and also on family inter-ests. Because of Herbert she was appointed to the Welfare Board of New York, to which Herbert had previously appointed her father, and got a special license plate, which I still use—16B.

<hr/>

LORD WILLIAM HOWARD GOODHART, *grandson of Herbert Lehman's eldest sister Hattie* – Herbert was still alive and active when I was at the Harvard Law School in 1957–1958, and so was the only one of the Lehman children I knew as an adult. I remember in particular going to his 80th birthday party at the Waldorf Astoria, a splendid tribute to his career. Herbert and Edith had me to lunch with them several times. I greatly liked and admired him. He was that unusual creature—a highly successful politician who was also a man of great integrity.

<hr/>

ROBERT M. MORGENTHAU, *grandson of Herbert Lehman's elder sister Settie* – Herbert used to go to din-ners carrying a clear glass medicine bottle with gin in it. I sat next to him at one dinner, and I remember him saying to the waiter, "I am required to take my medicine before I eat. Would you bring me a coffee cup with some ice in it?" He didn't want people to see him drinking a martini from a glass. He also liked to have a beer before he went to bed at night. When I ran for governor against Nelson Rockefeller, Herbert was very helpful to me. I remember we were over in Brighton Beach, and he climbed up the lifeguard tower to campaign for me. Even though Rockefeller won, he got only 48% of the vote against me.

—◆◆◆—

WILLIAM L. BERNHARD, *grandson of Herbert Lehman's elder brother Arthur* – Uncle Irving Lehman's death, according to his obituary, was precipitated by his tripping over a boxer dog given to him by Herbert (who had actually introduced German boxers into this country) and breaking an ankle. Also—and Judy [Loeb Chiara] confirms this—our grandfather Arthur Lehman had this boxer named Bubbie, given to him by

Herbert. The story goes that Bubbie jumped up on Grandpa, and Grandpa fell down and hurt his leg. He was told to stay in bed and rest as a result, but he was too active a person. He got up, and that led to the thrombosis in his leg going to his heart and killing him. So both Irving and Arthur died as a result of accidents involving boxers given to them by Herbert. Who would believe it?

—◆◆◆—

CAMILLA ROSENFELD, *niece of Herbert Lehman's wife, Edith* – We often visited at the Lehman apartment. If Uncle Herbert was resting in the afternoon and we were alone with Aunt Edith, laughing and having a wonderful time, he couldn't stand it. He'd come down the stairs in his robe because he didn't want to miss anything!

When I was young, my family spent time with Aunt Edith and Uncle Herbert at Lake Placid, where they rented a cottage at the Whiteface Inn for a month during the summer. Different members of the family would come, each for a week or so—and we did that for a long time. We also often spent time together at their weekend farm (Meadow Farm) in Purchase. It was one of the most beautiful retreats you can imagine—eighty acres of apple orchards, terraces running down to the swimming pool, and a tennis court.

ISADORE ROSENFELD, *Camilla Rosenfeld's husband and Herbert Lehman's physician* – If someone sent Uncle Herbert a gift—it could be as little as five dollars—he either politely turned it down or declared it on his income tax. . . .

He was famous, prominent, and much loved by all, but his family came first. Despite all the demands on his time, and his many important responsibilities, he was never too busy for his children, his grandchildren, other members of his family, or anyone who needed him. You never felt you were intruding or imposing. Family events, no matter how "unimportant" in the scheme of things, took priority. He took the better part of a day off

to travel to Sarah Lawrence to be present at Camilla's graduation.

CAMILLA ROSENFELD, *niece of Herbert Lehman's wife, Edith* – Uncle Herbert was a mensch. He really was. Everyone loved him. When he was campaigning, the crowds wanted to be near him, to touch him. He believed that things not only had to be right, they had to seem right. He never compromised with morals or his ethics. He probably was not political enough to have been elected president.

ISADORE ROSENFELD, *Camilla Rosenfeld's husband and Herbert Lehman's physician* – The day President Kennedy was shot (November 22, 1963), Uncle Herbert called to tell me he wasn't feeling well. He sounded and said he was disturbed, and asked me for a sedative. The next day he called me again, this time to tell me he'd had chest pain during the night. I had him come to the office immediately. His electrocardiogram was unchanged, as were the results of his physical exam. I didn't find any difference in him. I monitored him closely the next few days, but the chest pain never returned and his EKG remained normal.

About two weeks later, at 8:30 on the morning of December 5, 1963, Aunt Edith called to tell me that Uncle Herbert had collapsed suddenly while shaving in the upstairs bathroom. She was downstairs and heard a thump. She went upstairs and found him lying on the floor, motionless. I was there within five minutes. He was dead. His limo and chauffeur were waiting for him outside his apartment to take him and Aunt Edith to Washington, where he was to have received the Medal of Freedom. It had been conferred on him by President Kennedy. After Kennedy died, President Johnson honored that commitment to Uncle Herbert and was to present him with the medal the day he died. (The president attended the funeral in New York, despite Aunt Edith's pleas that he not do so because she was worried about his safety,

given the assassination of President Kennedy a few days earlier.)

———◆———

DEBORAH JANE WISE SHERIDAN, *granddaughter of Herbert and Edith Lehman* – I adored my Gramps. He never seemed too busy for us. Staying at 820 was the best. While Granny had her breakfast in bed, my brother Peter, my sister Stephanie, and I met Gramps in the dining room, where he made "snooks" for us—pieces of English muffins with strawberry jam, honey, sugar, and anything else on the table. We each got to toss a saccharin tablet in his coffee as he sang "Down went McGinty to the bottom of the sea. Up came McGinty; what a wise boy was he." At the "Up" part, somehow these little tablets always seemed to fizz. We were delighted.

He and Granny had a wonderful marriage. Often when we were watching some news show or *The Defenders*, one of his favorites, I could see them quietly holding hands. When we visited them in Washington, we stayed with

"Whiteface Mountain, 1948. Back row (left to right): Uncle Herbert, Jean Poletti (the lieutenant governor's wife), Jonathan Bingham, me. Front row (left to right): Penny Lehman, Sherry and Micki Bingham, Wendy Lehman, Claudia Bingham. Inexplicably missing are Edith Lehman and Tim Bingham." —June Rossbach Bingham Birge (June Rossbach Bingham Birge)

them at the Wardman Park and enjoyed watching Granny's pet canary flying around the living room, landing on Gramps's bald head. He seemed to enjoy it as much as we did.

I was always so proud when people stopped Gramps on the street when we were out walking to tell him how much he meant to them; he always responded courteously. When I went with them to a restaurant, Herbert often had a cigarette in his mouth, which some waiter was eager to light. I was amused each time when he told them he actually didn't smoke cigarettes, though he did smoke a pipe. Recalling the smell of his pipe can practically transport me back to him.

Christmas at Granny and Gramps's was magic. We all gathered with the rest of the family upstairs until the moment when the living room doors opened and we could go in, see the tree, and find our presents. One time I found a box with a double heart pin in it. Gramps told me it was his heart and mine forever. It is my most treasured piece of jewelry.

PENELOPE LEHMAN, *granddaughter of Herbert and Edith Lehman* – I remember going down to Washington to see him and being able to ring the bell for the train that goes from the Senate building to the Capitol. I remember meeting Everett Dirksen—whom he didn't like and used to call the "Wizard of Ooze"—and Alban Barclay, when he was vice president—whom he liked very much. I remember once using a derogatory term for the French people, and Gramps told me in no uncertain terms that we don't do that, that we were lucky enough to be born into the Lehman family, and now we should do something in return instead of thinking we are better than other people.

PETER LEHMAN WISE, *grandson of Herbert and Edith Lehman* – I grew up in Cleveland, Ohio. When I was in the fifth or sixth grade, I wrote to my grandfather and told him that we were learning about the United States government and its workings in history class. Knowing that he was a United States senator, I wrote and asked him to tell about how a bill moves through Congress and becomes law. He wrote back: "Dear Peter, I've enclosed a copy of an actual bill, which I hope you will find interesting." I didn't appreciate until years later that the bill he had authored and sent me introduced the Saint Lawrence Seaway Project.

My grandfather was a very sweet man who would find ways to include me in his life. One time, while visiting my grandparents in New York, my grandfather said to me, "I would like you to meet a former president of the United States." As simply as that, we walked nearby to the Carlyle Hotel, where he introduced me to Harry Truman. Former president Truman pulled a red and white plastic pen out of his lapel pocket and gave it to me as he shook my hand. On the pen was inscribed, "I had the pleasure of meeting Harry S. Truman." He appeared to have had a pocketful of these pens.

I don't know why I was always surprised by their political celebrity, but I was. I think it was my mother's influence—she was very humble, all things considered. I met a lot of prominent

people through my grandparents. I remember being introduced to Mamie Eisenhower in the White House Rose Garden, and Lyndon Johnson attended my grandfather's funeral. That was the first time the new president had been in public since the assassination of JFK about three weeks earlier. Six of the nine Supreme Court justices were at my grandfather's funeral, together with innumerable congressmen and other dignitaries. That day I began to understand the breadth and depth of my grandfather's public life.

I was only six or seven years old when my grandfather was in the United States Senate. I remember having lunch with him once in the U.S. Senate dining room. My grandfather ordered chicken livers, so I did as well, having never tried them before. When we were served, I took a bite and then vomited, right in the Senate dining room. My grandfather's reaction was very loving and not without humor. "It's quite alright," he said. "Let's see if we can find something that's better suited to your taste." I was both embarrassed and afraid that I had embarrassed him, but he didn't look the least bit concerned. As an adult I will sometimes order chicken livers, and I always think about the indignity and humor of that experience. Maybe that's why I only order chicken livers from time to time and why I enjoy them so much when I do.

Portrait of Edith Altschul Lehman as a young lady painted by Harrington Mann, c. 1922. (Wendy Lehman Lash)

Edith Altschul Lehman

1889–1976

New York Times, March 9, 1976

EDITH LEHMAN, PHILANTHROPIST, IS DEAD

By ALBIN KREBS

Edith Altschul Lehman, widow of former Gov. Herbert H. Lehman of New York and, in her own right, a leading philanthropist, died early yesterday. She was 86 years old.

Mrs. Lehman, whose husband also served as a United States Senator, died of a heart attack, following a long illness, at her home at 820 Park Avenue. Despite her age, she had remained active in a number of social-service organizations until her final illness.

Although Mrs. Lehman preferred to take a back seat to her husband when he was active in politics, she did so with unfailing grace, enthusiastically performing the sometimes dreary social duties expected of a political figure's wife.

At the same time, her activities in behalf of organizations such as the Henry Street Settlement and the Play Schools Association, of which she was board chairman from 1966 until her death, remained unabated. While her husband was in office, she regularly registered her opposition to his continued role in politics.

Many Political Campaigns

"For his family, it is the world's worst life," said the always genteelly outspoken Mrs. Lehman. "He's busy from morning until night, with scarcely a minute to see his own children." In 1937 she put the matter more bluntly in an interview, saying: "My husband has spent nearly 10 years in the service of the people. It has been a wonderful experience, but I feel that at the end of his term the Governor should be permitted to withdraw from public life and lead his own life."

Such, however, was not to be the case. Altogether, Mr. Lehman spent two terms as Lieutenant Governor and four as Governor. The Lehmans finally moved out of the Executive Mansion in Albany in 1942, but there were other political campaigns to come.

The former Democratic Governor ran unsuccessfully for United States Senator in 1946, but he filled an unexpired year in the Senate in 1949 and was elected Senator in 1950. It was not until 1956, when he was 78, that Mr. Lehman retired from public life. He died in 1963.

A native of San Francisco, Mrs. Lehman was the daughter of Charles Altschul and the former Camilla Mandelbaum. Her father was an official of Lazard Frères & Company, the investment banking concern, and when she was 11, he moved the family to New York, where he was to serve as managing partner of the Wall Street office.

Here young Edith attended Dr. Sach[s]'s Girls School and another private school, Miss Jacobi's, now known as the Calhoun

School. As a girl she was active in sports, including swimming, tennis and fishing. Her interest in fishing was practically lifelong, and in 1931 she hooked a 130-pound tarpon, which, she said, "gave me something to talk about for years."

She was also extremely fond of music, and as a young woman liked to compose melodies for the piano.

In 1910 the former San Franciscan was married to Herbert Lehman, a partner in the investment banking concern of Lehman Brothers and a member of an influential New York family with a long tradition of giving aid to welfare work and religious and philanthropic causes.

[In 1912 they purchased a farm as a second home in Westchester County just north of White Plains belonging to a family that acquired it by land grant before the Revolution.]

She joined her husband in the work of organizations such as the Federation of Jewish Philanthropies and the United Jewish Appeal and the cause of establishing a Jewish national homeland in Palestine.

Mrs. Lehman also worked as a fund raiser for the Henry Street Settlement, in which her husband had become interested while still in his teens.

The settlement, devoted to improving the living conditions of the poor on the Lower East Side, is now supported by a $5 million annual budget, and provides such services as a day-care center for preschool children of working mothers, a junior high school for pupils unable to get through the public school system, a center for the elderly, and living quarters for teenagers from broken or disadvantaged homes.

Mrs. Lehman's association with the settlement lasted more than 50 years. In 1948, with her husband, she donated a building dedicated in the memory of their son Peter, a pilot killed in World War II.

Another organization to which Mrs. Lehman devoted much of her efforts is the Play Schools Association. She had been a charter member since its founding in 1917 as "a consultation and training agency utilizing play activities as an educational, therapeutic, and recreational tool to benefit children." The association's work is carried out in partnership with the city's Board of Education and other public and private groups.

At her death, Mrs. Lehman was also an honorary trustee of Mount Sinai Medical Center, whose board she joined in 1921. She was a founding sponsor of the Mount Sinai School of Medicine, and in 1969 established a Lehman Chair in Pediatrics there in her husband's memory.

Suite at Columbia U.

Following her husband's death, Mrs. Lehman contributed in his memory $100,000 to the United Jewish Appeal, and made substantial gifts to other institutions, including Williams College, which Mr. Lehman attended. Most of Mrs. Lehman's philanthropic giving was not made public.

Mrs. Lehman took a particularly close interest in the establishment of the Herbert H. Lehman Suite at Columbia University's School of International Affairs. She financed and endowed the suite, which is the repository of the Lehman papers and memorabilia. Until her illness, she often visited the suite and helped the staff collect letters and other documents dealing with her husband's career.

Of Mrs. Lehman's three children, only one survives. He is John Robert Lehman, managing director of Lehman Brothers. Other survivors include a brother, Frank Altschul of Stamford, Conn., the retired financier and noted bibliophile; five grandchildren and three great-grandchildren.

The Lehman family will receive visitors tonight from 7 to 9 o'clock at Frank E. Campbell's, Madison Avenue and 81st Street. A funeral service is set at 11 A.M. tomorrow in the Beth-El Chapel of Temple Emanu-El, Fifth Avenue and 65th Street.

———✦———

Edith Altschul Lehman

[On VJ Day while all London seemed celebrating in the streets, the Lehmans had tea with George VI and Queen Elizabeth in Buckingham Palace.]

August 15, 1945

Claridge's [London]

Dearest Penny,

Gramps and I just came back from visiting the king and queen [George VI and Elizabeth] and I want to tell you all about it, and then you must tell Wendy [Penny's sister].

We drove to the palace and had a hard time getting through the crowds that were waiting to cheer the king and queen when they came out on the balcony. We were met by a very fancy looking gentleman with lots of gold ribbons decorating his suit. Then he took us to a room where the king and queen and the two princesses [Elizabeth and Margaret] were.

The queen had on a lovely pale blue dress and jacket, and the princesses wore light print dresses like you and Wendy wear. The king had on a dark blue uniform with lots of gold trimmings and many different color ribbons on the left side. After we had said how do you do, just like you and Wendy when you meet Mommy's friends, we all sat down at a big table for tea. It was covered with a pretty white cloth and lots of plates of sandwiches, cookies and cakes. It looked like your mommy's table when she has a birthday party—only there were no flowers. Instead, there was a beautiful big silver tea-set.

The princesses are very pretty and very sweet. They would like to come to America some time and I am sure you would love to see them. . . . Gramps and I had a lovely time with the king and queen and the princesses. It was just like being with any other very happy family, and it was nice that we were alone with them so that we could get to know them. Some day I hope you and Wendy will know them too. A big hug for each of you and one for Mommy too.

Your loving Granny

⧫

PENELOPE LEHMAN, *granddaughter of Herbert and Edith Lehman* – When they lived in D.C., there was a wonderful trick store where you could buy glasses that dribbled and whoopee cushions that made bathroom noises when you sat down on them. Granny would take us with the greatest glee to the trick store. She would love to pull the dribble cup trick on Gramps. Also the fake dog doo on the carpet.

At dessert, what looked like a Steuben bowl would be brought out with ice cream balls in it. The maid would come around first to Granny, who would break the bowl with the ice cream spoon. What some of the guests didn't know was that the bowl was made of candy. "Oh everyone, watch out," she would say. "I was so clumsy." And then she would put a piece of the glass (which was actually candy) in her mouth. It was great fun.

Grandma Edith was very erect in her bearing, but there was a softness to her face. She wasn't like the Duchess of Windsor. She was a comfortable queen interacting with people.

I'm sure you've heard of Josephine. She worked for Granny and Gramps forever. Nothing could function without her. She was family. If something needed mending, she knew how to mend it. If someone was sick, she knew where the hot water bottle was—or the Band-Aid. She was a majordomo who could make up beds. She was quiet, almost obsequious. If Josephine was around, everything was fine. She was the glue that kept the household together.

When Granny and Gramps were having their 50th wedding anniversary at the 21 Club,

Edith Altschul Lehman was greatly admired by family members. According to William Bernhard, "Edith was wonderfully wise and beautiful—strong," and according to Penelope Lehman, "There was a softness to her face. She wasn't the Duchess of Windsor. She was a comfortable queen. . . ." (Camilla Rosenfeld)

Mother [Peggy Lehman] kept pestering Granny to let her pick out a dress for the occasion. But Granny refused, saying, "I'm going to take care of this all by myself." When they appeared, Gramps was in his tuxedo and Granny in her wedding dress. My sister, Wendy, wore it when she got married in '64, and Abigail, her daughter, wore it last year at her wedding.

—•◇•—

PETER LEHMAN WISE, *grandson of Herbert and Edith Lehman* – One summer Edith took up residence at the Westchester Country Club, which had a reputation for being "restricted," a euphemism for not admitting Jews. Since Herbert was such a prominent citizen, admission to the club was not in question. My grandmother invited me to spend that summer with her. For nearly two months that summer, I played thirty-six holes of golf each day. It was their way of breaking down a barrier.

I remember on one occasion, while visiting my grandmother at her home on Park Avenue, I was asked to join her for lunch. A young man by the name of Hugh Carey had been invited to join us that day, as well. Carey was preparing to run for governor of New York for the first time, and he wanted her support as an elder stateswoman and contributor. During lunch the conversation turned somehow to Stephen Birmingham's book *"Our Crowd"* and I remember my grandmother was highly critical of Birmingham's depiction of the Lehmans. One story he told was that Herbert, as an undergraduate, had traveled to Williams College in a chauffeur-driven automobile. The fact that no such vehicle existed when Herbert went to college seemed only to prove my grandmother's point, that the author had a poor grasp on his facts. Later during lunch, when the Rockefeller name came up in conversation, I remember my grandmother referring to them as "nouveau riche." Even as a young man, I got a private chuckle from her comment, since people of wealth seemed all very much the same to me.

My grandmother could also be sarcastic, but she would always mask her comments with understatement. I remember her comment to a young lady who had dressed in the style of the day (early 1970s): "I like your costume," and the effect was quite deflating.

In retrospect, one of the most interesting conversations I remember having with my grandmother was about buying and selling stocks. My grandmother's view, and I suspect my grandfather's as well, was that buying stock in a company was a matter of simple patriotism, a way of helping to build America. They believed that part of the mission of Lehman Brothers was to help capitalize ventures that had the potential of strengthening our country. It was a "buy-and-hold" mentality. Selling a stock meant a loss of faith in the company in which one had made one's investment, an idea that seems foreign to the transactional society in which we live today.

Visiting my grandparents at their Park Avenue apartment was surreal to me, even as a young boy. When I would overnight there, I would usually find on my nightstand a small crystal glass filled with milk, placed upon a sterling tray, together with a few delicate lace cookies, which were served on a doily placed upon a plate. These items seemed to magically appear at bedtime, although I knew very well that they had been put there by a member of the household staff. I did not know how many staff members (servants) lived unobtrusively in small rooms there, but I do know that my grandparents had a cook for themselves and another who was responsible for feeding the live-in staff. The chauffeur would often take his meals there, as well. On the rare occasion that I would investigate this "upstairs/down-stairs" arrangement, I would find a series of small rooms—very austere, almost monastic—where mostly young Irish girls lived. Typically, they worked six days a week. They got Sunday mornings off to attend mass, and some took Sunday afternoons as well. A good number of people lived at 820 Park Avenue, but, with the exception of my grandparents, they were mostly out of sight. When I would go down to the kitchen to look for more lace cookies, my bedtime angels would say, "Master Peter, you mustn't be here," as I wasn't supposed to mingle with them.

—◆◇◆—

WENDY LEHMAN LASH, *granddaughter of Herbert and Edith Lehman* – I adored my grandmother. She was a fabulous person. She was always there. Even though she was in Washington a lot, I was very close to her. When my grandparents were in town, my sister Penny and I used to come over for breakfast any time. My mother would be aghast that I would walk down Park Avenue in my riding clothes to have breakfast with them, but Granny and Gramps would love it. They didn't care. When I was working, Granny would usually be on the phone at seven o'clock in the morning saying, "Do you want to come to dinner tonight?"

Before I married, I used to travel with Granny to Europe. We'd go to England and then to Switzerland and Italy. We'd eat, we'd drink, we'd take a walk. We were in Zermatt one summer when Granny said to me, "Go home. You're no fun to travel with." It was just

before my engagement to Stephen, and I missed him terribly. When we got married, she said, "I'll give you Smith (her chauffeur) to take you to the airport on your honeymoon." "That's very sweet of you," I said. We were leaving very early, and there she was, at six o'clock in the morning, in the car with Jay Jay her dog, going to the airport with us. We got there, she started to get out, and I said, "Don't get out of the car. We'll give you a kiss goodbye and we'll see you in a month." "I've got to get out of the car," she said. And out she gets and starts throwing rice all over us! She loved doing that. Months later we found rice in all the pockets of the coats we had worn.

She didn't really like to fly, but when Stephen and I were first married, she would fly to England all the time to see us. If she happened to be in New York, she would always call us up to wish us a happy anniversary at seven o'clock in the morning our time in London, and you know what time that was in America! She gave us our first dog. "You go pick out any dog," she said to Stephen, "as a birthday present." When we had dinner at Claridge's, where she always stayed when she was in London, she would ask us to bring the dog, because she just loved dogs, and would roll a ball down the halls of Claridge's for him.

She bought our apartment for us. "I might as well give it to you now," she said, "so you don't want me dead sooner." She gave a toast at our wedding rehearsal dinner saying, "I always loved Stephen. I just did not know if I was going to get him."

⤙⬥⬥⤚

New York World Telegram, November 1, 1934

The woman who organized the social service department of Mount Sinai Hospital, and who always helps captain the Federation of Jewish Charities Fund campaign, is frankly worried about the coming winter, about the relief problem and private charity. "The need is greater than ever," Mrs. Lehman said. "So many jobless families have come to the end of their rope. Every mail is filled with letters to both the Governor and

to me from people asking for jobs. It's sickening, heartbreaking. They don't want charity, nothing but the opportunity to work."

⤙⬥⬥⤚

New York Times, November 5, 1935

"TEN COMMANDMENTS" OF DEMOCRACY

Mrs. Lehman says her code restates moral and political ideals that we all profess.

By S. J. Woolf

It is only upon rare occasions that the wife of New York's Governor speaks in public. When she does speak, her words are listened to with more than ordinary attention. Recently, stirred by world conditions, she broke her usual silence and gave what she calls the "Ten Commandments of Democracy." . . .

"The Ten Commandments of the Bible are, after all, a complete moral code, and perhaps it is presumptuous of me to call by their name these modern principles which I have set down, for basically the biblical injunctions contain all that I have said. For example, my first commandment is 'Tell the truth,' which after all is the same as 'Thou shalt not bear false witness.' But where is this possible except in a democracy? I go on by suggesting that we treat others as we would wish to be treated, that we respect the religious beliefs of all, that we help those who suffer and who are persecuted, that we try to afford an equal opportunity to all to earn and learn. I then try to stress the fact that freedom of opinion is the basis of human liberty, that those who sow hatred are enemies of our form of government and that the hope of the world lies in peace and justice to all mankind.

"We have seen nations in Europe lose their rights of liberty, nations where justice no longer rules. This has not come about suddenly but it has been effected slowly, by degrees. With these nations as horrible examples, it becomes all the more necessary for us to guard our rights of freedom of press, speech, and thought.

"There is no doubt but that some who seek to destroy our form of government, those who would throttle this freedom had they the power, avail themselves of it to spread their doctrine of hate. Yet the very fact that they are unrestricted in the expression of their ideas makes those ideas less dangerous than if they were spread under cover.

"We must combat these sowers of dissension with the truth. We must stress the fact that America is not merely a country but an ideal; that race superiority, class hatred, group warfare have no place here where sympathy for the oppressed has ever been a cardinal characteristic."

⎯⎯⧓⬥⧔⎯⎯

ROBERT M. MORGENTHAU, *grandson of Herbert Lehman's elder sister Settie* – Edith Lehman's sister Hilda would take us to the park every Thursday afternoon, and she wanted to be called Hilda, which was unusual in those days. I remember saying to Aunt Edith one time, "How is Hilda?" She looked at me and said, "What do you mean?" And I said again, "How's Hilda?" And she said, "You mean Cousin Hilda." She was reprimanding me for referring to her sister by her first name.

———✦———

PETER JOSTEN, *grandson of Herbert Lehman's elder sister Settie* – When I was working in Washington for Naval Intelligence, I would go to Herbert and Edith's for lunch sometimes. Edith was a very handsome woman and a great hostess. She would really make you feel at ease. Everything was done perfectly. Herbert was rather quiet. He seemed shy. She, on the contrary, was not shy about voicing her opinions. She was really the dominant force, though I think they thought the same way.

———✦———

LAWRENCE B. BUTTENWIESER, *grandson of Herbert Lehman's elder brother Arthur* – I don't think any of the Lehmans were as influenced by their spouse as Herbert was by Edith. Edith lived in service to Herbert, but she was a person in her own right. She was very outspoken and I never heard Herbert disagree with her. She was a very wise and shrewd woman. At the 1956 Democratic National Convention, Ann and I, on our way home from our honeymoon, joined Herbert and Edith for lunch at the Blackstone Hotel in Chicago. As we were talking together, every third passerby would stop by the table to say, "Hello, Governor Lehman!" or "Hello, Senator Lehman!"—and Herbert would never know who the passerby was until Edith would whisper in his ear, filling in the blanks—and there were a lot of blanks to fill in. Herbert was very warm, affectionate, and friendly and a man of great courage, but I am not sure he would have had the courage to cross his wife. By electing Herbert, New York got two people in office for the price of one.

———✦———

WILLIAM L. BERNHARD, *grandson of Herbert Lehman's elder brother Arthur* – Edith was wonderfully wise and beautiful—and strong. She told me that once when Herbert was trying to get the

Edith and Herbert sharing a desk as they shared their lives. According to Lawrence Buttenwieser, "By electing Herbert, New York got two people in office for the price of one." (Camilla Rosenfeld)

nomination for governor at a state Democratic convention, the powers that be tried to ditch him. Herbert had to fight hard to stay on the ticket and, having achieved that, he knew exactly who the people were who fought against him. But it was not in his nature to hold grudges, so Edith stepped in by not letting Herbert forget or forgive those people who fought against him. She was very much a power player in their dynamic relationship.

When my cousin Peter Buttenwieser went to see Edith around holiday time, she told him she had separate holiday plans with the Lehman and Altschul sides of the family. Once when she was having a party, she told him he couldn't come because it wasn't for the Lehman side of the family.

At these wonderful Sunday lunches, which we were so lucky to go to, almost always the dessert would be ice cream. Edith felt that it was all right as long as it was chocolate. She loved chocolate ice cream—and I share her enthusiasm.

Aunt Edith once said to me that she was a very good political wife—she was totally devoted to Herbert—but that she was less good as a mother. They had children, all of whom were adopted, because everyone had children. The Lehmans were expected to have children, and I'm sure Edith and Herbert felt that way.

———※◆※———

JOHN L. LOEB JR., *grandson of Herbert Lehman's elder brother Arthur* – By the time I was about to run for Congress as a Republican candidate, Uncle Herbert had died, so I went to Aunt Edith to ask if she would support me, and instead she raked me over the coals. I was running against a man called Dick Ottinger, who was a staunch Democrat, and she said, "What business do you have running for Congress, and what do you know?" She really tore into me. So I finally said, "Look, would you just watch me, see how I do, and hold off your support for Dick Ottinger for the time being?" That much she finally agreed to do, reluctantly.

When Governor Nelson Rockefeller, for whom I served as a specialist on the environment, asked how he could help my run for Congress, I said the best thing he could do was to persuade my Aunt Edith to support me. He said he knew my Aunt Edith, and it would be difficult. But he would try.

Edith was a highly intelligent person, but I found her quite arrogant. I wasn't the only one. But she could be nice. On one occasion when I was still quite young, Aunt Edith called my mother and said Shirley Temple was coming by for a visit at their house in the country, and my cousins Bobby Bernhard and Dick Rossbach and I were invited to come and meet her. I still have a picture of us from that day, playing with Shirley Temple. We met again, many years later when Ambassador Shirley Temple Black (she served as the U.S. ambassador in Ghana) was one of my instructors at the State Department, preparing me for my own ambassadorship.

Toward the end of the lives of Edith Lehman and Grandma Adele Lehman, I happened to be at a luncheon with them. In the course of conversation we began discussing a play about a Catholic priest who had tried to help Jews and wound up in a concentration camp. That led me to ask Aunt Edith about criticism I had heard of wealthy American Jews, and especially its leaders such as Uncle Herbert, for not doing enough to help Jews during the Holocaust. "When did any of our family realize how bad things were in Germany?" I asked. She said, "We knew it was bad early on, about the harassment of the Jews, but did not know that Hitler planned to kill all the Jews in Europe."

She told me that Herbert—through my Aunt Dorothy Bernhard—had set up a foundation to bring every one of our distant Lehman cousins out from Germany. The foundation sent visas to almost 100 families, hoping they would all come to America. Sadly, only about 70 used them. The foundation supported the 70 families when they first came over, but within three years, every one of them was self-sufficient. The tragedy is that all of the 30 families who didn't use the visas were lost in the Holocaust.

Herbert Lehman having sherbet with Shirley Temple, who enjoyed visiting the governor and Edith at the Lehman home in Westchester County, c. 1938. (Herbert H. Lehman Suite & Papers, Columbia University)

Aunt Edith went on to say that not only did Jewish Americans not know the full extent of what was going on, but also in the late thirties, when Uncle Herbert was one of the Jewish leaders scheduled to speak at Madison Square Garden in support of the Jews in Germany and against Hitler, some of our relatives who lived in Würzburg, which is near Rimpar and where the Lehmans came from, sent him a telegram. They pleaded for him not to take part in the rally, as it would "only make things worse." Uncle Herbert went anyway. He knew it was very bad in Germany for the Jews, and he knew about the concentration camps, but this was in the late thirties. They did not know yet that what was at first only persecution would turn into genocide.

———>◆<———

CAMILLA ROSENFELD, *niece of Herbert Lehman's wife, Edith* – When I was growing up, my mother [Hilda Altschul Master], unlike her sister, Aunt Edith, was always very informal. Aunt Edith, the first lady of New York, was not. I remember that when we went to her home or with her to the theater in the evening, my mother would say, "Don't forget your gloves. We're going with Aunt Edith." My mother usually did not wear gloves but always carried a pair in her handbag whenever there was a chance that she would be going somewhere with my aunt. You had to be on your best behavior with Aunt Edith. It was an extraordinary family. Belonging to it made you feel a little uneasy, as if you could never measure up. Over the years, I remained very close to my aunt and uncle. After I married, I was so happy that they loved my husband too. He was not only their doctor, they loved him like a son— and it was mutual!

———>◆<———

ISADORE ROSENFELD, *Camilla Rosenfeld's husband and Herbert Lehman's physician* – You might say that Aunt Edith had a dual personality—her public face and her private reactions. In the company of strangers she was very much the first lady— formal and polite. Under those circumstances, she did not exude warmth. Some who didn't really know her might even have thought she was haughty. But with any of us, or with friends, she was always affectionate, demonstrative, considerate, relaxed—and funny! She used to get a great kick out of the practical jokes I played on her and Uncle Herbert. I'd call him up with an accent—Italian, Yiddish, whatever—introducing myself as a disaffected constituent. After I had him going for a while, Aunt Edith, laughing hysterically, would yell in the background, "Herbert, it's Is! It's Is!"

One night we went into Uncle Herbert's library. Sitting there together, we all became aware of a very foul odor in the room. I looked at Uncle Herbert, and he didn't seem distressed in any way; neither did it seem to bother Aunt Edith as the smell became more and more powerful. The mystery was solved when I finally got out of my chair. Edith's two wonderful dogs had been "using" my chair just before Camilla and I arrived. I sat down in the dog's poop! Boy, did I learn my lesson that day. For the next half hour everyone in that room (Aunt Edith, Uncle Herbert, Camilla, and I) was sure that someone else was incontinent—but we were too polite to say anything. When the explanation became apparent, we were all hysterical—and relieved.

One day, Aunt Edith, Uncle Herbert, and Camilla's mother returned by train from California to Grand Central Station. Aunt Edith always traveled with her poodle. Walking on the carpet that led from the train, the dog relieved itself. Very embarrassed, Aunt Edith picked up the poop and disposed of it. When I heard about this, I called her the next day as "McPherson" from the Department of Sanitation. "Mrs. Lehman," I asked her, "what do you or the Governor plan to do about this problem?" "What do you mean, what do I plan to do? I picked it up and put it away," she responded. And I said, "That's not good enough." We went on for fifteen minutes as she insisted she didn't know what more she could do! She admitted to being greatly relieved when I finally told her who I was, but from that time on we had a great time. She would call me with an accent and

Edith and Herbert photographed by their grandnephew Dick Rossbach, c. 1945. (Howard Rossbach)

"With love to Camilla and 'Is' from Aunt Edith and Uncle Herbert"—from a postcard to Camilla and Isadore Rosenfeld, c. 1955 (Camilla Rosenfeld)

accuse me of some misdemeanor—and ask me what I would do about it.

The Lehmans were extremely close. Uncle Herbert came absolutely first in her life. No matter whom they were entertaining and no matter what the hour, she would say, "I think my husband needs a rest." In other words, she was not concerned with protocol when he was concerned. He was "Number One."

While vacationing in Palm Springs in 1960, a few years before he died, Uncle Herbert fell and broke his hip. I went out there and brought a surgeon with me to do the necessary surgery. After a few weeks I returned to Palm Springs to accompany Aunt Edith and Uncle Herbert back on the plane. This was Edith's first flight—ever! Herbert had flown before when he was Director-General of UNRRA but never quite got used to it. They were both terrified, but their overriding overt reaction was to reassure the other that everything was okay. "This is nice," she would say, "isn't it, Herb?" "I love it," he replied. As soon as we landed, they ventilated their anxiety. Needless to say, neither of them ever wanted to fly again!

WENDY VANDERBILT LEHMAN, *former wife of Orin Lehman, grandson of Herbert's eldest brother Sigmund* – When we first married, we went to Aunt Edith's for dinner quite a few times. Guests often included Mrs. Arthur Sulzberger, various Altschul and Rossbach relatives, and so forth. I remember Aunt Edith as being very warm on those occasions. She asked me and my two-year-old daughter, Brooke, over for "Tea." Her apartment included a playroom for her grandchildren, equipped with everything a little child would want—slides and many climbing things. It was sweet of her to let Brooke come to play there. Aunt Edith was very welcoming to me as Orin's new wife.

——◆◆◆——

JUNE ROSSBACH BINGHAM BIRGE, *granddaughter of Herbert Lehman's elder sister Clara* – Edith Lehman was an artist. She loved to paint, mostly with oils but on occasion with watercolors. Her favorite subject was flowers. But she had little time for painting during most of her many happy years with Herbert. First they had adopted Peter, John, and Hilda Jane; then he went into politics, where Edith was of great help to him, mostly behind the scenes.

She was highly intelligent, like her brother, the successful financier Frank Altschul, and was far better at relating to other people than Frank was. She was gracious and a good listener; she had a quick sense of humor, which could, on rare occasion, convey an edge of ridicule. In her latter years she looked and acted the grande dame, not deliberately but simply because she was tall and regal in posture and demeanor. She loved dogs as well as people and always had a rather spoiled small animal at hand.

She was great friends with Herbert's brother Irving's wife, Sissie Lehman. Edith was also fond of Elinor Morgenthau whose mother Settie was Herbert's elder sister, in part because both their husbands were in public life and in part because Ellie could be very funny.

When Edith and Herbert's eldest son, Pete, and I got into mischief together (we stayed out all one night as mid-teenagers, for example), she was more understanding and forgiving than my

parents were. I remember visiting her and Uncle Herbert in the Executive Mansion during his time as governor. My mother and I spent the night. They were no different as governor and first lady than they had been before his election.

The time I got to know Edith best was when my husband ran for elective office. Jonathan Bingham challenged the then boss of the Bronx, Charles Buckley, for his seat in Congress in the Democratic primary of June 2, 1964. Because our congressional district included a high proportion of Jews, the endorsement by Uncle Herbert's widow was very important. But Aunt Edith resisted coming out publicly for Jonathan (though she did give his campaign a thousand dollars). Then Buckley made a serious tactical error. On the Barry Gray radio show, he said he knew "Hoybitt Layman" (instead of Herbert Lee-man) better than Bingham ever did. For her husband thus to be maligned by having his name mispronounced was finally too much. Aunt Edith came out publicly for Jonathan,

Edith Lehman between Jonathan and June Bingham in front of a portrait of Edith's husband,
Herbert H. Lehman, c. 1970. (June Rossbach Bingham Birge)

and he won in 1964 and again every two years for eighteen years.

By the latter part of the campaign, Aunt Edith agreed to come to the Bronx and publicly endorse Bingham. We invited her to Co-op City for an afternoon concert by our family orchestra. The jam-packed audience was so responsive that Aunt Edith got swept up in their enthusiasm and ended up dancing the hora, much to the amazement of her family members and, I strongly suspect, herself—though Uncle Herbert and Uncle Irving, I am certain, would have been delighted with her.

———◈———

New York Times, November 8, 1966

EDITH LEHMAN HIGH SCHOOL DEDICATED IN ISRAELI DESERT

Jerusalem (Israel Sector)—A comprehensive high school was dedicated today in the desert town of Dimona. It is one of 29 such schools being built in Israel by the American Jewish community. The new Edith Lehman High School, named after the wife of the late Herbert H. Lehman, New York governor and senator, will absorb 900 students when completed. Some are already attending classes in the three-story structure.

Afterword

JUNE ROSSBACH BINGHAM BIRGE in conversation with KENNETH LIBO

KL: As the granddaughter of Clara Lehman Limburg and the oldest living female descendant of Mayer and Babette Lehman, what comes to mind when you think of your family?

JRBB: As I've thought about my grandmother Clara and her generation, the word that leaps to mind is *claustrophobia*. Her life and those of her sisters were so limited to family and home. Part of that was emotional—they really wanted to be close to their family members—and part of it was societal, because New York society ghettoized them. So they were both externally and internally turned in upon themselves.

The letter from Arthur to Herbert that you found at the Lehman archive brought back that claustrophobia with such a rush that the hairs on my arms stood up. It was just terrible to go back there, even for a second. The first thing that everybody did was try to arouse guilt in somebody else. It was particularly true of parents toward children or grandchildren. And the guilt that Arthur is trying to arouse in Herbert lest Herbert want to go somewhere else for Christmas vacation hit me right in the face.

I've learned a lot about my grandmother in the process of working on this book, for which I am grateful. I am also feeling far more kindly toward her than I had. I truly sympathize with how limited life was for females like her and her sisters. It never occurred to them to go down to Henry Street and work with the people off the boat. It would have been scorned as what we today might call "leper kissing."

KL: How would you describe the Lehman women of your grandmother's generation?

JRBB: The Lehman women were matriarchal without necessarily being maternal. Part of the reason was that their children were brought up by nurses and governesses. Some of us learned more about life from our cook or chauffeur than we did from our parents. Given their situation in life, there was very little for my grandmother and her sisters to do.

KL: What do you remember most about your mother?

JRBB: My mother Mabel was very beautiful. She dressed out of Saks's Salon Moderne. She also went to Paris for her clothes. My mother never finished high school, though she spoke French and German fluently with her governess and read Schiller in the original. She knew a lot about art and music. She had what is called "a well furnished mind." Yet Mother was not even allowed to take Columbia extension courses. My grandmother's favorite expression, and my mother's, too, was: "Don't ever do that. Don't even think it." There was this narrowness of life—this imprisonment.

There was also, and this turns up in Mayer's letter to Herbert at Williams—a terrible enforced intimacy—"Tell me what you're thinking. It's my right to know because I'm your father!" is what he communicates. My mother read my diary. When I confronted her, she said, "As your mother it is my duty to know what you are thinking." So I never wrote another word of interest in it. I didn't stop the writing because that would have been rebellion, and

"My parents, Mabel and Max Rossbach, at my wedding, standing with my husband Jonathan's mother, Mrs. Henry Gregor, at his left." —June Rossbach Bingham Birge (June Rossbach Bingham Birge)

there would have been all hell to pay. I just never put anything of significance in it again.

Daddy, who was in many ways an adoring and dear and warm parent, would say, "Are you happy?" Shoot, I didn't want to be stopped in the middle of whatever I was doing to think about whether I was happy or not, and if not, I certainly didn't want to tell him. So I would say, "Oh yes, of course." One learns to fudge. You were imprisoned, and you were not safe in your prison.

KL: During their heyday when you were growing up, the Lehmans were just about the most important Jewish family in New York, with Arthur the senior partner of Lehman Brothers, Herbert the governor of New York, and Irving the highest-ranking judge in the state. What impact do you remember this having on the way you conducted yourselves?

JRBB: As I think back, more than seventy years after Granny's death, I marvel at how much appearances mattered, not only to her but also to the other Lehmans. Whether this was caused by fear of anti-Semitism, or by vanity, or by something else, I have no idea, but it was not mirrored among my WASP in-laws.

The Lehman attention to appearances meant that we children behaved well in public, or else, and that parlor maids were hired only if they were gifted in arranging large vases of fresh flowers, which they had to do almost daily. It meant that some female family members, like my mother and Peter Loeb (Frances Lehman), were fashion plates, and some male ones, like my father and Uncle Arthur Lehman, sported carnation boutonnieres and handsome hankies at the breast pocket.

Somebody, I think it was a Buttenwieser, once mentioned that in the John and Frances Loeb memoir the word *attractive* appeared more than any other. It didn't seem to matter if people were good, bad, or indifferent. What mattered was to be attractive in the sense of being socially viable. We felt ourselves always on show and therefore always under threat. One corollary might have been that you didn't drink too much. (There is remarkably little alcoholism in the Lehman family.)

My parents thrived in this world. They were extremely cultivated—elegant, sophisticated, socially sought-after within their circle and even by strangers, like, say, those on a cruise boat. They had impressive taste. In 1962 when the snooty Episcopalian parents of my daughter Sherry's fiancé came down from Boston (where else?) to visit Thirlsmere in White Plains, where I grew up and which Max and Mabel had bought just before I was born in 1919, the Bostonians were stunned by the tasteful antique furnishings and impressive library. They admitted to Sherry that they'd had no idea that Jews lived like that. So I guess we passed muster.

We had a greenhouse at Thirlsmere, and if carnations were not in season, my father would wear a gardenia. He wore spats, gray flannel in winter, and white linen in summer. He carried a cane, which my second husband, Bob Birge, now sports—a very handsome one. Max was a boulevardier in his appearance—very elegant. He used to walk me up to Park Avenue to kindergarten. It was heaps of fun.

KL: The word Lehman brings to mind the Robert Lehman wing of the Metropolitan Museum of Art, not to mention the distinguished collections of Philip Lehman, Arthur and Adele Lehman, John and Frances Lehman Loeb, and John Loeb Jr., just to name a few. How do you account for this?

JRBB: I think the interest in art by the Lehmans was based on the feeling that if they couldn't achieve greatness, at least they could own it, and talk about it. Also, collecting was nothing new to Jews. After all, many Jewish immigrants started out collecting junk. So they went from collecting junk to collecting art. It's also an area where Jews could compete with WASPS. In those days Jewish bankers were not allowed in WASP investment firms and Jewish lawyers were not allowed in WASP law firms, but with regard to collecting, it was a level playing field.

KL: When you were growing up, how conscious were you of being a Jew?

JRBB: I always knew there was an "us" and a "them." When I was very little, I thought that maybe if you spelled "Jew" like Winnie the Pooh—*J-o-o-h*—we would be more popular. But it never happened. When I was thirteen, Max, Mabel, and I went motoring with Arthur, Iphigene, and their daughter Manny (Marian) Sulzberger, Adolph Ochs's granddaughter who married Orvil Dryfoos and, subsequently, Andrew Heiskell, chairman of Time, Inc. We had reservations at the very tony Chatham Bars Inn on Cape Cod. Max and Arthur went in to claim our reservations. I'll never forget when they came back. Arthur's face was white with rage and Max's was red with rage. They were told, "No Jews."

So we went to a different hotel, a much less classy one, which Manny and I infinitely preferred because we didn't have to dress for dinner.

I was taken to the Brearley School, age five, by my mum to see if I could be admitted. I was a precocious brat who had taught herself to read, had been to kindergarten, and was reasonably well behaved. So Mother was quite sure I would be admitted. However, the headmistress said to my mother, after sending me from the room, "She seems like a nice child, but we already have a Jewess in that class." And the Jewess turned out to be my cousin Edie Altschul, daughter of Frank and Helen Goodhart Altschul. My parents sent me instead to the Lincoln School, into which the Rockefellers had put lots of money, plus four of their five sons. Lincoln was much more progressive than Brearley, and I loved it.

Perhaps half the students at the Lincoln School were Jewish. Marjorie Lewisohn was there. And Marian Sulzberger. Hilda Reis, subsequently Hilda Reis Bijur, was a pal of mine. Also Joan Heming, whose mother and father were very close friends of my parents. Their name was originally Heimerdinger. There's a story of Joan's father going home with a friend of his who introduced him as Charlie Heimerdinger to his grandmother, who was quite deaf. "Who?" she said, and he repeated and repeated, "Charlie Heimerdinger." Finally she said, "I keep hearing 'Heimerdinger,' but nobody could be called that." Anyway, Charlie and his brother Henry changed their name to Heming, but their mother, who was my grandmother Clara's best friend, never did.

There were also Jewish kids at Lincoln I hadn't known before. One was Tommy Goldberg, son of Rube Goldberg, the great cartoonist. Another was Tessim Zorach, son of the well-known sculptor. Not being "Our Crowd," they were possibly of East European Jewish background. They each invited me for a weekend, but my parents were adamant. Under no circumstances could I go. Nor was it well explained to me. Years later, during World War II, I was on a train with a lot of GIs, and Tommy Goldberg turned up among them. He told me he was still seething over my having been forbidden to visit, and I thoroughly agreed with him.

When I was in my early teens during the depths of the Depression, my father's export-import business was having problems, and my parents let go of their apartment in Manhattan to cut expenses. This meant I could no longer continue at Lincoln. Instead, I was sent to Rosemary Hall in Greenwich. It was the equivalent of Hotchkiss, which my two Limburg uncles, my two brothers, and four cousins attended.

Greenwich, Connecticut, like Rye, New York, as I discovered much later, had covenants running with the land, which meant that nobody could sell to a Jew. That's one reason why the Lehmans and the Century Country Club are all in Purchase and why we lived on North Street in White Plains, as did the Adolph Ochses, the Arthur Sulzbergers, the Charlie Hemings, and my uncle and aunt, Alan and Kay Limburg.

Next to us was the Maginnes family. Younger than I, Nancy Maginnes took my place riding with my father on weekends after I went off to Vassar. Much later, when her engagement to Henry Kissinger was announced, I sent her a note saying that I knew who the *first* charming man with a German accent was with whom she had been in love. She wrote back, "You're so right."

As far as I could tell, there was a total of three Jewish girls at Rosemary Hall when I got there. And once Bernard and Alva Gimbel's twin daughters, Hope and Caral (who married Hank Greenberg), graduated, I was left solo. Then Marian Sulzberger turned up. And Joanie Untermyer, daughter of Judge Irwin Untermyer and granddaughter of Samuel. And Jane Rosenthal. That was great, but meanwhile I was forced to make non-Jewish friends because there wasn't anyone in my class or the next class or the next class who was Jewish. In this sense my life was vastly different from that of Mabel and Clara, who had no choice but to socialize almost exclusively among people of German Jewish descent.

At the beginning of my eighth grade, my uncle Alan Limburg and his wife, Kay, invited me to bring along a school friend for dinner at a speakeasy, to be followed by a musical. I asked a girl from Greenwich. We were thirteen, so this was very exciting. She came back the next day looking glum. "Mummy and Daddy said I can't go because if you are seen in New York with Jews, then no one will dance with you at your debut." I didn't even know what a debut was, so I didn't say anything, but she said, "Don't invite anyone else just yet. I want to work on them." I wasn't about to ask anyone else, ever. A few days later she came back and said, "Mummy and Daddy say I'm still so young that people won't remember if I'm seen with Jews." So she came.

It was a formative experience for me because it gave me a sense of purpose I had never had before. By God, I would show these people what Jews are made of. The way to impress them, I thought at the time, was not to excel in my studies so much as in athletics. Because my family had a swimming pool and a tennis court, I was no stranger to sports by the time I entered Rosemary Hall. So I kept myself running around the track and made varsity in hockey and tennis. I also rode to hounds with the Fairfield-Westchester Hunt, from which I earned my hunt colors.

KL: How did "Our Crowd" Jews relate to their Jewishness?

JRBB: There was the sheepishness of being dumped on by the majority of society, but also a fierce pride in Jewish survival and intelligence. Einstein was Jewish, and so were Freud and Marx—not that my father approved of either of the latter two. Like many Jews of their class, my parents had no religion. As a result, they were left with the shell of being Jewish without the meat. Religion to them meant absolutely zero. They never went to Temple. I never heard of Chanukah, but I did hear of the Day of Atonement. That's the day when fat people dieted, I was told.

Many, if not most of my cousins and friends were brought up the same way. Marian Sulzberger was a bit more exposed to religion because her mother, Iphigene [granddaughter of Isaac Mayer Wise, founder of American Reform Judaism, and wife of *New York Times* publisher Arthur Hays Sulzberger] set up a Bible class for Marian and her sister Ruth, future publisher of the *Chattanooga Times*, and a few of their friends on Friday afternoons. I begged Mother to let me go to it because I had a vacuum where other people had a religion, but Mother said, "Oh no," because Bible class on Friday afternoons would get in the way of our commuting on weekends to White Plains with the servants and the food and the dogs.

KL: The father of your children, Jonathan Bingham, who died in 1986, was a Christian. Bob Birge, your present husband, is also a Christian. How do you account for your attraction to Christians and Christianity in the light of your Jewish heritage? Wasn't there a conflict?

JRBB: Not really. At Rosemary there stood this beautiful little Gothic chapel that filled a need not only in me but also in many girls. We had Evensong daily and two services on Sunday. By the time I was a sixth former (a senior in high school), they elected me head of the chapel committee. I don't think this upset my parents at all. Some people would think it should have, but their indifference to religion was profound. I had been brought up in a Jewish family without any religion, sent to an Episcopal school where the chapel was a part of everyday life, and I resonated to it—especially to the Bible readings and the hymns, organ music, and candlelight.

Because I have roots in the Jewish community but religious involvement with the Christian community, I define myself as Judeo-Christian. The word Christian is a bad word for many Jews. It's synonymous with "enemy." But it also happens to be a faith grounded in Hebrew scriptures as expounded by a Jew speaking, at least in the early part of his ministry, solely to other Jews. Jesus was not only a Jew. He was a good Jew. If there's any chance of anybody in today's world having Mary's DNA, it's the Jews. As one of today's leading Protestant theologians, Jürgen Moltmann, has said, the principal responsibility of Christianity is to bring the message of Judaism to the world at large.

KL: What do you recall of the day of your wedding to Jonathan Bingham?

JRBB: It probably provided a culture shock for some of the two hundred guests because the service was in the Rosemary Hall chapel in Greenwich, complete with cross on the altar, while the reception was ten minutes away in the Port Chester house of Irving and Sissie Lehman, complete with a menorah on the mantel. Although a Jewish-Christian wedding was unusual in those days, there was no feeling of Capulet/Montague; everyone seemed to mingle cheerfully (helped, no doubt, by first-class champagne and a several-course dinner). Jonathan Bingham and I were happily dancing when my mother came up and told us that Aunt Sissie [Judge Irving Lehman's wife] was tired and we should leave. So we changed our clothes and departed (in the Lehmans' car driven by their chauffeur). Apparently some of the younger guests were having such a good time that they refused to go home. So my brothers took a case of champagne in the rumble seat of their roadster and lured the guests over to the carriage house on the Whitelaw Reid estate (Reid had been publisher of the New York *Herald Tribune*), where they continued to party for most of the night. Our marriage was off to quite a liquid start.

"Walking toward the Rosemary Hall chapel in Greenwich on my wedding day with my father."
—June Rossbach Bingham Birge (June Rossbach Bingham Birge)

KL: What were the consequences of marrying "out"?

JRBB: Well, one result was that when our engagement—and, subsequently, our wedding (in 1939)—was announced in the *New York Times,* both Jonathan and I received hate mail from strangers. Some letters were signed, and some not. We just pitched them all out. A year later, a friend informed us that Jonathan's name had been dropped from the *Social Register.* We had a good laugh. What has been going on since then is what Alice Roosevelt Longworth referred to cheerfully as the "mongrelization" of America. I think it's wonderful because of all the contrasts and enrichment that can occur when people of different backgrounds unite. In retrospect, what I obtained from marrying out was more security for myself and my children, escape from over-emotionality (WASP emotions tend to be deep but not loud), and learning to be more relaxed about appearances.

My mother-in-law, a Tiffany, who had been married to Hiram Bingham, the discov-erer of Machu Picchu and a U.S. senator from Connecticut, wore whatever she felt like, whether it was fashionable or not. It was a mar-velous form of independence that she had, bor-dering on a superiority complex. WASPs also tend to give people privacy. Nobody reads your diary or asks you if you are happy. All in all, my Bingham in-laws exemplified a lack of self-pity and a refusal to complain. Instead there was sto-icism, the stiff upper lip I had been exposed to at Rosemary. "She has learned to dry her tears before they fall" is the last line of a school song. I tried to model myself on that because I thought it was dignified.

The older members of "Our Crowd" were happy to discuss money: who was making it, who was losing it, who was marrying it, who was managing it and in what manner. In con-trast, my parents-in-law, the Binghams, treated money rather like sex, as something that lots of people were interested in but should not be mentioned at the dinner table.

Of the children of my Lehman grandmoth-er and her siblings, only Margaret Fatman and

Arthur Goodhart married out. In my generation the list is much longer—Orin Lehman and Ellen McCluskey; all of Hattie's grandchildren, with the exception of Margaret Altschul Lang; Bob Morgenthau; Myles, Phyllis, and Peter Limburg; Judy, John, and Debbie Loeb; Bob and Bill Bernhard; and me. Though the number of professing Jews in succeeding generations is negligible, the young seem to maintain an overwhelmingly positive attitude toward their Jewish background. One example is my son, Tim Bingham. Being a lawyer, he was able to draft the document at the General Convention of the Episcopal Church apologizing to the Jews for the dreadful things done to them by Episcopalians over the centuries. This resolution was passed by acclaim. Later he went around to Jewish groups and told them, "I don't expect you to grant us pardon or perform any other action; we just feel the need to apologize in all sincerity to you."

Many years after my oldest daughter graduated from Milton Academy, her headmistress told her, "Sherry, you will never know how lucky you are that you come from both WASP and Jewish traditions. The WASPs repress their feelings, and this leads to great unhappiness, while the Jews show a great joy in life." Sherry said, "Oh?" because Milton was not exactly un-anti-Semitic, and she was one of the few even half-Jewish students there.

KL: Marrying out is a two-way street. What does it look like from the other side?

JRBB: I had lunch the other day with Wendy Vanderbilt Lehman and her first cousins, Elsie Vanderbilt Aidinoff, and Flora Biddle, whose mother was Gertrude Vanderbilt Whitney. They are direct descendants of the "Commodore." I asked them how come two of them had racked up three marriages to Jews. Flora said to Wendy, "Did you know Orin was Jewish?" And Wendy said, "Of course." But then she said, "He was a WASP at heart and handsome as can be. He had been to Taft and Princeton. He knew all the right people and was totally comfortable in the WASP world." And then Elsie said she just fell in love with her two Jewish husbands. A few relatives of hers had turned up their noses, but she didn't care.

I asked them how many Vanderbilt descendants were coupon clippers who did absolutely nothing, and they asked, "How do you define "nothing?" I said if people do nothing, they don't have anything serious to do or care about. So Wendy said, "My father was a gentleman sportsman. Is that okay?" I said, "Sure. That's fine." (Her father raised and raced horses and her uncle raced yachts; they were serious sportsmen who did not sit still and were called upon for decisions every day.)

"The picture that I get from you guys," I said, at the end of lunch, "is that my family was busy getting established and keeping from being unwanted in America, whereas your family was busy trying to be British aristocrats." They laughed, and one of them said, "More like landed gentry."

KL: Summing up, what have the descendants of Mayer and Babette Lehman accomplished in their lives?

JRBB: Members of my extended family certainly register a wide range of fascinating careers, paid and volunteer. Of those who behaved heroically during World War II, Peter Lehman was killed in action; Robert Morgenthau had two destroyers torpedoed out from under him and won the Silver Star and the Bronze Star; Orin Lehman earned a Silver and Bronze Star but lost one leg, the other being badly injured; and my brother, Dick Rossbach, won the Silver Star for gallantry in action plus two Bronze Stars. He kept saying, "I never was so goddamn gallant." He was captured by the Axis four times and escaped each time, until the fifth, when the Nazis imprisoned him in Posen. A year later he escaped again. Fear, Dick said, was better than a martini.

By and large the Lehman family comprises strong men as well as strong women married to successful men. Among these are a governor; a U.S. senator; New York's chief judge; a U.S. secretary of the Treasury; a member of the House of Lords; a member of the House of Commons; a member of the House of Representatives; the Manhattan district attorney; two ambassadors (one to the U.N. Economic and Social Council and one to Denmark); two presidents of Temple Emanu-El; and many investment bankers, educators, judges, lawyers, doctors, philanthropists, artists, art dealers, writers, and interior decorators; a successful restaurateur; a bookstore owner; two heads of major American corporations; a New York State Parks commissioner; and several foundation executives.

What else does our family contain? A few ardent members of AA and Al-Anon, no full-time coupon clippers, at least as far down as my generation, and many people involved in a wonderful variety of volunteer work. We remain indebted to Mayer and Babette Lehman for bequeathing us some viable DNA and also sufficient money so that some of us can use it to make more and others can feel "comfortable" enough to allow ourselves the luxury of not thinking about it. For these and other reasons unknown to me, I conjecture that we have fewer conflicts about money than do many families. As for the very few gays and lesbians among us, they are finally out of the closet. As for the young adult Lehman descendants, I was fascinated to be told recently that two of my cousins have become Orthodox Jews. As Adlai Stevenson used to say, "No generation can predict the weapons the next one will use against it."

Contributors Who's Who

—◆—

Bernhard, Dorothy L. (1903–1969) – Civic worker and philanthropist. Daughter of Arthur Lehman and Adele Lewisohn Lehman. Horace Mann School, Wellesley College. Husband: Richard J. Bernhard (d. 1961). Two children. Member, State Board of Social Welfare. Chair, Advisory Committee of the Hunter College School of Social Work. Vice chair, Institute of International Education. Trustee, Federation of Jewish Philanthropies and NYU Institute of Fine Arts. Active in the Child Welfare League of America. Headed the Lehman Fund to help German Jews immigrate to America to escape the Nazis, saving seventy families. Founder of the Arthur Lehman Counseling Service.

Bernhard, Robert A. (1928–) – Investment adviser and philanthropist. Son of Richard J. Bernhard and Dorothy Lehman Bernhard. Grandson of Arthur Lehman and Adele Lewisohn Lehman. Lawrenceville School, Williams College, Harvard School of Business. Wife (1): Frances Wells. Four children. Wife (2): Joan Mack Sommerfield. Partner, MB Investment, New York. Founded Bernhard Association, Ltd., 1982, which merged to become Munn, Bernhard & Association, 1990. Partner at Salomon Brothers and Lehman Brothers. Headed investment management division of Lehman Brothers. Board member, Lehman Corporation and One William Street Fund. Chairman of the board and trustee, The Cooper Union for the Advancement of Science and Art. President and trustee, Temple Emanu-El. Trustee and vice chairman, Montefiore Medical Center. Board of Overseers, Albert Einstein School of Medicine. Trustee, Lincoln Center Institute. Member and former president of the Century Country Club. Member of the New York Yacht Club.

Bernhard, William L. (1931–) – Foundation executive, historic preservation activist. Son of Richard J. and Dorothy Lehman Bernhard. Grandson of Arthur Lehman and Adele Lewisohn Lehman. Schools in New York City, Lawrenceville School, Yale '54, U.S. Air Force, University College, Oxford. Wife: Catherine Cahill. Worked at Lehman Brothers, the Council on Foreign Relations, and the Institute of International Education. Secretary of the International Council of the Museum of Modern Art. Board member: Federation Employment and Guidance Service, New York Landmarks Conservancy, Yale University Art Gallery, Film Society of Lincoln Center, Naumburg Orchestral Concerts and the Winston Churchill Foundation of the United States. Past president of J.F.S., Inc. and president of the Bernhill Fund. Trustee: Preservation League of New York State. Fellow: Pierpont Morgan Library, NYU Institute of Fine Arts. Clubs: Knickerbocker, Century Association, Yale, and the Devon Yacht Club.

Bingham, Jonathan (1914–1986) – U.S. representative from New York. Son of Connecticut Governor and Senator Hiram Bingham and Alfreda Mitchell Bingham. Groton School, Yale College, Yale Law School. Wife: June Rossbach. Four children. Liberal Democrat representing the Bronx in Congress, 1965–1983. In Congress he was a member of the House Foreign Affairs Committee, where he wrote the Soviet Jewish Refugee Assistance Act of 1972 and co-wrote the Nuclear Nonproliferation Act of 1978. Served as U.S. representative to and president of UN Trusteeship Council with rank of minister, 1961–1962. Served as U.S. representative to UN Economic and Social Council with rank of ambassador, 1963–1964. Served as U.S. delegate to four UN General Assemblies. Served in State Department, 1945–1946. Wrote *Shirt Sleeve Diplomacy: Point 4 in Action* (1954) and co-wrote *Violence and Democracy* (1970) with brother Alfred.

Birge, June Rossbach Bingham (1919–) – Author and playwright. Daughter of Max Rossbach and Mabel Limburg Rossbach. Granddaughter of Richard Limburg and Clara Lehman Limburg.

Lincoln School, Rosemary Hall School, Vassar College, Barnard College, honorary doctorate from Lehman College. Husband (1): Jonathan Bingham (d. 1986), a member of Congress for eighteen years. Four children. Husband (2): Robert B. Birge, who went to Andover, Yale, and Union Theological Seminary, and worked in the fur trade and in mergers and acquisitions, before cofounding *The Living Pulpit*, a journal for preachers. June wrote biographies of Reinhold Niebuhr and U Thant. Author of four plays, including *Asylum: The Strange Case of Mary Lincoln*, produced off-Broadway, 2006. Coauthor of books on health. Trustee: Barnard College, Riverdale Mental Health Association, and the Franklin and Eleanor Roosevelt Institute.

Birmingham, Stephen (1931–) Author of *"Our Crowd": The Great Jewish Families of New York*, a social history of New York's German Jewish elite in which many Lehman family members figure prominently, including Hattie Lehman Goodhart, who is portrayed as a major figure in the world of "Our Crowd."

Bronfman, Ann Loeb (1932–) – Philanthropist. Daughter of John L. Loeb and Frances Lehman Loeb. Granddaughter of Arthur Lehman and Adele Lewisohn Lehman, Town School, Dalton, Potomac, Spence, Rosemary Hall School, Bennington College. Husband (until 1973): Edgar Myles Bronfman, head of Seagram's, World Jewish Congress. Five children. Benefactor: Hillel, the Greater Washington D.C. Jewish Community Center, the Jewish Council for the Aging, the Visiting Nurse Service, the New York Public Library, Rosemary Hall, plus a multicultural high school in Washington, D.C., the "fistula pilgrims" of Ethiopia, and Have Justice–Will Travel, an organization that provides legal aid to abused wives.

Buttenwieser, Helen L. (1905–1989) – Lawyer and civic leader. Daughter of Arthur Lehman and Adele Lewisohn Lehman. Horace Mann School, Connecticut College, New York School of Social Work, New York University Law School. Husband: Benjamin Buttenwieser (d. 1992), a partner in Kuhn, Loeb & Company. Four children. Among the first women admitted to the City Bar Association in New York. First chairwoman of the Legal Aid Society. President, New York Federation of Jewish Charities. Trustee, Connecticut College.

Buttenwieser, Lawrence B. (1932–) – Lawyer and civic servant. Son of Benjamin Joseph Buttenwieser and Helen Lehman Buttenwieser. Grandson of Arthur Lehman and Adele Lewisohn Lehman. George

School, University of Chicago, Yale Law School. Wife: Ann Lubin Buttenwieser. Four children. Chairman of the board and director, General American Investors Company; trustee and past chair, Citizens Budget Commission; director and past chairman of the board, Montefiore Medical Center; vice chairman and trustee, Playwrights Horizons; honorary officer and life trustee, UJA–Federation of New York; life trustee, University of Chicago; past chairman of the board and past trustee, American Jewish World Service; past president and past trustee, Associated YM–YWHAS of Greater New York; past vice president and past director, Citizens Housing and Planning Council of New York; past treasurer and past director, City Center of Music and Drama; past director, Council on Social Work Education; past trustee, Dalton School; past president, past chairman of the board, and past trustee, Federation of Jewish Philanthropies of New York; past governor, New York Academy of Science; past general campaign chairman, United Jewish Appeal–Federation of Jewish Philanthropies Joint Campaign; past counsel and past director, United Neighborhood Houses of New York.

Buttenwieser, Paul A. (1938–) – Novelist and psychiatrist. Son of Benjamin Buttenwieser and Helen Lehman Buttenwieser. Grandson of Arthur Lehman and Adele Lewisohn Lehman. Putney (Vermont) School, Harvard College, Harvard Medical School. Wife: Catherine Frum. Three children. Faculty member, Harvard Medical School and Boston Psychoanalytic Society and Institute. Chairman of the board, Family-to-Family Project and Institute of Contemporary Art, Boston; member of the board of overseers, Harvard University; member and former chairman of the board, American Repertory Theater; trustee, Museum of Fine Arts, Boston; trustee, Boston Symphony Orchestra. Author, *Free Association* (1981) and *Their Pride and Joy* (1987).

Buttenwieser, Peter L. (1935–) – Educational consultant and activist. Son of Benjamin Buttenwieser and Helen Lehman Buttenwieser. Grandson of Arthur Lehman and Adele Lewisohn Lehman. Columbia University. Wife (1): Elizabeth Worthen. Two children. Wife (2): Terry Marek. Head, Peter L. Buttenwieser and Associates. Inner-city Philadelphia school principal for ten years. Major contributor to the Democratic Party. Supporter of gun control, abortion rights, and public education.

Chiara, Judith Loeb (1927–) – Captain of vintage yacht *Susanna* and philanthropist. Daughter of John L. and Frances Lehman Loeb. Granddaughter of Arthur Lehman and Adele Lewisohn Lehman. Brearley School, Madeira School, Vassar College. Husband (1): Richard Beaty, d. 1965. Five children. Husband (2): Marco Chiara. One child. Chair, Exponents, an organization providing services for people affected by drug addiction, incarceration, or HIV/AIDS. Chair: Friends of the Housing Authority Symphony Orchestra and Council on Hemispheric Affairs (COHA), an organization concerned with human rights issues.

Edelstein, Julius (1912–2005) – Educator and close aide to New York Governor Herbert Lehman. One of the architects of CUNY's "open admissions" policy. Served as deputy mayor to Robert F. Wagner and as aide to Presidents Franklin Roosevelt and Harry Truman.

Flexner, Carolin – Longtime secretary to New York Governor Herbert Lehman.

Forbush, Gabrielle (1890–?) – Treasury Department official. Friend of Elinor Fatman Morgenthau. Secretary to Louis Howe, a close aide to President Franklin Roosevelt, 1932–1936.

Friedman, Peter (1936–) – Author, teacher, and lawyer. Grandson of Evelyn Lehman Ehrich. Grandnephew of Harriet Lehman Lehman. Walden School, Swarthmore College, Harvard Law School. Received Fulbright grant to Freie Universität, Berlin, and Columbia University. Author, *Ideal Marriage* (2004), as well as short stories, articles, and light verse in *Harper's, Saturday Review, New York Times,* and *The Wall Street Journal.* Writing instructor, The New School. Counsel to former New York City Mayor Robert F. Wagner Jr., at the New York State Constitutional Convention, 1967.

Gerst, Hans – One of dozens of refugees from Nazi Germany helped by the Lehman Fund to reestablish themselves and their families in America.

Gertler, Ann Elizabeth Straus (1922–) – Activist. Daughter of Hugh Grant and Flora Stieglitz Straus. Niece of Irving Lehman and Sissie Straus Lehman. Lincoln School, Vassar College, Columbia University, Cambridge University. Husband: Maynard Gertler. Five sons. Vice chair of the Canadian Crown Corporation for International Peace and Security and an executive officer of the Canadian branch of "Pugwash."

Goodhart, Sir Philip (1925–) – British conservative member of Parliament and author. Son of Arthur Goodhart and Cecily Carter Goodhart. Grandson of Philip Goodhart and Hattie Lehman Goodhart. Cambridge University. Wife: Valerie Forbes Winant. Seven children. Member, House of Commons, 1957–1992. Army minister in Mrs. Thatcher's first government. Author of various books and pamphlets, including *Fifty Ships That Saved the World* (1965), *Referendum* (1971) and *The Royal Americans* (2004).

Goodhart, Lord William Howard (1933–) – Lawyer, member of the House of Lords. Son of Arthur Goodhart and Cecily Carter Goodhart. Grandson of Philip Goodhart and Hattie Lehman Goodhart. Cambridge University. Wife: Celia McClare Herbert. Three children. Vice president, International Commission on Jurists, a human rights group. Appointed Queen's Counsel, 1979. Served as head of chambers, 1978–1995. Knighted for political and public service in 1989 and made a life peer by Queen Elizabeth II in 1997.

Gordan, John D., III (1945–) – Lawyer. Son of John D. Gordan Jr. and Phyllis Goodhart Gordan. Great grandson of Philip Goodhart and Hattie

Lehman Goodhart. Phillips Academy, Harvard University, Harvard Law School. Wife: Catherine Morot-Sir. Two children. Litigation partner, Morgan, Lewis & Bockius. Partner, Lord Day & Lord, Barrett Smith. Executive assistant U.S. Attorney, Southern District of New York. President, New York Law Institute. Trustee, William Nelson Cromwell Foundation.

Gordan, Phyllis Goodhart (1913–1994) – Incunabulist and benefactor. Daughter of Howard Goodhart and Marjorie Walter Goodhart. Granddaughter of Philip Goodhart and Hattie Lehman Goodhart. Bryn Mawr College, Radcliffe College. Husband: John D. Gordan II (d. 1968), curator of New York Public Library's Berg Collection of English and American Literature. Four children. Chairwoman, New York Public Library's committee of research libraries. Trustee, New York Public Library, 1974–1985.

Hirschhorn, Joan Morgenthau (1922–) – Physician, professor, and activist. Daughter of Henry Morgenthau Jr. and Elinor Fatman Morgenthau. Granddaughter of Morris Fatman and Settie Lehman Fatman. B.A., Vassar College, with distinction in history; M.D., Columbia College of Physicians and Surgeons. Husband: Fred Hirschhorn. Three children. Joan is a professor of clinical pediatrics and associate dean, Mount Sinai School of Medicine. Assistant professor, Cornell University Medical School; professor, clinical pediatrics, Mount Sinai School of Medicine; visiting scholar/professor/fellow in pediatrics: Stanford University, University of California at San Diego, Yale University School of Medicine. Professor of psychology, Smith College. Founder and director, Adolescent Health Center at Mount Sinai Hospital. Member, External Advisory Committee, Columbia University Center for Ethics. Trustee: Madeira School, Vassar College. Henry J. Kaiser Family Foundation.

Josten, Peter (1922–) – Restaurateur, quail farmer, philanthropist. Son of Werner Josten and Margaret Fatman Josten. Grandson of Morris Fatman and Settie Lehman Fatman. Eaglebrook, Los Alamos Ranch School, Deerfield Academy, Bard College, Johns Hopkins University, University College, Oxford. Worked for the Jewish Agency for Palestine, Carl M. Loeb, Rhoades & Company, Goldman Sachs. Founding partner of Griggstown Quail Farm, in business for twenty-five years and specializing in raising quail, pheasants, duck, and chicken, primarily for restaurants.

Lash, Wendy Lehman (1942–) – President, Edith and Herbert H. Lehman Foundation. Daughter of Peter G. Lehman and Peggy Rosenbaum Lehman. Granddaughter of Herbert Lehman and Edith Altschul Lehman. Brearley School, Bennett College, Connecticut College. Husband: Stephen S. Lash, chairman, Christie's in New York City. Two children. Chair, board of fellows of Lyman Allan Museum, New London, Connecticut. Trustee, Connecticut College and Animal Medical Center. Assistant to director of admissions, Bennett College. Assistant to high school director, Dalton School. Responsible for publishing an extensive genealogy and family tree of the Lehmans.

Lehman, Arthur (1873–1936) – Banker and philanthropist. Son of Mayer Lehman and Babette Neugass Lehman. Sachs Collegiate Institute, Harvard College. Wife: Adele Lewisohn Lehman (d. 1965). Three children. Senior member, Lehman Brothers. President, Federation for the Support of Jewish Philanthropic Societies. Member of board of directors, Merchants Association of New York. Member of board of trustees, New School for Social Research. Trustee, Museum of the City of New York. Member of the board of trustees, City Housing Corporation and the Andrew Freedman Home.

Lehman, Babette Neugass (1838–1919) – Daughter of Isaak and Friederike Goldschmidt Neugass. Husband: Mayer Lehman (d. 1897). Mother of seven siblings featrured in this book. Immigrated to the United States in 1850s. Board member, Jewish Home and Hospital for the Aged. Member, Temple Emanu-El.

Lehman, Edith Altschul (1889–1976) – Philanthropist. Daughter of Charles Altschul and Camilla Mandlebaum Altschul. Dr. Sachs Girls School, Miss Jacobi's (later, Calhoun School). Husband: Herbert H. Lehman (d. 1963). Three children. Honorary trustee, Mount Sinai Medical Center. Founding sponsor, Mount Sinai School of Medicine. Board chairwoman, Play Schools Association and the Henry Street Settlement. A competent amateur painter.

Lehman, Herbert (1878–1963) – Son of Mayer Lehman and Babette Neugass Lehman. Sachs Collegiate Institute, Williams College. Wife: Edith Altschul (d. 1976). Three children. U.S. senator from New York, 1949–1956. Head of UNRRA, 1943–1946. Governor of New York, 1933–1942. Lieutenant Governor of New York, 1929–1932. Fundraiser, Federation of Jewish Philanthropies and the United Jewish Appeal. Organizer, Palestine Loan Bank and Palestine Economic Corporation.

Lehman, Irving (1876–1945) – Son of Mayer Lehman and Babette Neugass Lehman. Sachs Collegiate Institute, Columbia University, Columbia Law School. Wife: Sissie Straus Lehman (d. 1950). Judge of New York State Court of Appeals, 1924–1939. Justice of New York Supreme Court, 1st District, 1909–1924. Member, American Bar Association and New York State Bar Association. Honorary member, Association of the Bar of the City of New York. Enthusiastic fisherman.

Lehman, Mayer (1830–1897) – Merchant, banker, philanthropist. Father of the seven Lehman siblings featured in this book. Würzburg Bavarian public schools. Wife: Babette Neugass Lehman (d. 1919). Immigrated to the United States, 1850. Appointed by the Alabama governor to visit Confederate soldiers confined in Northern prisons. Partner, Lehman Brothers. Director, Hamilton Bank. Member, Temple Emanu-El.

Lehman, Orin (1920–) – Son of Allan Lehman and Evelyn Schiffer Lehman. Grandson of Sig

Lehman and Harriet Lehman Lehman. New York University. Wife (1): Jane Bagley (d. 1988). One child. Wife (2): Wendy Vanderbilt. Two children. New York State Commissioner of Parks, Recreation and Historic Preservation, 1975–1993. Chairman, New York City Board of Correction. Founder and chairman of the board of trustees, Just One Break, an organization that aids disabled people in finding employment. Member, Public Advisory Board of the Economic Cooperation Administration. Served as a U.S. Army pilot in World War II. Badly wounded in Germany. Recipient of the Distinguished Flying Cross, the Silver Star, and the Bronze Star. Supporter, New York Landmarks Conservancy.

Lehman, Penelope (1940–) – Daughter of Peter Lehman and Peggy Rosenbaum Lehman. Granddaugher of Herbert Lehman and Edith Altschul Lehman. Nightingale-Bamford, Bennett Junior College, Parsons School of Design. One child. Board of directors, Hill House (senior residence). Active in community efforts for the elderly.

Lehman, Wendy Vanderbilt (1944–) – Artist. Direct descendant of Commodore Cornelius Vanderbilt. Ex-husband: Orin Lehman. Two children. Sculptures and paintings in major collections, such as the University of Santa Barbara Museum, Herbert and Dorothy Vogel, Jeanne Thayer, Ambassador John Loeb Jr., and Flora Miller Biddle. Public installation venues include Clifton (New Jersey) Municipal Sculpture Park; Summit (New Jersey) Village Green; University of Delaware, Newark; *Sculpture in the Park*, Albany; Veterans' Park, Stamford (Connecticut); Dante Park, New York City. Mrs. Lehman's works have been exhibited at Yeager Museum, Hartwick College (Oneonta, N.Y.); Albany Institute of History and Art; Guggenheim Museum Invitational at Chesterwood (Stockbridge, Massachusetts); Andre Emmerich's Tom Gallant Farm Sculpture Park, (Pawling, New York); and The Century Association, On Line at Feigen Contemporary, and Hunter College Gallery, all of New York. She attended Truman Capote's Black and White Ball at the Plaza and has been chosen by *Hampton Style* as one of the five hundred people who have had the most impact on the Hamptons.

Lewisohn, Marjorie (1918–2006) – Physician and professor. Daughter of Samuel Lewisohn and Margaret Seligman Lewisohn. Granddaughter of Adolph Lewisohn on her father's side and Isaac Newton Seligman on her mother's side. Johns Hopkins Medical School. Professor, New York

Hospital–Weill/Cornell Medical Center. Elected first woman trustee at Johns Hopkins University, 1971; Emerita, 1988. JHU Professorship in Ambulatory Medicine named in her honor. Board member, United Negro College Fund and New York Philharmonic.

Limburg, A. Myles (1925–) – Sales representative to schools, hospitals, industrial plants. Grandson of Richard Limburg and Clara Lehman Limburg. The Brunswick School, Pomfret School, Dalton High School, University of Miami. Ex-wife: Margaret Estes. Three children. Joined Marine Corps during World War II. Fought at Iwo Jima. Active in Moral-Rearmament.

Limburg, Peter (1929–) – Author. Grandson of Richard Limburg and Clara Lehman Limburg. St. Bernard's School, Hotchkiss School, Yale University, Georgetown University, Columbia University. Wife: Margareta Fischerstrom. Four children. Wrote, among other books, *Deep-Sea Detectives*, *Deceived: The Story of the Donner Party*, *WEIRD! The Complete Book of Hallowe'en Words*, and *The Story of Your Heart,* designated an Outstanding Science Book for Children by the National Science Teachers Association and the Children's Book Council.

Loeb, Arthur Lehman (1932–) – Bookseller and philanthropist. Son of John Loeb and Frances Lehman Loeb. Grandson of Arthur Lehman and Adele Lewisohn Lehman. Dalton School, Sidwell Friends, The Harvey School, Hotchkiss School, Collegiate School, Harvard University. From 1973 to 2000 he was the owner of the Madison Avenue Bookshop. He is a supporter of, among other organizations, New York Landmarks Conservancy, Preservation League of New York State, Planned Parenthood of New York City, and Harvard University.

Loeb, Frances Lehman (1906–1996) – Public servant and philanthropist. Daughter of Arthur Lehman and Adele Lewisohn Lehman. Attended Vassar College, honorary degree from New York University. Husband: John Loeb (d. 1996). Five children. Benefactor, Barnard College, Central Park, New York University, Harvard College, the Collegiate School, and Vassar College, to which she donated the Frances Lehman Loeb Art Center. Principal benefactor, East Side International Pre-School and the United Nations School. Trustee, Vassar College and Cornell University. Overseer, New York Hospital–Cornell Medical Center.

Head of New York City Commission for the United Nations, Consular Corps & Protocol.

Loeb, John L., Jr. (1930–) – Philanthropist, investment banker, and ambassador. Son of John L. Loeb and Frances Lehman Loeb. Grandson of Arthur Lehman and Adele Lewisohn Lehman. Collegiate School, Harvey School, Hotchkiss School, Harvard College, Harvard Business School. Honorary LLD from Georgetown University. First Lieutenant, U.S. Air Force. Wife (1): Nina Sundby. One daughter. Wife (2): Meta Harrsen. One son. Chairman, Loeb, Rhoades, & Co.; chairman, Winston Churchill Foundation of the United States; trustee, Langeloth Foundation and American-Scandinavian Foundation. Past trustee, Educational Testing Service. Past member, seven Harvard visiting committees. Past chairman of the board, Holly Sugar. Director, MGM Rio Grande Industries and John Morrell & Company. Owner, Russian Riverbend Vineyards (Sonoma-Loeb Wines). Former U.S. ambassador to Denmark and delegate to the 38th Session of United Nations General Assembly. Adviser to Governor Rockefeller on environmental and economic affairs. Chairman, New York State Council of Environmental Advisors. Recognitions include the Justice Louis D. Brandeis Award, C.B.E. bestowed by H.R.H. Elizabeth II, and Knight of the Grand Cross of the Order of Dannebrog from H.R.H. Margrethe II of Denmark.

Loeb, John L., Sr. (1902–1996) – Son of Carl M. Loeb and Adeline Moses Loeb. Banker, art collector, and philanthropist. Married Frances Lehman and fathered five children. Honorary degrees from Harvard University and New York University. Harvard's President's House and Drama Center named in his honor. Major donor to New York University's Institute of Fine Arts. Co-founder of Carl M. Loeb & Co and senior partner at Loeb, Rhoades and Company. Director of Dome Petroleum, Allied Chemical, Seagram, General Instrument, Arlen Realty, and Empire Trust Co.

Lowe, Eileen Josten (1925–) – Violist, wife, and mother. Daughter of Werner and Margaret Fatman Josten. Granddaughter of Morris Fatman and Settie Lehman Fatman. Ethel Walker School, Bennington College. Ex-husband Charles Lowe, professor of pediatrics at the University of Buffalo. Four children. Red Cross volunteer, Suburban Hospital, Buffalo. Volunteer, Albright-Knox Art Museum.

Mayer, William (1925–) – Composer. Grandson of Jules Ehrich and Emanuel Lehman's daughter, Evelyn.

Lincoln School, Taft School, Yale, Mannes College of Music. Wife: Meredith Nevins. Three children. His opera, *A Death in the Family,* was cited at the Kennedy Center as the best musical theater work of 1983. Dawn Upshaw has sung the lead in this opera, which has been performed frequently. Eleanor Roosevelt narrated his *Hello, World!* for RCA Recordings. Recipient of Guggenheim and MacDowell fellowships, National Endowment for the Arts grants, and a Lifetime Achievement citation from the Center for Contemporary Opera. Interestingly, the works of both Peter Josten's father, Werner Josten, and William Mayer were performed at Carnegie Hall under the baton of Leopold Stokowski.

Morgenthau, Henry, III (1917–) – Author, television producer, and activist. Son of Henry Morgenthau Jr. and Elinor Fatman Morgenthau. Grandson of Morris Fatman and Settie Lehman Fatman. Lincoln School, Deerfield Academy, Princeton. Wife: Ruth Schachter (d. 2006). Three children. Author, *Mostly Morgenthaus: A Family History.* Producer for Public Television. His documentaries have won Peabody, Emmy, UPI, and Flaherty Film Festival awards. Active in cause of exposing Armenian genocide in Turkey. President emeritus, Harvard Hillel. Fellow, Joan Shorenstein Center on the Press, Politics & Public Policy at the Harvard University John F. Kennedy School of Government.

Morgenthau, Robert M. (1919–) – Manhattan district attorney (1975–). Son of Henry Morgenthau Jr. and Elinor Fatman Morgenthau. Grandson of Morris Fatman and Settie Lehman Fatman. Amherst College, Yale Law School. Wife (1): Martha Pattridge (d. 1972). Five children. Wife (2): Lucinda Franks. Two children. U.S. attorney for the Southern District of New York (1961–1970). Associate and then partner, Patterson, Belknap & Webb (1948–1961). Chairman, Museum of Jewish Heritage. President and chairman, Police Athletic League. Trustee, Temple Emanu-El, the Federation of Jewish Philanthropies, and the Anti-Defamation League. Served in the U.S. Navy during World War II; awarded a bronze star and a gold star in lieu of a second bronze star; rose to the rank of lieutenant commander.

Roosevelt, Franklin Delano (1882–1945) – U.S. president. When FDR was New York State governor (1928–1932), Herbert Lehman was his lieutenant governor. When FDR was president (1933–1945), Henry Morgenthau Jr. served as his treasury secretary.

Rosenfeld, Camilla Master (1935–) – Activist. Daughter of Hilda and Dr. Arthur Master. Niece of Edith Altschul Lehman. Dalton School, Sarah Lawrence College. Husband: Isadore Rosenfeld, M.D. Four children. Active in Citizens' Committee for Children and Meals on Wheels.

Rosenfeld, Isadore (1926–) – Physician. Son of Mr. and Mrs. Morris Rosenfeld. McGill University, McGill Medical School MD, CM. Wife: Camilla Master. Rossi distinguished professor of clinical medicine and attending physician, New York Hospital–Presbyterian Hospital–Weill Cornell Medical Center. Health editor, *Parade Magazine*; medical consultant, Fox News Network; advisory committee, White House Conference on Aging; overseer, Weill Cornell Medical College. Author of twelve books, including *Symptoms, Best Treatment, Dr. Rosenfeld's Guide to Alternative Medicine,* and *Live Now, Age Later.* President, New York County Medical Society. Member, Practicing Physicians Advisory Council for the Secretary of Health and Human Services. Received the United Nations Citizen of the World Award and the Maurice Greenberg Award for Distinguished Service.

Rossbach, Mabel Limburg (1894–1967) – Philanthropist. Daughter of Richard Limburg and Clara Lehman Limburg. Husband: Max Rossbach (d. 1963). Three children. President, Auxiliary of the City Hospital at Elmhurst, Queens. Chair, Central Council of Hospital Auxiliaries. Benefactor, Auxiliary of the James Ewing Hospital. Trustee, Bank Street College of Education. Vice president of the Board of Managers, Inwood House. Director, Westchester County Children's Association and the Andrew Freedman Home. Co-wrote 1949 pamphlet (with Jessie Stanton) for New York State Division of Housing called "Learning by Experience." Wrote book reviews of new novels for the Sunday *New York Times* in 1930s and 1940s.

Sheridan, Deborah Jane Wise (1947–) – Educator of learning-disabled children. Daughter of Hilda Jane Lehman Wise. Granddaughter of Herbert Lehman and Edith Altschul Lehman. Hathaway Brown School for Girls, Shaker Heights High School, Western College for Women (Oxford, Ohio), American University. One child. Head, Junior High English Department of Lab School of Washington. Board member of Edith and Herbert Lehman Foundation.

Straus, Irving Lehman (1921–) – Nephew of Sissie Straus Lehman. Son of Nathan Straus Jr., first U.S. housing commissioner under FDR. Grandson of Nathan Straus, founder of Macy's and Dr. Barnard Sachs who identified Tay Sachs disease. Taft Preparatory School, Amherst College. Navy night fighter pilot in Pacific during WWII. Awarded Air Medal, 1944. Founder and chairman of Straus Corporate Communications providing investor and public relations skills in developing businesses and organizations. Awarded Silver Anvil by Public Relations Society of America for Investor Relations program he implemented in 1978 for the Federal Home Loan Association (Freddie Mac) when it went public. Advisory board, Museum of American Finance, New York City. Enjoys fly fishing, golf, tennis, and attending theater and concert performances.

Sulzberger, Louise Blumenthal (1898–2001) – Philanthropist and sportswoman. Daughter of Hugo and Estelle Blumenthal. Hugo numbered among Morris Fatman's best friends. Miss Jacobi's School. Husband: David Hays Sulzberger (d. 1962). Volunteer nurse's aide at Roosevelt Hospital in both World Wars. Founder and director, Yorkville Neighborhood Club. Sister-in-law of former *New York Times* publisher Arthur Hays Sulzberger and his wife Iphigene.

Tananbaum, Duane (1949–) – Associate professor of history and former chair of the History Department, Lehman College (named after Herbert H. Lehman). Author, *The Bricker Amendment Controversy* (1988); "I Will Not Compromise with My Conscience: The Essence of Herbert H. Lehman" in Herbert H. Lehman Remembered: Historical and Personal Perspectives, a 2003 Lehman College Symposium; and "'I Can Leave the Combination of My Safe to Colonel Lehman': Herbert Lehman and Franklin Roosevelt—Working Together to Improve the Lives of New Yorkers and People All Over the World," *New York History*, Winter 2006.

Wise, Peter Lehman (1949–) – Senior vice president and general manager, Major Accounts Division for the National Market, Liberty Mutual Group. Son of Hilda Jane Lehman and Edward Wise. Grandson of Herbert Lehman and Edith Altschul Lehman. Colgate University. Wife: Marylou Wise. Two children.

Reader's Guide to
The World of the Mayer Lehman Family

—◆—

Contributors are identified in the preceding section.

Altschul, Frank (1887–1981) – Husband of Helen Goodhart, the only daughter of Philip and Hattie Lehman Goodhart; only brother of Herbert Lehman's wife, Edith. Investment banker and a senior partner at Lazard Frères & Company until 1945. He also founded and ran Overbrook Press. "One of the most successful financiers of his time, Frank Altschul was in many ways a Renaissance man. He possessed a keen interest in international relations, rare-book collecting and politics." —*New York Times*, May 30, 1981.

Altschul, Helen Goodhart (1887–1985) – Only daughter of Philip and Hattie Lehman Goodhart; wife of Frank Altschul. Trustee emerita of Barnard College, which she had attended. Her daughter Edith married Robert Graham of the Graham Gallery, the oldest art dealership in New York City.

Ambassador Hotel – Located at Park Avenue and 51st Street in Manhattan; where Clara Lehman Limburg lived as a widow until her death in 1932. "An aristocratic structure, it differed from some of its contemporaries in having individually designed rooms and suites. The furnishings and interior ornamentation, loosely inspired by eighteenth and nineteenth century English and French styles, were supplied by John Wanamaker." —*The Encyclopedia of New York City.*

American Jewish Committee – A Jewish defense agency formed in 1906 in response to pogroms in Russia. Arthur, Herbert, and Irving Lehman, along with other wealthy Jews of German descent, were early supporters of the American Jewish Committee. Irving served on its executive committee when the AJC fought the American Ku Klux Klan, advocated anti-lynching laws, and opposed the restrictive Immigration Act of 1924. The Committee became a strong defender of Israel after its founding in 1948.

American Joint Distribution Committee – An organization to help displaced East European Jews. Herbert Lehman was a founder in 1914 of the AJDC. One of the most effective institutions of its kind, the "Joint" over the years has helped millions of Jews worldwide.

Bernhard, Richard J. (1894–1961) – Husband of Dorothy Lehman Bernhard. Investment banker, art collector, and civic leader. Yale University. Partner, Bernhard, Scholle & Co. Partner, Wertheim & Co.; Member, Bankers Club of America, City Midday Club, Harmonie Club, Stock Exchange Luncheon Club, Yale Club, Century Country Club. Fellow, Pierpont Morgan Library. Founder and vice president, Federation Employment and Guidance Service, a nonprofit job placement organization affiliated with the Federation of Jewish Philanthropies. Served in the U.S. Navy in both World Wars. Was also an enthusiastic golfer and farmer.

Bingham, Hiram (1875–1956) – June Bingham Birge's father-in-law. After discovering the Incan ruins at Machu Picchu, he served as a U.S. senator from Connecticut until 1933, overlapping Herbert Lehman's service as lieutenant governor of New York under FDR.

Blumenthal, George (1858–1941) – Banker, art patron, and card-playing companion of Morris Fatman. Headed the New York office of Lazard Frères. As trustee and, later, president of Mount Sinai Hospital, Blumenthal contributed $2,000,000 to it. The first Jewish president of the Metropolitan Museum of Art, serving from 1934 to his death in 1941, he donated a collection of masterpieces; the collection was named by the museum in his honor. A plaque in the entrance foyer of Mount Sinai Hospital is inscribed: "Erected on the occasion of the eightieth birthday of George Blumenthal by his fellow trustees to record their grateful appreciation of his inspired leadership during forty-six years as trustee and twenty-seven as president."

Buttenwieser, Benjamin (1900–1992) – Husband of Helen Lehman; son of Joseph L. Buttenwieser and Caroline Weil Buttenwieser. An investment banker, civic leader, and philanthropist. He received an honorary doctorate from Columbia University. Served as president of the Federation of Jewish Philanthropies of New York from 1938 to 1940 and was also an executive member of the American Jewish Committee. Other charities included Lenox Hill Hospital, Columbia Presbyterian Medical Center, Fisk University, New York Philharmonic Symphony Society, and the Parkinson's Disease Foundation. He was assistant U.S. high commissioner in Germany from 1949 to 1951, a general partner at Kuhn, Loeb from 1932 to 1949, and a limited partner at Kuhn, Loeb from 1952 to 1977.

Cardozo, Benjamin (1870–1938) – U.S. Supreme Court associate justice from 1932 to 1938. A bachelor, Cardozo visited regularly with Irving and Sissie Lehman at their home in Port Chester. Cardozo is related to John L. Loeb Jr. and his family through Adeline Moses Loeb, Carl M. Loeb's children's Southern grandmother, who was a member of the Daughters of the American Revolution (DAR).

Century Country Club – America's first and most exclusive Jewish country club, founded in Pelham in 1898. Until the 1920s, Century was located west of White Plains, next to the Warburg estate. It then moved to across the street from Ridgeleigh, Arthur and Adele Lehman's estate in Purchase. The Lehmans, along with other "Our Crowd" families, were charter members.

Cullman, Joseph, 3rd (1912–2004) – Husband of Susan Lehman Cullman; CEO of Philip Morris from 1957 to 1978. Guided the company from sixth, and last, place in the cigarette industry to the leading tobacco company in the United States, largely as a result of Cullman developing a new Marlboro cigarettes package and promoting the "Marlboro Man." A golf, fishing, and wildlife enthusiast and conservationist, Cullman set up and supported projects in East Africa to benefit people and wildlife. A tennis aficionado, Cullman chaired the International Tennis Hall of Fame from 1985 to 1988 and was U.S. Open chairman from 1969 to 1970. He was a graduate of Hotchkiss and Yale and served in the U.S. Navy as a commander in the South Pacific during World War II.

Cullman, Susan Lehman (1914–1994) – Daughter of Harold and Cecile Seligman Lehman; granddaughter of Sigmund and Harriet Lehman. Horace

Mann School graduate in 1932; attended Vassar College 1932–1934; awarded a B.A. with honors from New York University in 1962. A Japanese language decoder during World War II and an editor of cryptogram publications for many years, Cullman served on the board of directors of Philips Memorial Hospital, Mount Sinai Hospital, and the Federation of Jewish Philanthropies. She was president of the Blythedale Hospital for over fifty years and also served on the advisory council of Rockefeller University.

Delmonico's Restaurant – New York City restaurant that catered many a Lehman event, including Irving and Sissie's wedding in 1901. Drawing its customers from the city's elite, Delmonico's became known for the elegant presentation of such culinary innovations as baked Alaska and lobster Newburg. Famous patrons of the restaurant included Charles Dickens and Diamond Jim Brady.

Federation of Jewish Philanthropies – An umbrella organization for New York Jewish charity organizations; founded in 1917 by Felix Warburg and Arthur Lehman (its first two presidents), and Joseph Buttenwieser. Adele Lewisohn Lehman served as honorary chairperson for many years, and her eldest daughter, Dorothy L. Bernhard, was also active in the federation. By the 1950s, with an annual budget exceeding $30 million, New York Federation, as it is sometimes called, had become the single largest local philanthropic organization in the world.

Flade, Roland (1951–) – Author of *The Lehmans: From Rimpar to the New World, A Family History.* Dr. Flade was born in Bavaria and holds a doctorate from Julius-Maximilians-Universität in Würzburg. A newspaper editor since 1979, he has published various scholarly books and numerous articles on past Jewish life in Bavaria. For his work as a journalist and historian, Dr. Flade was awarded the Bavarian Constitutional Medal. He continues to publish articles about the Lehman family.

Goodhart, Arthur Lehman (1891–1978) – Younger son of Philip and Hattie Lehman Goodhart. A leading authority on international law, and the master of University College, Oxford. A graduate of Hotchkiss and Yale, Goodhart was tutored in economics by John Maynard Keynes. The first American to head an Oxford college, he was offered a knighthood in 1948 but refused it. His wife, Cecily, however, continued to be addressed as Lady Goodhart.

Goodhart, Howard (1884–1951) – Elder son of Philip and Hattie Goodhart. A bibliophile and philosopher who attended Hotchkiss and Yale, Goodhart was a collector of fifteenth-century tomes. Member of the Grolier Club and partner in P. J. Goodhart and Son. Goodhart Hall at Bryn Mawr College is dedicated to the memory of Goodhart's wife, Marjorie Walter. A year before his death, he donated much of his fifteenth-century book collection to Bryn Mawr in memory of his wife.

Gottheil, Gustav (1827–1903) – Senior rabbi of Temple Emanu-El. A German university graduate, Rabbi Gottheil officiated both at the burial of Mayer Lehman in 1897 and the marriage of Mayer's son Irving to Sissie Straus four years later. Unlike most of his congregants, Rabbi Gottheil was an ardent Zionist, as was his son Richard, a Columbia University professor who founded and headed the Semitic division of the New York Public Library for many years.

The Harmonie Club – Social club formed in 1852 as the Harmonie Gesellschaft. The first men's club to admit women at dinner. A select German Jewish counterpart to the other social clubs in New York City, the club hung the Kaiser's portrait in its hall for many years. In 1906 a clubhouse designed by Stanford White was constructed at 4 East 60th Street. The club still meets there.

Hellman, Isaias (1842–1920) – Husband of Babette Neugass Lehman's sister Esther and a close friend and associate of Mayer Lehman. A pioneer California entrepreneur, Hellman instituted the Farmers and Merchants Bank in 1871. He later served as president of the Wells Fargo Bank.

Henry Street Settlement – Institution founded in the 1890s by Lillian Wald to provide medical care to the indigent of the Lower East Side. Herbert, Edith, and Irving Lehman numbered among its principal supporters. First institution of its kind to have a visiting nurse service. Developed into a center for civic, social, and philanthropic work at which Herbert coached basketball and debating teams and Irving served as a volunteer social worker until his first election to the bench in 1908. Herbert and Edith's eldest son, Peter, was killed in England while on duty with the Army Air Force; in 1948 the Lehmans honored his memory by dedicating a youth center at the Henry Street Settlement called Pete's House.

Herbert H. Lehman Suite – Located at Columbia University's School of International Affairs. Came into being through the efforts of the governor's widow, Edith Altschul Lehman, who sought to bring all of her late husband's public and private papers into one central location. Mrs. Lehman oversaw the development of the Lehman Suite space. The facilities include a replica of Governor Lehman's personal study in his Park Avenue home. The dedication of the suite in 1971 attracted over 500 guests, including many members of the Lehman and Altschul families and former colleagues of Governor Lehman.

Hotchkiss School – What in England would be called a public school, Hotchkiss in Litchfield County, Connecticut, was attended by many Lehman descendants. "My great aunt Hattie's two sons, my two Limburg uncles, my two brothers, and four cousins attended Hotchkiss. Howard Rossbach loved it, but Dick hated it." – *June Rossbach Bingham Birge.*

"When I arrived at Hotchkiss in the fall of 1944, I met a great deal of hostility because I was Jewish. I remember toward the end of the war when they showed the first pictures of the Holocaust, the entire school cheered. Anti-Semitism was prevalent at all the top boarding schools in New England at the time." – *John L. Loeb Jr.*

Ickelheimer/Isles – "Robert Lehman's sister, Pauline, married Henry Ickelheimer. Their son Phil's wife, Lil Fox, got him to change his name to Isles. Phil Isles is chairman of the Lehman Foundation, which helps to run the Lehman Wing at the Metropolitan Museum of Art. Young Phil's sister Tina Barney is a well-known photographer." – *John L. Loeb Jr.*

Jewish Home and Hospital for the Aged – Incorporated in 1870, the Home has been located for over a century at 120 West 106th Street. For years, Babette Neugass Lehman and her daughter Hattie Lehman Goodhart numbered among its principal contributors.

Jewish Theological Seminary – Opened in 1887 to train conservative rabbis and preserve traditional Judaism in the United States. Attracted some of the best faculty in the world, inspiring students to see Judaism as an evolving religion. Irving Lehman served as honorary secretary and in 1936 was awarded an L.H.D.

Jewish Welfare Board – From 1921 to 1940, Irving Lehman was president of JWB, parent organization of what today comprises several hundred Jewish Community Centers and Young Men's Hebrew Associations throughout the country. For years Irving also served as president of the Y's flagship institution, New York's 92nd Street Y.

Josten, Margaret Fatman (1888–1976) – Settie Lehman Fatman and Morris Fatman's eldest daughter. Studied singing and acting with the celebrated French singer Yvette Guilbert. Using the name Margaret Farman, she performed several times at the Metropolitan Opera House before marrying Werner Josten (1885–1963), a symphonic composer who for many years headed the music department at Smith College.

Kildare – A 10,000-acre camp in the Adirondacks bought jointly in the 1890s by Emanuel Lehman's daughters, Harriet Lehman (who married Sigmund Lehman, the son of Emanuel's brother Mayer) and Evelyn Lehman Ehrich. The camp is still owned and used by Lehman descendants.

Kohler, Rabbi Kaufman (1843–1926) – As spiritual leader of Temple Emanu-El, Rabbi Kohler blessed the marriage of Irving Lehman to Sissie Straus in 1901, two years before assuming the presidency of Hebrew Union College. Holding that post for eighteen years, Rabbi Kohler was regarded by many as American Reform Judaism's foremost scholar.

Lashanska, Hulda (1908–1971) – A student of Marcella Sembrich, Madame Lashanska performed in New York as a concert soprano for many years. Her daughter, Peggy Rosenbaum, married Herbert and Edith Lehman's elder son, Peter, who was killed in action in World War II.

Lazard Frères & Co. – Lazard's origins date back to 1848, when the founders moved to the United States from France and formed a dry goods business in New Orleans before moving to San Francisco, where the business expanded into banking and foreign exchange. Edith Altschul Lehman's father, Charles, and her brother, Frank, were senior partners of the San Francisco and New York operations, respectively.

Lehman, Adele Lewisohn (1882–1965) – Philanthropist and art collector. Daughter of Adolph Lewisohn and Emma Cahn Lewisohn. Annie Brown School; attended Barnard College. Husband: Arthur

Lehman (d. 1936). Three children. Honorary chair, Federation of Jewish Philanthropies. Board member, New York Service for the Orthopedically Handicapped. Founder and board member, Arthur Lehman Counseling Service. A competent amateur painter.

Lehman, Emanuel (1825–1907) – With his brothers, Mayer and Henry, founded Lehman Brothers in Montgomery, Alabama, in 1850. In 1858, a few years after Henry's untimely death, thirty-two-year-old Emanuel relocated to New York City to run the firm's first New York office, at 119 Liberty Street. Nine years later Mayer followed. The brothers remained partners until Mayer's death. Emanuel Lehman and his descendants are mentioned only peripherally in this book.

Lehman, Henry (1822–1855) – Mayer's elder brother and the first of his family to travel from Rimpar, Bavaria, to Montgomery, Alabama. Followed by his brothers, Emanuel and Mayer, Henry founded Lehman Brothers on Montgomery's Court Square in 1850. Only a few years later, Henry died of yellow fever. Henry Lehman and his descendants are mentioned only peripherally in this book.

Lehman, John (1920–1994) – The younger son of Herbert and Edith Altschul Lehman, John Lehman was a lieutenant colonel in the U.S. Army during World War II. He subsequently maintained an office for many years at Lehman Brothers.

Lehman, Peter Gerald (1917–1944) – The elder son of Herbert and Edith Altschul Lehman, Peter Lehman had flown fifty-seven missions over Germany as a fighter pilot when he was shot down and killed. He is buried in Cambridge, England's American cemetery.

Lehman, Philip (1862–1947) – The only son of Emanuel and Pauline Sondheim Lehman and a nephew of Mayer Lehman, Philip Lehman was among the leaders of the second generation of Lehman Brothers financiers and a notable art collector, acquiring works by El Greco, Goya, Rembrandt, Bellini, and Memling, as well as Gothic tapestries. A dedicated philanthropist, he was active in the Hebrew Orphan Asylum, Mount Sinai Hospital, and Temple Emanu-El.

Lehman, Robert (1891–1969) – The only son of Philip Lehman and one of the most powerful and famous of the Lehmans, Robert "ate art and drank finance," according to friends. A graduate of Hotchkiss and Yale, where he was managing editor of the *Yale Daily News* and a chum of Cole Porter's. Robert Lehman was an art collector of impeccable taste who expanded his father's art collection to include works by Cezanne, Renoir, Monet, Botticelli, Dürer, Van Gogh, Matisse, and Picasso. The Lehman Wing of the Metropolitan Museum of Art houses his collection.

Lehman-Stern – The New Orleans affiliate of Lehman Brothers, Lehman-Stern was headed by Maurice Stern, the younger brother of Abraham Stern of Liverpool. Abraham was married to Betti Neugass, sister of Babette Neugass Lehman and Esther Neugass Hellman, wife of the president of Wells Fargo.

"Edgar Bloom Stern, the son of Maurice Stern, married Edith Rosenwald, the daughter of Sears Roebuck tycoon and eminent philanthropist Julius Rosenwald. The Edgar Stern home in New Orleans is now a museum called Longue Vue House and Gardens. Surrounded by eight acres of gardens and fountains, it still houses the original Stern furnishings and collections. Edgar Bloom Stern Jr., the son of Edgar Stern and Edith Rosenwald, is one of the founders of Aspen, Colorado, as well as two ski resorts in Utah: Deer Valley and Park City." — *John L. Loeb Jr.*

The Lehmans: From Rimpar to the New World, A Family History – A history, written by Roland Flade, of the Lehman family from its origins in the Bavarian village of Rimpar to the establishment of Lehman Brothers in antebellum Montgomery, Alabama, to becoming one of the most prestigious banking firms on Wall Street. What happened to those who stayed behind is conveyed in a recounting of the ordeal of Eva Thalheimer, a first cousin of Mayer Lehman's children, who was killed at Treblinka.

Lewisohn, Adolph (1849–1938) – Father of Adele (Mrs. Arthur) Lehman, Lewisohn made a fortune in the mining business. He devoted much of his wealth to cultural and philanthropic causes. In addition to donating Lewisohn Stadium to the College of the City of New York, he promoted prison reform and American ORT (Organization for Rehabilitation and Training), a Jewish organization founded in 1922 for the development of skilled trades and agriculture among Jews.

Lewisohn was a distant cousin of the Hambros, merchant bankers of Denmark and England.

Limburg, Alan (1899–1984) – Younger son of Richard and Clara Limburg; Alan's wife, Kathryn Bernhard, was a cousin of Dorothy Lehman Bernhard's husband, Richard. Serving in the U.S. Marine Corps during World War II, he subsequently ran a hand-painted wallpaper business.

Limburg, R. Percy (1895–1977) – Elder son of Richard Limburg and Clara Lehman Limburg. Attended Swiss boarding schools and Yale before going to fight in France during World War I. Percy was married to Adele Lewisohn Lehman's niece Edith Reckford and, after she died, to the widowed Janet Reckford, who had been married to Edith's brother, Joe. Percy was a stockbroker–bond specialist who was in charge of Selective Service for New York State during World War II. He was a board member of Montefiore Hospital and a supporter of the Federation of Jewish Philanthropies and Yale.

Marshall, Louis (1856–1929) – Irving Lehman's predecessor as the president of Temple Emanu-El. He was also an outstanding lawyer. Marshall was president of the American Jewish Committee, in which both Irving Lehman and Herbert Lehman were active from 1912 to 1929. He was also chairman of the board of the Jewish Theological Seminary, which awarded Irving Lehman an L.H.D. in 1936.

Montefiore Hospital – Founded in the north Bronx in 1884 by Sigmund Lehman and other New York Jewish community leaders to treat patients with tuberculosis and other chronic illnesses. Named after renowned philanthropist Sir Moses Montefiore. Affiliated today with the Albert Einstein School of Medicine, Montefiore Hospital is one of the largest health-care systems in the United States.

Morgenthau, Elinor Fatman (1892–1949) – Younger daughter of Settie Lehman Fatman and Morris Fatman. Elinor studied drama at Vassar (1913) and went on to Columbia University. In 1916 she married childhood friend Henry Morgenthau Jr., who for eleven years served FDR as U.S. secretary of the Treasury. When not in Washington, Elinor, Henry, and their children—Henry III, Robert, and Joan—enjoyed their 1,700-acre apple farm and dairy in East Fishkill, New York.

Morgenthau, Henry, Sr. (1856–1946) – Elinor Fatman Morgenthau's father-in-law. Amassed a fortune as a real estate developer in northern Manhattan and the Bronx. A supporter of President Woodrow Wilson, he served as American ambassador to the Ottoman Empire from 1913 to 1916 and also helped to establish the American National Red Cross and Bronx House.

Morgenthau, Henry, Jr. (1892–1967) – Husband of Elinor Fatman Morgenthau; father of Henry Morgenthau III, Robert Morris Morgenthau, and Joan Morgenthau Hirschhorn. An alumnus of Phillips Exeter and Cornell, he was FDR's secretary of the Treasury from 1934 to 1945. Morgenthau was instrumental in taking refugee policy out of State Department hands and transferring it in 1944 to the War Rescue Board, thereby saving thousands of Jewish lives.

Mostly Morgenthaus: A Family History – An intimate portrait written by Henry Morgenthau III of an extraordinary American family whose members have included an ambassador, a cabinet member, prominent businessmen, and a Pulitzer Prize–winning historian. The Morgenthaus are connected to the Lehmans through Mrs. Henry Morgenthau Jr.

(nee Elinor Fatman), whose mother was Mayer and Babette Lehman's daughter Settie Lehman Fatman. Her son is Manhattan District Attorney Robert Morgenthau.

Mount Sinai Hospital – Incorporated in 1852 as the Jews' Hospital in the City of New York. Until the Civil War, when it opened its doors to a large number of Union soldiers, it admitted only patients who were Jewish. Mayer Lehman was a major supporter. In 1898, a year after his death, land was purchased at Fifth Avenue and 100th Street, where a 456-bed hospital opened in 1904 and has been there ever since. Babette Lehman, Settie Fatman, Edith Lehman, and Philip Goodhart all served on the board. In addition to organizing Mount Sinai's Social Service Department, Edith was a founding sponsor of the Mount Sinai School of Medicine, and in 1969 established a Lehman Chair in Pediatrics there in her husband's memory.

National Association for the Advancement of Colored People (NAACP) – Established in 1909 to fight racial injustice by judicial and legislative means. Herbert Lehman was an active board member and a major financial contributor.

National Council of Jewish Women – Dedicated to furthering human welfare in the Jewish and general communities through service, education, and social action. Nationwide membership of over 100,000 and hundreds of chapters. Sissie Straus Lehman served as president of the New York chapter in 1922 and 1923.

Neugass, Benjamin (1839–1921) – Babette Neugass Lehman's younger brother. After the civil War he headed Lehman, Neugass & Co. in New Orleans when it "handled nearly a third of all the cotton shipped from American ports, much of it going through Benjamin's hands. . . . In 1872 the New Orleans firm owned three warehouses for the storage of cotton. In 1872 Benjamin Neugass left New Orleans and settled in Liverpool, the English cotton center there, to establish his own firm. In 1886 Benjamin Neugass had left Liverpool. Benjamin, according to his nephew, Herbert H. Lehman, 'made and lost several fortunes. Whenever he saw anything cheap, he could not resist it. A lace store in Venice, for example, might be for sale at a bargain. He took possession though he had no idea what he could do with it.' When he died, Benjamin Neugass left a fortune of 228,000 pounds." — *Roland Flade,* The Lehmans

New York Cotton Exchange – In 1870, Mayer Lehman numbered among the founders of the NYCE, which developed into the leading cotton futures market in the nation.

New York State Court of Appeals – The state's highest court, on which Irving Lehman sat from 1923, serving as chief judge from 1939 until 1944. During his tenure he earned a reputation as a brilliant legal scholar. An opinion by Lehman written in 1928, almost a decade before the right of collective bargaining came to have general statutory recognition, won wide attention. The reasoning set forth in the opinion was largely responsible for shaping New York's labor policy for many years.

Play School Association – Founded in 1917 as "a consultation and training agency utilizing play activities as an educational, therapeutic, and recreational tool to benefit children." Edith Lehman was a director.

Prospect Point – "Prospect Point was just down the lake from Fish Rock Camp, owned by Guta Seligman, which my parents and I visited with Guta's granddaughter and my close friend and contemporary Marjorie Lewisohn. Prospect Point was owned by Adolph Lewisohn, who built separate houses for his children. Aunt Adele loaned her house to the Rossbachs several times for several weeks. The only payola was that we had to listen to Mr. Lewisohn sing in the late afternoon and not giggle." —*June Rossbach Bingham Birge*

Ridgeleigh – An 85-acre Westchester estate bought by Arthur and Adele Lehman from Oliver Harriman in 1923. Their children and grandchildren—the Loebs, Buttenwiesers, and Bernhards—spent much of their time there. Ridgeleigh is owned and occupied today by John L. Loeb Jr.

Rosemary Hall School – A girl's preparatory school in Greenwich, Connecticut, attended by a number of Lehman descendants, including June Rossbach Bingham Birge and Ann Loeb Bronfman, who donated the building that houses the school's day care center for faculty.

Rossbach, J. Howard (1913–1975) – Elder son of Max and Mabel Rossbach. Attended Hotchkiss. Commissioner of the Securities and Exchange Commission; headed the New York Legal Aid Society. Later, became a New York judge.

Rossbach, Max (1883–1963) – A skins and hides importer, Rossbach was the son of Joseph H. Rossbach and Ida Kopp Rossbach. After attending the University of Lausanne, University of Berlin, and University of Munich, he married Mabel Limburg, the daughter of Richard Limburg and Clara Lehman Limburg. Rossbach was the president of J. H. Rossbach & Brothers and Rossbach Brazil Co., and also headed the Hide and Leather Association and the National Association of Importers of Hides and Skins. He founded the Rye Riding Association.

Rossbach, Richard (1915–1987) – Younger son of Max and Mabel Rossbach. A graduate of Hotchkiss and Yale, Rossbach was awarded the Silver Star, two Bronze Stars, and the Purple Heart for heroism during World War II. He was a stockbroker at Ingalls and Snyder, vice president of the board of trustees at the Museum of the City of New York and, like his brother Howard, an outstanding fly fisherman.

The Sachs Schools – Male and female college preparatory schools (now called the Dwight School) run by Dr. Julius Sachs, a cousin of the Goldman, Sachs & Co. Sachses. These schools were attended by Arthur, Irving, and Herbert Lehman and by future spouses Edith Altschul and Sissie Straus.

Salem Fields Cemetery – Located at 775 Jamaica Avenue in Brooklyn. Founded in 1852 and served as the final resting place for such Jews of German descent as mining industrialist Meyer Guggenheim, financier and philanthropist Felix M. Warburg, and Mayer and Babette Lehman, until it was replaced by Kensico in Westchester, where the eldest Lehman sibling, Sigmund, is buried in a mausoleum constructed in 1931.

The Sherry-Netherland – Where Harriet Lehman lived for many years as a well-tended-to widow. "Built in 1927 at 59th Street and Fifth Avenue, it contained 525 rooms in forty stories. As the first graceful skyscraper hotel in the area, it was one of the country's most distinguished addresses. It was largely a residential hotel, advertised as 'more than a place to live—a new way of living.' Like other hotels of the time, the Sherry-Netherland became known for its opulent interiors and elegant appointments and helped to make luxury high-rise apartments fashionable." —*The Encyclopedia of New York City*

Smith, Alfred E. – "As early as 1920 Herbert Lehman was one of the staunch supporters of New York Governor Al Smith. In 1924 Smith appointed him to mediate disputes in the garment trades. During Al Smith's campaign for the presidency, Herbert Lehman acted as National Democratic Committee finance chairman." —*Roland Flade,* The Lehmans

Stieglitz, Dr. Leopold – Lehman family doctor and brother of famed photographer Alfred Stieglitz, husband of Georgia O'Keeffe.

Straus, Nathan (1848–1931) – Father of Sissie Straus Lehman (Mrs. Irving) and co-owner with his brother, Isidor, of Macy's. Nathan was so stricken by Isidor's death on board the *Titanic* that he retired from business to devote himself to philanthropy. Among his many achievements was the introduction of pasteurization to America. In addition to serving as New York City commissioner of parks and New York City commissioner of education, Straus financed a Well Babies Clinic that is now a part of Hadassah Hospital in Jerusalem. In 1923, on the 25th anniversary of Brooklyn's incorporation into New York City, Straus was named New York City's most generous benefactor.

Straus, Nathan, Jr. (1889–1961) – Brother of Sissie Straus Lehman; son of the elder Nathan Straus. Served from 1921 to 1926 in the New York state legislature and headed the U.S. Housing Authority from 1937 to 1942.

Straus, Oscar (1850–1926) – Uncle of Sissie Straus Lehman; minister to the Ottoman Empire when Irving and Sissie visited him in Constantinople on their honeymoon trip. Straus became the first Jewish member of a presidential cabinet when he was appointed secretary of commerce and labor by President Theodore Roosevelt. In 1912 he ran unsuccessfully for governor of New York State. Twenty years later, his niece's brother-in-law, Herbert Lehman, won election to that office.

Sulzberger, Marian ("Manny") Effie – Childhood friend of June Rossbach Bingham Birge. Daughter of Arthur Hays and Iphigene Ochs Sulzberger, Marian was first married to Orvil E. Dryfoos, publisher of the *New York Times* from 1961 until his death in 1963. She then married Andrew Heiskell, chairman of Time, Inc. Her father, Arthur Hays Sulzberger; her grandfather, Adolph Ochs; her brother, Arthur O. Sulzberger; and her nephew Arthur O. Sulzberger Jr., have all served as publisher of the *New York Times*.

Temple Emanu-El – American Reform's cathedral synagogue in which Lehman connections date back to Emanuel Lehman's joining in 1857. On January 10, 1930, Irving Lehman, who succeeded Louis Marshall as president of the congregation, dedicated the present art deco structure on Fifth Avenue at 65th Street. One of the largest synagogues in the world, Temple Emanu-El features a stained-glass rose window facing Fifth Avenue, donated by Mayer and Babette Neugass Lehman's seven children in their parents' memory. In addition to Irving Lehman, Robert Bernhard has served as president of the congregation and John L. Loeb Sr. served as trustee for many years.

United Jewish Appeal – An American organization established in 1939, the UJA became the central American Jewish organization for the resettlement of Jews in Palestine, which Herbert and Edith Altschul Lehman supported wholeheartedly.

United Nations Relief and Rehabilitation Administration – Created at a forty-four-nation conference at the White House on November 9, 1943. UNRRA's mission was to repatriate and assist the Allied refugees who came under Allied control. The organization was directed by Herbert Lehman from 1943 to 1946. UNRRA assisted in the repatriation of millions and managed hundreds of displaced persons' camps in Germany, Italy, and Austria after the war. Under Governor Herbert Lehman's leadership, the organization aided more than 500 million war victims.

Warburg, Felix (1871–1937) – A partner in Kuhn, Loeb and Co. and a founder in 1917 with Arthur Lehman and Joseph Buttenwieser of the Federation for the Support of Jewish Philanthropies. Felix's wife, Frieda Schiff Warburg, and Adele Lewisohn Lehman were close friends.

Wertheim, Maurice (1886–1950) – Husband of Elinor Fatman Morgenthau's sister-in-law Alma Morgenthau. Publisher of *The Nation*, director of the Theatre Guild, founder and president of Wertheim & Co. Father of noted historian Barbara Tuchman.

Wise, Hilda Jane Lehman (1921–1974) – Only daughter of Herbert and Edith Altschul Lehman. Attended the Holmquist School in New Hope, Pennsylvania, and Bennett Junior College in Millbrook, Pennsylvania. Hilda Jane served in the Women's Army Auxilliary Corp (WAAC) in World War II, was married three times, and had three children.

Young Men's and Young Women's Hebrew Association (YM/YWHA) – A nonsectarian cultural, educational, and recreational center formed in New York City in 1874 and known today as the 92nd Street Y. Irving Lehman served as president for many years. His wife, Sissie Straus Lehman, was an active board member. Mayer Lehman's great-great-grandson Matthew Bronfman served as president from 2002 to 2003 and now serves on the board of trustees.

Descendants of Mayer and Babette Lehman

Note: The numbers that precede the individual's name indicate the generation into which the person was born. Each successive generation is indented further to the right. Spouses are indicated by plus signs and subsequent spouses are indicated by asterisks. Birth date is preceded by "b," marriage date by "m," and death date by "d." Information is up-to-date as of October 2006. Some information was not available.

1 Mayer Lehman b: Jan 1830; d: Jun 1897
..+Babette Neugass b: Apr 1838; d: Aug 1919

..........2 Sigmund Lehman b: Feb 1859; d: Apr 1930
............+Harriet Lehman b: 1861; d: Jan 1944; m: Jan 1884
................3 Allan Sigmund Lehman b: Jan 1885
....................+Evelyn Schiffer b: Aug 1894
..........................4 Ellen Lehman b: Nov 1913
..............................+Richard Matthew McCluskey b: May 1914
....................................5 Maureen McCluskey b: Apr 1943
......................................+ Robert Oxenberg b: Dec 1949
....................................5 Sharon, Countess Sondes b: Mar 1946
......................................+James Hammond

....★2nd Husband of Sharon McCluskey:

....+Henry, The Earl Sondes b: May 1939

....5 Orin A. Lehman McCluskey b: Jan 1951

....+Ellen Regan b: Aug 1952

............................★2nd Husband of Ellen Lehman:

............................+Preston Long

........................4 Orin Lehman b: Jan 1920

........................+Jane Reynolds Bagley b: Apr 1932; d: Apr 1988

........................5 Susan Lehman b: Nov 1964

..........................+Trent Carmichael b: Aug 1965; m: Sep 1992

........................6 Avery Jane Carmichael b: Jan 1995

........................6 Haley Anne Carmichael b: Dec 1996

........................6 Ryan Trent Carmichael b: Mar 1999

........................6 Whitney Susan Carmichael b: Dec 2002

....................★2nd Wife of Orin Lehman:

....................+Wendy Vanderbilt b: Mar 1944

......................5 Brooke Lehman b: May 1972

......................5 Sage Lehman b: May 1975

..................★2nd Wife of Allan Sigmund Lehman:

..................+Anne Roche

................3 Harold Lehman b: 1889

................+Cecile Seligman

............4 Susan Lehman b: Dec 1914; d: 1994

............+Joseph F. Cullman b: 1912; d: 2004

........5 Dorothy Cullman b: Dec 1939

........+Norman Treisman

........6 Joel Harold Treisman b: Jun 1961

........+Marjorie Jacobson b: 1964; m: 1996

....7 Rachel Jacey Treisman b: 1997

....7 Maya Elizabeth Treisman b: 1999

....7 Jordana Rose Treisman b: 2006

....6 Jeffrey David Treisman b: Jul 1963

.............................4 Betty Lehman b: Sep 1918; d: Oct 1999

...............................+E. Nelson Asiel b: Jul 1917

.................................5 Harold Nelson Asiel b: Feb 1944

.....................................+Cynthia Christensen b: 1949

....6 Carrie Asiel b: Feb 1971

....+Dennis Grammas; m: Nov 1995

....7 Alexandria K. Grammas; b: 1999

....6 Scott N. Asiel b: Apr 1973

....+Maureen Flynn b: May 1974

....7 Kathryn Taylor Asiel b: Jul 2006

....*2nd Wife of Harold Nelson Asiel:

....+Patricia Gagne b: Dec 1943

.................................5 Terri Lee Asiel b: Jan 1946

.................................5 John Howard Asiel b: Jun 1949

..........2 Hattie Lehman b: 1861; d: 1948

............+Philip J. Goodhart b: 1857; d: Apr 1944; m: 1882

.................3 Howard L. Goodhart b: Feb 1884; d: 1951

...................+Marjorie Walter

...........................4 Phyllis Walter Goodhart b: Oct 1913; d: Jan 1994

.............................+John Dozier Gordan Jr. b: Nov 1907; d: Mar 1968; m: Jun 1938

.................................5 Marjorie Gordan b: Nov 1942

....+Adrian Harold Houston Bowden b: Jun 1938; d: 1995

....6 Alexander Gordan Houston Bowden b: May 1972

...............................6 Stephanie Florence Houston Bowden b: Apr 1976
...............................+Nicholas Reynolds; m: 2004
...............................7 Daniel Adrian Bowden Reynolds b: 2006
...............................6 Richard Waring Baylor Houston Bowden b: May 1979
...............................5 John Dozier Gordan III b: Sep 1945
...............................+Catherine Morot-Sir b: Nov 1946; m: Jun 1967
...............................6 Elizabeth Gordan b: Dec 1975
...............................+Stewart Ellis; m: 2002
...............................6 John Dozier Gordan IV b: Aug 1978
...............................+Robin Allan; m: 2003
...............................5 Lucy Latane Gordan b: Jan 1948
...............................+Luciano Rastelli b: Mar 1939
...............................6 Veronica Deborah Rastelli b: Jan 1975
...............................6 Rebecca Phyllis Rastelli b: Jul 1980
...............................+Emilio Oliveti; m: 2006
...............................5 Virginia Baird Gordan b: Oct 1950
...............................3 Helen L. Goodhart b: May 1887; d: Jun 1965
...............................+Frank Altschul b: Apr 1887; d: May 1981
...............................4 Charles Altschul b: Jan 1913
...............................4 Margaret Altschul b: Nov 1915
...............................+Daniel Lang b: May 1913; d: Nov 1981
...............................5 Frances Lang b: Aug 1947
...............................+ Robert Labaree b: Jan 1944
...............................6 Aaron Lang Labaree b: Nov 1978
...............................6 Hannah Rose Labaree b: Jul 1981
...............................6 Sophie Elizabeth Labaree b: Mar 1987

...................................5 Helen G. Lang b: Jun 1949

...................................6 Isaiah Orozco Lang b: Dec 1974

...................................+Dinorah Matias; m: 2005

...................................6 Daniel Everardo Lang b: 1998

...................................6 Joaquin Lang b: 2000

...................................5 Cecily Lang b: May 1953

...................................+Eric Kooijman b: Aug 1961

...................................6 Nicholas Kooijman b: Nov 1991

...................................6 Olivia Kooijman b: Dec 1994

...........................4 Edith Altschul b: Nov 1917; d: May 2003

...........................+Robert Claverhouse Graham b: Apr 1913; d: Mar 1994

...................................5 Robert Claverhouse Graham b: Sep 1941

...................................+Christine Denny; m: Jun 1963

...................................6 Elizabeth Ashley Graham b: Jun 1964

...................................+Adam Lindemann b: Aug 1961; m: Oct 1989

...................................7 Helen Christine Lindemann b: Apr 1991

...................................7 Charlotte I. Lindemann b: Jul 1992

...................................7 Frances Lindemann b: Feb 1997

...................................6 Kathryn Graham b: Jul 1966

...................................★2nd Wife of Robert Claverhouse Graham:

...................................+Julia Clarice Moran b: Sep 1953; m: May 1982

...................................6 James Wesley Hawkes Graham b: Feb 1993

...................................5 Michael Charles Graham b: Apr 1943

...................................5 Kathryn Goodhart Graham b: Feb 1947

...........................4 Arthur Goodhart Altschul b: Apr 1920; d: Mar 2002

...........................+Stephanie Wagner b: Mar 1932; d: Jan 1961

......................................5 Stephen Altschul b: Feb 1957

.....................................+Caroline Kershaw James b: May 1956; m: Apr 1995

.....................................6 James Wagner Altschul b: Jul 1996

.....................................6 William Kershaw Altschul b: Jun 1998

.....................................5 Charles Altschul b: Aug 1958

.....................................+Charlotte Dixon b: 1966; m: Jul 2005

.....................................6 Stephanie Ivy Altschul b: Oct 2006

.....................................★2nd Wife of Arthur Goodhart Altschul:

.....................................+Siri von Reis b: Feb 1931; m: 1963

.....................................5 Arthur G. Altschul b: Mar 1964

.....................................5 Emily Altschul b: May 1966

.....................................+John J. Miller b: May 1958; m: Nov 2002

.....................................6 Caroline Goodhart Miller b: Apr 2003

.....................................6 Rex Altschul Miller b: Nov 2006

.....................................5 Serena Altschul b: Oct 1970

.....................................★3rd Wife of Arthur Goodhart Altschul:

.....................................+Diana Landreth b: Jul 1946; m: 1980

.....................................★4th Wife of Arthur Goodhart Altschul:

.....................................+Patricia Dey Fleming; m: 1996

..................3 Arthur L. Goodhart b: Mar 1891; d: Nov 1978

...................+Cecily Carter b: Apr 1896; d: Apr 1985

.....................4 Sir Philip Carter Goodhart b: Nov 1925

.....................+Valerie Winant b: Mar 1926; m: 1950

.....................5 Arthur Winant Goodhart b: Feb 1952

.....................+Jacqueline Lewis; m: 1998

.....................6 Grace Ivy Goodhart b: Nov 1999

.....................5 Sarah Cecilia Goodhart b: Nov 1953

.....................+ George Mitton Kershaw b: Oct 1952; m: 1976

.....................6 Samuel Goodhart Kershaw b: Dec 1982

.....................6 John A. Crookenden Kershaw b: Feb 1986

..............................6 Harry Clinton Kershaw b: Oct 1988
.......................5 David Forbes Goodhart b: Sep 1956
.......................+Lucy R. Kellaway b: Jun 1959; m: 1990
..............................6 Rosamond Cecily Goodhart b: Feb 1991
..............................6 Matilda Katherine Goodhart b: Oct 1992
..............................6 Arthur Kellaway Goodhart b: Nov 1994
..............................6 Stanley William Goodhart b: Nov 1997
.......................5 Rachel Goodhart b: Oct 1957
.......................+Adrian D. Richardson b: Jul 1943; m: 1978
..............................6 Thomas Donald Richardson b: Mar 1981
..............................6 Victoria Emma Richardson b: May 1983
..............................6 Edward Philip Richardson b: Aug 1987
.......................5 Harriet Goodhart b: Apr 1961
.......................+Richard Owen Roberts b: 1964; m: 1988
..............................6 Richard Christopher Roberts b: Apr 1989
..............................6 Peter Lewis Roberts b: Aug 1992
..............................6 Matthew Carter Roberts b: Sep 1993
.......................5 Rebecca Goodhart b: Dec 1964
.......................+David Michael Billings b: Aug 1962; m: 1994
..............................6 Jacob Goodhart Billings b: Oct 1998
..............................6 Daniel Carter Billings b: Jul 2000
..............................6 Simon Forbes Billings b: Oct 2002
..............................6 Thomas Winant Billings b: Jun 2005
.......................5 Daniel Lehman Goodhart b: Apr 1966
.......................+Amanda Jane Moonie b: May 1967; m: 1993
..............................6 Hattie Georgina Goodhart b: Nov 1996
..............................6 Wilfred James Goodhart b: Nov 1998
..............................6 Florence Jemima Goodhart b: Nov 1999

..........................4 Lord William Howard Goodhart b: Jan 1933

............................+Celia McClare Herbert b: Jul 1939; m: 1966

....................................5 Annabel Frances Goodhart b: 1967

....................................+James Andrew Dallas b: Feb 1968; m: 1995

....6 Josephine Juliet Dallas b: 1997

....6 Beatrice Charlotte Dallas b: 2000

....6 Katharine Claudia Dallas b: 2004

....................................5 Laura Cristabel Goodhart b: Jan 1970

....................................+William Edward Kenneth Watts b: 1969; m: 1999

....6 Matthew Urban Watts b: 2000

....6 Kenneth Lando Watts b: 2002

....6 Fletcher Clement Watts b: 2005

....................................5 Benjamin Herbert Goodhart b: Sep 1972

..........................4 Charles Albert Eric Goodhart b: Oct 1936

............................+Margaret Ann Smith b: May 1938; m: Jul 1960

....................................5 Lucy Margaret Goodhart b: Oct 1962

....................................+Gordon Eric Bennett b: Oct 1961; m: Aug 1997

....6 Theodore Asa Bennett b: Feb 2001

....6 Eli Morrison Bennett b: Jul 2004

....................................5 William Eric Goodhart b: Jul 1964

....................................+Kate Elizabeth Hill b: Jun 1970; m: Mar 1995

....6 Eve Elizabeth Goodhart b: Apr 1998

....6 George Eric Goodhart b: Dec 2000

....6 Sarah Margaret Goodhart b: Dec 2000

....................................5 Alice Jessica Goodhart b: Mar 1968

....................................+M. James Snelling b: Feb 1964; m: Jul 1997

....................................5 Sophie Judith Goodhart b: Jun 1970

..........2 Settie Lehman b: Jan 1863; d: Feb 1936

............+Morris Fatman b: 1858; d: Sep 1930

................3 Margaret Fatman b: May 1888; d: Aug 1976

...................+Werner Josten b: Jun 1885; d: Feb 1963

.........................4 Peter W. Josten b: Apr 1922

...........................4 Eileen Josten b: Feb 1925

...........................+Charles Upton Lowe b: Aug 1921

.....................................5 Sarah Margaret Lowe b: Sep 1956

....+Elisabeth E. Smith b: 1956

....6 Simon M. Lowe b: 2000

......................................5 Elizabeth Lowe b: Jan 1958

......................................5 Josten Stephen Lowe b: Feb 1959

....+Jane Ceraso b: Feb 1959

....6 Jessica Sage Lowe b: Nov 1991

....6 Rory J. Lowe b: 1995

......................................5 Susannah Cambria Lowe b: Oct 1960

....+Devin Alexander Hess b: Jan 1955

................3 Elinor Fatman b: Feb 1892; d: Sep 1949

...................+Henry Morgenthau Jr. b: May 1891; d: Feb 1967; m: Apr 1916

.........................4 Henry Morgenthau III b: Jan 1917

...........................+Ruth Schachter b: Jan 1931; d: Nov 2006; m: May 1962

.................................5 Sarah Elinor Morgenthau b: Jun 1963

...................................+Carlton Edward Wessel b: May 1961; m: Sep 1993

......................................6 Edward Carlton Wessel b: Oct 1996

......................................6 Henry Morgenthau Wessel b: Oct 1998

......................................6 Mizia Claire Wessel b: Nov 2000

.................................5 Henry Morgenthau IV b: Aug 1964

.................................5 Kramer Morgenthau b: Dec 1966

..........................4 Robert Morris Morgenthau b: Jul 1919
............................+Martha Pattridge b: Oct 1919; d: Oct 1972; m: Dec 1943
...............................5 Joan Morgenthau b: Feb 1945
.................................+Eugene R. Anderson b: Oct 1927; m: Nov 1986
...............................5 Anne Morgenthau b: Apr 1947
.................................+Paul R. Grand b: Dec 1933; m: Sep 1970
.....................................6 Hilary Morgenthau Grand b: May 1972
....+Benjamin H. Harris b: Jun 1970; m: Jun 1999
....7 Sam Grand Harris b: Mar 2001
....7 Daisy Morgenthau Harris b: Feb 2004
....7 Noah Grand Harris b: Aug 2006
.....................................6 Noah Morgenthau Grand b: Jul 1975
....+Alicia Gabica b: 1989; m: Aug 2006
...............................5 Elinor Morgenthau b: May 1951
...............................5 Robert Pattridge Morgenthau b: Mar 1957
.................................+Susan Moore b: Dec 1959; m: Jun 1983
.....................................6 Harry Morgenthau b: Sep 1989
.....................................6 Martha Bryce Morgenthau b: Sep 1993
...............................5 Barbara E. Morgenthau b: Dec 1962
.................................+Hanmin Lee b: Sep 1965; m: Jul 2001
.....................................6 Mimoh Martha Morgenthau Lee b: Jul 2003
...........................★2nd Wife of Robert Morris Morgenthau:
............................+Lucinda Franks b: Jul 1946; m: Nov 1977
...............................5 Joshua Franks Morgenthau b: Mar 1984
...............................5 Amy Elinor Morgenthau b: Aug 1990
..........................4 Joan Morgenthau b: Oct 1922
............................+Fred Hirschhorn b: May 1919
...............................5 Elizabeth Scharps Hirschhorn b: Jul 1960
.................................+Bruce Hugh Wilson b: Dec 1957; m: 1995

......................................6 Josephine Wilson b: 1996

......................................6 Frederick Wilson b: 1998

......................................6 Amalya Wilson b: 2001

....................................5 Joan Morgenthau Hirschhorn b: Jul 1961

......................................+David Evan Bright b: May 1957; m: 1989

......................................6 Jennifer Morgenthau Bright b: Mar 1991

......................................6 Katherine Hirschhorn Bright b: Apr 1994

....................................5 Elinor Hannah Hirschhorn b: Dec 1962

......................................+Michael Carroll; m: 1996

......................................6 Hannah Carroll b: 1999

......................................6 Henry Carroll b: 2001

..........2 Benjamin Lehman b: 1865; d: 1865

..........2 Clara Lehman b: 1870; d: 1932

............+Richard Limburg b: 1857; d: Feb 1916

................3 Mabel Minne Limburg b: Mar 1894; d: Feb 1967

....................+Max Rossbach b: Feb 1883; d: Aug 1963; m: Jan 1913

..........................4 J. Howard Rossbach b: Dec 1913; d: Sep 1975

............................+Eleanor Frank b: Nov 1916; d: Jul 2005; m: Dec 1947

....................................5 Anne Clara Rossbach b: Apr 1950

......................................+Ernest R. Munch b: May 1947; m: Dec 1974

......................................6 Lucia Eleanor Marquand Munch b: Dec 1979

......................................6 Nicholas Reid Hayward Munch b: Sep 1983

....................................5 Sarah Frank Rossbach b: May 1952

......................................+Douglas Morrison Fleming b: Aug 1948; m: Oct 1985

......................................6 Benjamin Elliot Max Fleming b: Jun 1992

......................................6 Charlotte Eleanor Currie Fleming b: Dec 1992

.....................................5 Howard Max Rossbach b: Oct 1954

.....................................+Kathleen Ellen Fulgham b: 1956; m: Aug 1992

.....................................6 Max Russell Rossbach b: Apr 1997

.....................................6 Audrey Joan Rossbach b: Dec 2000

.....................................4 Richard Max Rossbach b: Mar 1915; d: Jul 1987

.....................................+Susan Goodman b: Jul 1919; d: Apr 2001

.....................................5 Cynthia Richards Rossbach b: May 1943

.....................................+James Flood Stebbins b: Jul 1931; m: Aug 1973

.....................................5 James Michael Rossbach b: Oct 1946

.....................................+Patricia Elisabeth Gould b: Jan 1938; m: Jan 1976

.....................................4 June Rossbach b: Jun 1919

.....................................+Jonathan B. Bingham b: Apr 1914; d: Jul 1986; m: Sep 1939

.....................................5 Sherrell Bingham b: Apr 1941

.....................................+James Edward Bland b: May 1940; d: Aug 1974; m: Jun 1962

.....................................6 Edward B. Bland b: May 1965

.....................................+Juliette Robbins b: Apr 1965

.....................................★2nd Wife of Edward B. Bland:

.....................................+Rebecca Young b: Sep 1960; m: Jun 1998

.....................................7 Jackson Bingham Bland b: Mar 1999

.....................................7 Eva Young Bland b: Jun 2000

.....................................6 Theodorick Bland b: Jan 1968

.....................................+Nancy Frost b: Jan 1968; m: Jun 1992

.....................................7 Nicholas Frost Bland b: Jan 1995

.....................................7 Emily Bingham Bland b: Mar 1996

.....................................7 Mary Brereton Bland b: Mar 1996

.....................................6 Richard Bland b: Mar 1973

.....................................+Katharine Brandi b: Jun 1974; m: Jun 2003

......................................★2nd Husband of Sherrell Bingham:
......................................+Richard Hill Downes b: Jul 1938; m: Mar 1976
......................................5 June Mitchell Bingham b: Oct 1942; d: Oct 1999
......................................+Erik Canfield Esselstyn b: Apr 1937; m: Aug 1967
......................................6 June Eriksson Esselstyn b: Dec 1970
......................................+Jeffrey George Aten b: Sep 1970; m: Jul 1997
......................................7 June Edith Aten b: Dec 2001
......................................7 Sarah Eriksson Aten b: May 2004
......................................6 Blakeman Bingham Esselstyn b: Mar 1973
......................................+Cindy Ann Sanger b: Mar 1969; m: Dec 2004
......................................7 Mitchell Esselstyn b: May 2006; d: May 2006
......................................5 Timothy Woodbridge Bingham b: Feb 1945
......................................+Susan Adams Hulsman b: May 1944; m: Jun 1969
......................................6 Katherine Ellis Bingham b: Sep 1970
......................................+J. Donald Moorehead b: May 1962; m: Aug 1994
......................................7 Luke Moorehead b: Sep 1998
......................................7 Jacob Moorehead b: Sep 2000
......................................7 Max Moorehead b: Oct 2004
......................................6 Jonathan Brewster Bingham II b: Dec 1972
......................................+Caroline April Colette; m: Jun 1999
......................................7 William Woodbridge Bingham b: Sep 2002
......................................7 Charles Walker Bingham b: Jul 2005
......................................5 Claudia Rossbach Bingham b: Feb 1947
......................................+Robert Hall; m: 1968
......................................6 Harbhajan Taiki M. Hall b: Aug 1968
......................................7 Sunderta Khalsa b: Dec 1997

..............................★2nd Husband of Claudia Rossbach Bingham:

.............................+Thomas A. Meyers b: May 1939; m: Mar 1972

.....................................6 Gurubhajan Khalsa b: Dec 1973

.....................................6 Satbhajan Khalsa b: Jun 1976

.........................★2nd Husband of June Rossbach:

..............................+ Robert B. Birge b: Dec 1914; m: Mar 1987

.............3 Richard Percy Limburg b: Nov 1895; d: Oct 1977

.............+ Edith Reckford b: Oct 1900

.....................4 Peter R. Limburg b: Nov 1929

.....................+Margareta Fischerstrom b: Mar 1932

.........................5 Richard Peter Limburg b: Apr 1953

.............................+Mary Rose Dowd b: Jun 1961; m: 1988

.................................6 Rosemary Karin Limburg b: Aug 1990

.................................6 Nicholas Percy Limburg b: Jul 1992

.................................6 Peter John Limburg b: Oct 1993

.........................5 Karin Edith Limburg b: Jun 1954

.........................+Dennis Peter Swaney b: May 1953

.........................5 David Alan Limburg b: Jul 1956

.........................5 Ellen Margareta Limburg b: Nov 1964

.............................+ Mark Ambrose Santistevan b: Mar 1957

.................................6 Margareta Elena Santistevan b: Nov 1992

.................................6 Dorothe Karin Santistevan b: Sep 1994

.................................6 Mark Santistevan b: Dec 1999

.............★2nd Wife of Richard Percy Limburg:

.............+Janet Reckford b: Dec 1911

.............3 Alan Mayer Limburg b: Jan 1899; d: Mar 1984

.............+Kathryn Bernhard b: Jan 1900

...........................4 A. Myles Limburg b: Dec 1925

..........................+Marjorie Estes b: Jul 1930

...................................5 Karen Limburg b: Mar 1951

....6 Joti S. Smith b: Sep 1982

....6 Jali Smith b: Jun 1987

....6 Jaia Smith b: Dec 1992

....6 Kiyahna Smith b: Sep 1995

...................................5 Fred Limburg b: Mar 1953

...................................5 William Limburg b: Nov 1955; d: May 1978

...........................4 Phyllis Limburg b: Jan 1930

..............................+ Peter Beeman

..........2 Arthur Lehman b: Jun 1873; d: May 1936

............+Adele Lewisohn b: May 1882; d: Aug 1965; m: 1901

.................3 Dorothy Lehman b: Apr 1903; d: Mar 1969

..................+Richard J. Bernhard b: Jun 1894; d: Feb 1961

...........................4 Robert Arthur Bernhard b: May 1928

............................+Frances Wells b: Sep 1929; m: Dec 1949

...................................5 Adele Bernhard b: Nov 1950

....+Peter Neufeld b: Jul 1950

....6 Shane Bernhard Neufeld b: Sep 1982

....6 Lena Neufeld b: Dec 1985

...................................5 Michael Bernhard b: Nov 1952

....+Nancy Doll b: Apr 1951

....6 Anna Bernhard b: May 1986

....6 Andrew Bernhard b: Jan 1991

......................................5 Susan Bernhard b: Aug 1954

....+Donald Collins b: Oct 1952

....6 Ashley Collins b: Mar 1978

....6 Brian Clifford Collins b: Aug 1979

....6 Garrett Thomas Collins b: Aug 1982

......................................5 Steven Bernhard b: Oct 1957

....+Sheryl Niebuhr b: Aug 1957

....6 Jessica Bernhard b: Jun 1985

....6 Matthew Bernhard b: Nov 1989

...................................★2nd Wife of Robert Arthur Bernhard:

.............................+Joan Mack Sommerfield b: May 1931; m: Aug 1970

.......................4 William Lehman Bernhard b: Dec 1931

.........................+Catherine G. Cahill

.................3 Helen Lehman b: Oct 1905; d: Nov 1989

...................+Benjamin Joseph Buttenwieser b: Oct 1900; d: Dec 1991

.......................4 Lawrence Benjamin Buttenwieser b: Jan 1932

.........................+Ann Harriet Lubin b: Nov 1935; m: Jul 1956

......................................5 William Lawrence Buttenwieser b: Apr 1957

....+Lisa Gould Rubin b: Feb 1955; m: Nov 1982

....6 Indiana Gould Buttenwieser b: May 1985

....6 Hallie Gould Buttenwieser b: Apr 1990

....6 Liberty Gould Buttenwieser b: Jul 1993

...................................★2nd Wife of William Lawrence Buttenwieser:

......................................+Eugenie Deserio b: Sep 1963; m: Apr 2000

....6 Jake E. Deserio b: Jan 1989

....6 Luke William Buttenwieser b: Nov 2000

......................................5 Carol Helen Buttenwieser b: Apr 1959

.....................................+John Rubin Sharp b: Nov 1960; m: May 1987

....6 Ashley Lehman Sharp b: Mar 1990

....6 Else Weil Sharp b: Apr 1992

......................................5 Jill Ann Buttenwieser b: May 1961

 ....+Richard Perry Schloss b: Mar 1960; m: Mar 1989

....6 Nicholas Benjamin Buttenwieser Schloss b: Sep 1990

....6 Samuel Lawrence Schloss b: Nov 1992

....6 Julia Bier Schloss b: Sep 1996

......................................5 Peter Lubin Buttenwieser b: Apr 1965

.....................................+Susan Helen Upton b: 1965; m: Jun 1995

....6 Zachary Upton Buttenwieser b: May 1997

....6 Annabelle Sage Buttenwieser b: May 2000

....6 Charlotte Leah Buttenwieser b: Mar 2003

..................................4 Carol Helen Buttenwieser b: Jun 1933; d: Oct 1955

...............................+ Michael A. Loeb b: Nov 1928

..................................4 Peter Lehman Buttenwieser b: Dec 1935

.................................+Elizabeth Werthen b: Jan 1939

......................................5 Sarah Werthen Buttenwieser b: Aug 1963

......................................+Hosea Baskin b: Dec 1968; m: Oct 1993

....6 Ezekiel Baskin b: Sep 1995

....6 Lucien Baskin b: May 1998

....6 Remiel Baskin b: Sep 2002

......................................5 Julie Buttenwieser b: Apr 1966

....+Maurice Suh; m: May 1991

....6 Daphne Suh b: Mar 2001

....6 Charlotte Suh b: May 2003

....6 Kate Suh b: May 2003

..............................★2nd Wife of Peter Lehman Buttenwieser:

..............................+Terry Marek b: 1945

..............................4 Paul Arthur Buttenwieser b: Apr 1938

..............................+Catherine Frum b: Nov 1938; m: Aug 1963

.....................................5 Susan Catherine Buttenwieser b: Aug 1965

.....................................+Andrew Blackman b: Jan 1965

....6 Rae Buttenwieser Blackman b: 1997

....6 Lola Buttenwieser Blackman b: 2002

.....................................5 Stephen Paul Buttenwieser b: Sep 1967

.....................................+Rachel Harrington-Levey b: Sep 1970

....6 Maya Harrington-Levey b: 2005

.....................................5 Janet Adele Buttenwieser b: Apr 1971

.....................................+Matthew Wiley b: 1971

.................3 Frances Lehman b: Sep 1906; d: 1996

.................+John Langeloth Loeb Sr. b: Nov 1902; d: Dec 1996

..........................4 Judith Helen Loeb b: Sep 1927

..............................+Richard Norton Beaty b: Jan 1920; d: Feb 1965; m: May 1948

.....................................5 Richard Norton Beaty b: Apr 1949

.....................................+Karin Brackett b: Jun 1955; m: Sep 1980

....6 Ryan Thomas Beaty b: Mar 1981

....6 Kristin Adele Beaty b: Jan 1984

....6 Christopher Evan Beaty b: Apr 1991

.....................................5 Frances Dawbarn Beaty b: Dec 1950

.....................................+William Perry b: Nov 1948

....6 Jessica Rose Perry b: Jun 1976

.....................................5 Anne Phillips Beaty b: Nov 1952

....6 James Julian Beaty b: Oct 1982

....................................5 John Loeb Beaty b: Apr 1957

....................................+Joy Parmley b: Jan 1950

....6 Alysia Danielle Beaty b: Jun 1989

 ....6 Aliana Rae Beaty b: Aug 1998

....................................5 Charles Arthur Chiara b: Oct 1959

....+Rene Garry b: Jun 1963; m: Apr 1992

....6 Julian Arthur Chiara b: 1995

....6 Lucas Marco Chiara b: 1997

....6 Sophie Valentine Chiara b: 2000

............................★2nd Husband of Judith Helen Loeb:

............................+Marco Chiara b: Jul 1937; m: May 1967

....................................5 Daniela Chiara b: May 1969

....................................+Chris Mason

....6 Karma Mason b: Dec 2005

...........................4 John Langeloth Loeb Jr. b: May 1930

...........................+Nina Sundby b: Jan 1939; m: Apr 1960

.................................5 Alexandra Loeb b: Aug 1961

......................................+Joseph Edward Driscoll b: May 1964; m: Oct 1994

....6 Aiden Edward Driscoll b: Sep 1998

....6 Allegra Frances Driscoll b: Oct 2000

..............................★2nd Wife of John Langeloth Loeb Jr.:

...........................+Meta Martindell Harrsen b: Jul 1949; m: Jan 1976

.................................5 Nicholas Mears Loeb b: Aug 1975

......................................+Anna Elizabeth Viola Pettersson b: Dec 1978

...........................4 Ann Margaret Loeb b: Sep 1932

..............................+Edgar Miles Bronfman Sr. b: Jun 1929

....5 Samuel Bronfman II b: Oct 1953

.............................+Melanie Mann b: Jan 1954; d: Dec 1991; m: Mar 1976

..................................6 Maxwell Peter Bronfman b: Sep 1984

..................................6 Dana Luisa Bronfman b: Dec 1986

.............................★2nd Wife of Samuel Bronfman II:

.............................+Kelly Johnston Conner b: Jun 1959; m: Jul 1994

..................................6 Ann Wright Bronfman b: Nov 1996

.......................5 Edgar Miles Bronfman Jr. b: May 1955

.............................+Sherry Marcina Brewer

..................................6 Vanessa Sherry Bronfman b: Aug 1980

..................................6 Benjamin Zachary Bronfman b: Aug 1982

..................................6 Hannah Marcina Bronfman b: Oct 1987

.............................★2nd Wife of Edgar Miles Bronfman Jr.:

.............................+Clarissa Alcock b: Mar 1966; m: Feb 1994

..................................6 Aaron Edgar Bronfman b: Sep 1996

..................................6 Bettina Isabel Bronfman b: Feb 1998

..................................6 Erik James Bronfman b: Feb 1998

..................................6 Clarissa Emilia Bronfman b: Oct 2000

.......................5 Holly Bronfman b: Aug 1956

.............................+Ross Hoffman

..................................6 Lauren Amrit Hoffman b: Jun 1977

..................................6 Lilli Emily Hoffman b: Mar 1980

.............................★2nd Husband of Holly Bronfman:

.............................+Bharat Lev; m: May 2000

.......................5 Matthew Bronfman b: Jul 1959

.............................+Fiona Woods b: May 1959

....6 Jeremy Samuel Bronfman b: Nov 1986

....6 Eli Miles Bronfman b: Sep 1988

....6 Gabriela Talia Bronfman b: Nov 1992

....★2nd Wife of Matthew Bronfman:

.....................................+Lisa Belzberg b: May 1961

....6 Sasha Eliana Bronfman b: Mar 1996

....6 Tess Emmanuelle Bronfman b: Jan 1998

....6 Ezekiel Belzberg Bronfman b: Nov 1999

....★3rd Wife of Matthew Bronfman:

.....................................+Stacey Kaye b: Jun 1966; m: Jan 2005

....6 Coby Benjamin Bronfman b: Nov 2005

.....................................5 Adam Rodgers Bronfman b: Mar 1963

.....................................+Cynthia Marie Gage b: May 1964; m: Jun 1984

....6 Joshua Bronfman b: May 1987

....6 Zachary Rosner Bronfman b: Jun 1989

....6 Samantha Bronfman b: Mar 1992

....6 Jacob Bronfman b: Mar 1994

..........................4 Arthur Loeb b: Sep 1932

..........................4 Deborah Loeb b: Feb 1946

..........................+David Davies

.....................................5 Taran John Davies b: Oct 1970

.....................................+Natalie Munk b: Nov 1974; m: 2004

....6 Rowan John Davies b: Mar 2006

..........................★2nd Husband of Deborah Loeb:

..........................+John James Brice b: Jul 1945

..........2 Irving Lehman b: Jan 1876; d: Sep 1945

............+Sissie Straus b: 1879; d: 1950; m: Jun 1901

..........2 Herbert Henry Lehman b: Mar 1878; d: Dec 1963

...........+ Edith Altschul b: Aug 1889; d: Mar 1976

.................3 Peter Gerald Lehman b: Jan 1917; d: Mar 1944

...................+Peggy Rosenbaum b: Dec 1919

..........................4 Penelope Lehman b: Apr 1940

...........................+Stanley Karp b: Jun 1924

..................................5 R. Christopher Lehman Karp b: Feb 1970

..........................4 Wendy Lehman b: Apr 1942

..........................+Stephen Sycle Lash b: Feb 1940; m: Oct 1967

.................................5 Abigail Sycle Lash b: May 1970

....................................+Austin Victor Shapard b: Jan 1971; m: Mar 2004

......................................6 Harriet Lehman Shapard b: Mar 2005

.................................5 William Lehman Lash b: Nov 1971

.................3 John R. Lehman b: Feb 1920; d: Jan 1994

.................3 Hilda Jane Lehman b: Mar 1921; d: May 1974

...................+ Eugene Lee Paul b: 1919

.........................4 Deborah Jane Wise b: Feb 1947

...........................+Peter Sheridan

.................................5 Elizabeth Jane Sheridan b: Nov 1979

.........................4 Stephanie Lee Wise b: Dec 1951

...........................+Eugene Tulchin

.........................4 Peter Lehman Wise b: Feb1949

...........................+Sharon McAuliffe

.................................5 Catherine Jane Wise b: Oct 1980

...........................*2nd Wife of Peter Lehman Wise:

...........................+Marylou Hanover b: Jun 1953

.................................5 Matthew Lehman Wise b: Jan 1986

Index